EQUAL TO MYSTERY

To my wife, Alison and three stalwart sons, Kamu, Kaimare and Kazakao. To the Ladoo family and the villagers of McBean. To the incredible dedication and devotion of Dennis Lee, Peter Such and all those who helped ensure that Harold's Caribbean talent, audacity, and spirit could not be quenched by the vicious events of the night of 16 August 1973 on the silent roads of Central Trinidad.

CHRISTOPHER LAIRD

EQUAL TO MYSTERY

PEEPAL TREE

First published in Great Britain in 2023
by Peepal Tree Press Ltd
17 King's Avenue
Leeds LS6 1QS
England

ISBN13: 97818452325628

Thanks are due to Dennis Lee for kind permission to quote
extensively from his poem "The Death of Harold Ladoo" from *Heart
Residence*.

Supported using public funding by
ARTS COUNCIL
ENGLAND

# CONTENTS

# INTRODUCTION
## FIERCE RECKONING

Only by dying brutally can man become equal to mystery.
— "A Short Story", Harold Sonny Ladoo, 1973

I never met Harold Ladoo. I discovered his writing almost by accident; it was in 1974, in Port of Spain, and I was working on a soon-to-be-launched periodical called *KAIRI*.[1] One morning a book landed on my desk for review – and to this day I have no idea how it got there, or who sent it. But from the first, staccato paragraph, I was hooked.

> Pa came home. He didn't talk to Ma. He came home just like a snake. Quiet.

What followed was so spare, so violent, so *human* that I can still feel the shockwaves it produced. The book was *No Pain Like This Body* (1972), Harold Sonny Ladoo's first novel. It exploded in our midst, and set me on a quest that has lasted for nearly fifty years.

Who *was* this man, glowering from the back cover of the book with such coiled intensity? The biographical note gave only the skimpiest clues; it said

*Harold Sonny Ladoo: cover photo by Graeme Gibson.*

Ladoo was born in Trinidad in 1945, and emigrated to Canada in 1968. Given his surname and the author photo, he was clearly of Indian descent – like half the people in Trinidad. Then in 1974, when his second novel *Yesterdays* appeared, there was a new biographical detail on the back cover: Ladoo had been killed, in Trinidad, in 1973. He was 28.

How could such a meteoric talent be snuffed out just like that? And what did it mean for the larger cultural awakening we were exploring at *KAIRI*? Neither question had an answer, of course. But to even consider the second question, some background is necessary.

Trinidad won its independence from Great Britain in 1962, and for a few years a patriotic optimism prevailed on the island. But the slogans rang increasingly hollow – especially among the young, who were "still waiting for Independence to happen."[2] Much of our land and industry remained foreign-owned, and colonial racial discrimination was still entrenched – overwhelmingly favouring whites, though they made up less than 2% of the population. Meanwhile, a drop in oil prices had depleted the economy, and unemployment was rising. And in the spring of 1970, with streets constantly jammed by thousands of young people protesting, the army mutinied in support, refusing to take up arms against the demonstrators. After more turmoil, a number of racial and colour barriers were officially removed, and parts of the economy, particularly in the oil and banking sectors, were nationalized. That whole chain of events came to be known as the 1970 Revolution.

Part of this seismic shift took place in the cultural field. There was a grassroots movement to revitalize traditional forms in music, dance and theatre – to address the experience of the young nation by re-imagining, in contemporary terms, forms previously considered too parochial and unsophisticated to be taken seriously.

Our aim at *KAIRI* was to analyse and celebrate this turn towards our roots, in Trinidad and across the Caribbean. And we covered all aspects of culture: music, writing, theatre, carnival arts, photography, visual art.

Ladoo's novels landed slam-bang in the midst of this ferment. They opened up areas missing from the canon till then. In *No Pain Like This Body* we were given a raw, unfiltered glimpse of a vital element in our heritage – the peasant world of the formerly East Indian indentured labourers, the so-called "coolies", in the years when an increasing proportion of them escaped the regimentation of indentured labour on sugar and coconut estates for a peasant existence that was highly precarious for many of them. I was nagged by the question, "How come no one has written about these things in this way before?" It felt like the harbinger of a more searching, more ruthless examination of ourselves – a new kind of writing, from a new generation of writers.

In part, these novels of Ladoo's were remarkable for what they *didn't* do.

Unlike most previous Caribbean fiction, they weren't designed to fit comfortably into Eurocentric models and markets. Nor did his characters express themselves in the "perfect sentences" of a Naipaul. And though V.S. Naipaul had hinted at this kind of existence at the beginning of *A House for Mr Biswas*, his portrayal is at a distance and not extended. Ladoo was following his own path; not only had he staked out new content, he portrayed it with a new kind of storytelling. His writing was often cinematic. He braided stories within stories within stories. If anyone *had* written about these downtrodden lives before, it was with contempt or ridicule, certainly not with the stark, spare energy of Ladoo, who captured the rhythms, the mischievousness, the hurt, the humour, the despair, the cut-and-thrust of creole speech[3] with unsurpassed confidence and verve.

Ladoo's novels were gifts to our purpose; we rejoiced in their fierce originality. Add the drama of his death and the glowering cover photograph, and we were in awe. We ran lengthy reviews of both Ladoo's novels in *KAIRI*; they remain, with all their youthful naivety, the most comprehensive appreciation of his writing published in the West Indies at the time.[4] Sections of the Caribbean literary establishment took little notice of Harold Ladoo. If it acknowledged him at all, it was as an oddity, or a dead-end rebel.

It seemed incomprehensible to me that, quite apart from Ladoo's literary accomplishments, no one was asking: how come, as Ladoo might have put it, "a little coolie boy from Trinidad" had, within three years, earned a university degree in Canada, published two landmark novels, was later the subject of a long poem by Toronto's first poet laureate,[5] had a prize for creative writing established in his name at the University of Toronto, and an art project dedicated to him by a major Canadian artist who had never met him?[6] What would a biography of Ladoo reveal about this unlikely trajectory?

I decided to pursue the question myself. It was slow going, but in 2017, after having worked on a screenplay for *No Pain Like This Body*,[7] and then on a six-part television documentary on Ladoo's life and work (both of which stalled for lack of funding), I decided to tackle the legend of Harold Ladoo in a book, a new medium for me as a filmmaker, so this extraordinary story wouldn't be lost.

I had the videotaped interviews from the stalled documentary. But apart from reviews, I'd found only two biographical sources in print form. One was a memorial essay from 1974, "The Short Life and Sudden Death of Harold Sonny Ladoo."[8] This was a touching, detailed piece by the novelist Peter Such, a mentor and close friend of Ladoo's in Toronto. The other significant source was a 17-page poem, "The Death of Harold Ladoo",[9] by Dennis Lee, who had edited *No Pain Like This Body*. The poem is both an elegy and a philosophic meditation, exploring the conflicted emotional void left by Ladoo's death.

Based on these sources, which relied on Ladoo's own accounts of his early years, the accepted story went like this. Harold Ladoo was an orphan, adopted by a desperately poor peasant family.[10] He spent part of his childhood in hospitals, and was abused by Canadian missionaries in primary school. Put to work in the rice-fields from the age of eight, he later emigrated to Canada, intent on re-inventing himself as a great poet. As he would later declare in a letter to Dennis Lee, "I had no formal schooling. ... I began to work when I was eight years old and I knew that one day I was going to leave the rice-fields and go out into a greater world."[11]

In Toronto, the story continues, he worked as a dishwasher and short-order cook. But he soon destroyed every word he'd written and took to writing fiction in all-night binge sessions. His ambition was titanic; he was planning a sequence of 200 novels, spanning five centuries. But in August 1973 he travelled home to settle some painful family business. A week later, on August 17, his battered body was found at the side of a road about a mile from the family home, near the junction of Exchange Extension and the Southern Main Road.

Ladoo's body found here

The tragic, indeed grisly circumstances of his death remained shrouded in rumour and suspicion. His legacy apparently included six or seven novels he left in manuscript – which were subsequently removed by an acquaintance, and never returned.

So the story went.

Over the past half century, I've often been asked why I'm so obsessed with this man's dark and violent vision. I knew that answering this question would drive me deeper into the riddle of Ladoo, and perhaps into myself.

What made Ladoo something more than just another promising Caribbean writer? It was partly his rage against centuries of brutality and denial. But it was also the stubborn and audacious originality of his work, which made it hard for many readers to pigeonhole it, let alone embrace it. He wasn't trying to excel as one more writer from the colonies, packaging his fiction in the familiar categories of the metropolis. He was making a fresh start – telling our story the way he saw it, which at times required new approaches.

He was poised to become a significant and defiant voice of his birthplace, his people – in fact, of any region where imperial depredations have scarred the lives of the colonised, i.e. much of the planet. And his portrait of a rootless Indo-Trinidadian peasantry was so savage that even his own people shied away. But in the long arc of a complete writing life, that resistance typically subsides. In Ladoo's case, however, the process was cut short almost as soon as it began; neither his writing nor his readers' grasp of what he was doing had a chance to fully mature. Yet the power and tang of his vision was unmistakable, and I couldn't shake it.

We who grew up in the optimism of Federation and Independence were traitors if we criticised Trinidad. We had to deny the negative, and promote the positive. Ladoo was a child of Independence, too, but he sensed its dark side. He experienced it viscerally, and fled Trinidad knowing it would always be there. More specifically, Independence had not embraced the Trinidadian Indian community. In the later 1960s and early 1970s, many politicised young Indo-Trinidadians saw themselves as an oppressed minority.

What was Ladoo so intent on bringing to light? Any truthful account of Trinidad must include three horrific chapters. First, the near-annihilation of indigenous peoples by Europeans, from 1498 on. Next, the abduction of Africans to serve as slaves on the sugar plantations during the 18th and 19th centuries; this lasted until slavery was abolished in 1838. And finally, there was the conscription of Indians into the near-slavery of indentured labour, from 1845 to 1917. When Indians were offered land grants as a means of inducing them to stay in Trinidad, as a body of reserve labour, when their indentureships ended, this did nothing to calm latent Creole hostility to the Indian presence.[12] Ethnic divisions have remained endemic in Trinidad's politics.

As of Trinidad & Tobago Independence Day, however – on August 31, 1962 – those chapters were papered over. Sealed off. Optimism and sunshine were now the order of the day; what place did recollecting such massive crimes have in the new Trinidad?

But Ladoo was having none of this willed amnesia. His calling was to strip away the façade – to tell ugly counter-truths on an epic scale. To "mash up" the colonial furniture. So I was drawn to his work, not in spite of its "dark and violent vision", but *because* of it. Someone was finally getting down to business in our literature – making the fierce reckoning we needed. Ladoo had a kind of pure rage on tap – a connection to the elemental, to a raw power he rode – which he could release and wrestle into art.

What did this mean for us and our literature? That I didn't know. But as a reader, and as a biographer, I was going to ride it with him.

This book will document the story of a young man from rural Trinidad in his audacious bid to out-write V. S. Naipaul and other Caribbean writers – in fact, to out-write all writers anywhere. It's a story of personal courage, grave flaws and driven talent, one that deserves a place among the legends of Caribbean, Canadian, and – if only as a poignant footnote – world literature. I also hope to locate the man behind the myths he cultivated, and perhaps exorcize the glowering mask that has occupied some corner of my own life for nearly half a century.

Along with excerpts from Ladoo's writing (many unpublished till now), and interviews with family, friends and colleagues, I lean on published reviews and memories, notably those by Such and Lee, and voices from the small community where Ladoo grew up: teachers, relatives, neighbours and others. As the years have passed, many in the community have become intrigued by this possibly famous native son. They're fascinated, too, by the story of the whole Ladoo family, which has entered the realm of legend since the death of its respected *patron*, Ladoo's father, Sonny. The family's descent into near oblivion provides a lurid yet riveting soap opera of drama and intrigue, which has left few standing.

It is by interweaving these strands, leavened with his letters and bound by my interpretations, that I hope to build a portrait of a young man for whom Canada, and the literary circle into which he found himself cata-pulted, offered a blank page on which to realise his ambition, and test his concept of the writer as mythmaker and hero – both through his writing and through the personas he presented to his new friends and colleagues. And to himself.

Ladoo's sister Meena once described him as "a knight in shining armour". And it was *this* persona – the hero, with his sense of historic injustice and family loyalty – that led Harold Ladoo to his untimely death, and to becoming, in the words of one of his characters, "equal to mystery."

## Endnotes

1. KAIRI ran for half a dozen issues between 1974-75 – including artwork, creative writing and a 45rpm recording.
2. Sunity Maharaj of the Lloyd Best Institute of the Caribbean: private discussion in September 2020.
3. The term "creole" refers to the modified version of the European colonisers' language (whether English, French, Spanish or Dutch) that was developed by the people they enslaved. There were two Trinidadian creoles – one French-African, the other English-African, both utilising African language structures and grammar. As the dominant form, the English Creole absorbed elements from the French. When East Indian labourers were imported after 1845, they adopted the Afro-Trinidadian creole that was already in place, adding their own Hindi terms for cultural items (food, plants, musical instruments etc.) particular to their traditions.
4. These reviews can be read in Appendices Six and Seven.
5. Dennis Lee, *The Death of Harold Ladoo* (San Francisco & Vancouver: The Kanchenjunga Press, 1976). A revised version appears in Lee's Collected poems, *Heart Residence* (Toronto: Anansi, 2017).
6. See Chapter Eight, p. 93.
7. For Channel 4 in the UK, in collaboration with dramatist Tony Hall and actor Errol Sitahal.
8. Peter Such, "The Short Life and Sudden Death of Harold Sonny Ladoo", *Saturday Night* (Toronto), 89, 5, 1974; and *BIM* (Barbados), Volume 16 No 63, 1978.
9. See note 5 above.
10. Thus the Ladoo site on *Wikipedia* declares that he was "born into extreme poverty," and "grew up in an environment very much like the world of his novels."
11. See Selwyn Ryan, *Race and Nationalism in Trinidad and Tobago* (Toronto: University of Toronto Press, 1972), pp. 190-194.
12. For a general history of indentured immigration, see Hugh Tinker, *A New System of Slavery: The Export of Indian Labour Overseas 1830-1920* (London: Oxford University Press, 1974).

## CHAPTER ONE
## GROWING UP IN MCBEAN

"He used to have a massive fantasy of his own, you know, a fellow who could create a story now for now, even if something didn't happen to him like that."
— Ramsoondar Parasram

Harold Sonny Ladoo was born on February 4, 1945, to Sonny and Hamidhan Ladoo. They lived in McBean, a small settlement in central Trinidad, in the middle of the sugarcane-farming region. The village straddled the Southern Main Road, which connects the capital, Port of Spain, in the north, with the industrial capital, San Fernando, in the south.

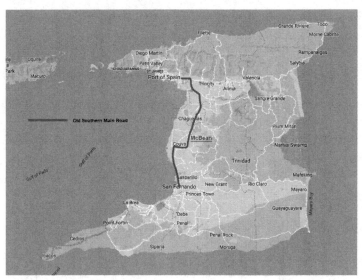

Today McBean is a bustling community of over 4,000. In the 1950s and 1960s, however, it was barely a village. With only a few hundred inhabitants, it supported two stores: a dry-goods outlet, selling hardware, pulses and rice, etc; and a bar/rumshop and 'parlour', selling drinks and snacks.

The inhabitants of McBean and the surrounding countryside were almost completely Indo-Trinidadian, and mainly Hindu[1] (with Muslim and Christian minorities). Nearly 144,000 East Indians had been brought to Trinidad after the emancipation of African slaves, to serve as cheap and "bonded" labour on the sugarcane plantations. By 1960, they constituted

36.5% of the country's population. A few had become independent farmers, but most were still hybrid peasant-labourers, with small plots of land,
but still dependent on seasonal labour on the sugar estates.

Among these Indo-Trinidadians in McBean was the Ladoo family.

The head of the family, Harold's father Sonny, was short in stature but
formidable in nature. Villagers in McBean describe him as very strong[2] and
very serious, a stern disciplinarian but well-known for his integrity and
generosity. He was a farmer, highly respected in the community, growing
vegetables and citrus on ten acres that his father and mother had been
granted at the end of their second indentureship. The farm stretched
behind the Ladoo home, off the Sonny Ladoo Trace[3] east of the Southern
Main Road. One end of the trace joined the Southern Main Road by Sonny
Ladoo Road – the latter designation being one of several indications of the
father's standing in the community.

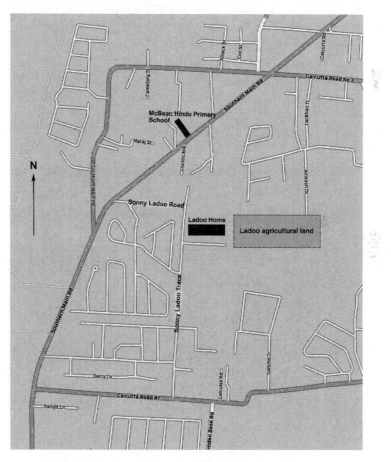

*The Ladoo home in McBean*

*Sonny Ladoo Trace becomes Sonny Ladoo Road as it joins the Southern Main Road (2019)*

The area between Sonny Ladoo Trace and the Southern Main Road was planted in sugarcane at one time, but has since become a housing development. In 2003, Trinidad's sugar industry closed down and by 2007 the last sugar factory had shut.

*Ladoo residential gardens*

With the proceeds from these ten acres, Sonny, Harold's father, rented more land. His crops of vegetables and citrus flourished, and according to Harold's youngest sister, Meena, he was able to acquire further land in nearby

Gran Couva. Villagers describe his holdings as one of the largest vegetable plantations in the country, yielding tomatoes, cabbage, pumpkin, aubergines, etc. They describe Sonny Ladoo as "the richest man in the area", and his plantation as "the food basket of the country".

What did this mean? The more I spoke with Harold's neighbours and family in McBean the clearer it became that the real story of Harold and the Ladoo family directly contradicted the "accepted story" mentioned in my Introduction, on Wikipedia, and in every biographical sketch by reviewers and critics. It became evident that Harold had created an alternate personal history for consumption by his Canadian colleagues and the literary establishment.[4]

Harold was the third child of Sonny and Hamidhan.[5] There were two older sisters, Sylvia and Ballo/Llalouci (both now deceased). After Harold came another sister, Geeta, who committed suicide in her mid-teens. Next was a brother, "Toy" or Ramesh, who, following a car accident in the late 1960s, suffered from mental illness and spent much of his later years at St. Ann's Mental Hospital in Port of Spain. He too is deceased. Ramesh was followed by a final sister, Meena or Kusum, the sole survivor among the siblings.

There was an older half-brother as well: Cholo/Balkaran, by Sonny's first marriage. But he lived with an aunt and, according to Meena, was not treated as part of the immediate Ladoo family. Thus Harold was the oldest male child, the number one son. When the time came, he would be expected to take over the role of Sonny, the stern, upright, yet generous patriarch of the clan. Harold first rebelled against these expectations, and then later, to his cost, tried to fulfil them.

In 1952, Harold began attending the Exchange Canadian Mission Indian School (CMI) in the town of Couva, two miles south of McBean – the only primary school in the area at the time. He was seven, two years past the recommended age for enrolment. (While five was the official age for starting school, children in outlying areas often began later, because of the difficulty of walking the miles to and from school at age five.)

Contrary to what Harold would later tell his Canadian friends, and describe in his novel *Yesterdays,* people who attended the school at the same time (his sister-in-law Phyllis Siewdass, and a neighbour, Hugh Ramdeen) insist that CMI was a pleasant and good school. There were no Canadian teachers, and no punishment rooms or untoward disciplinary measures. Nevertheless, Harold's father, a devout Hindu, was not happy sending his children to a Presbyterian school, where entrance to the Canadian Mission secondary schools was conditional on conversion to Christianity, and the teachers at both levels had to be Christian.[6] We can assume that Harold was aware of his father's objections, and his criticism of the Canadian missionaries whose work was entirely focused on the Indian community. This antagonism no doubt fuelled Harold's later portrayal of such a school in his novel, *Yesterdays.*

Sonny even offered to donate land for the establishment of a Hindu school in McBean. Eventually, land and funds were provided by other donors and in March 1955, the McBean Hindu School opened. Harold was transferred immediately, having just turned ten. Here is his teacher, Ramsoondar Parasram, whom I interviewed in 2003:

*McBean Hindu School (2003)*

*RP*: As a student, Harold was the third child I believe in the family if I am not wrong. So when this school McBean here opened, he came into I think the Second Standard.[7] He was a sort of middle student. By the term middle, I mean average student. But he used to have a massive fantasy of his own, you know, a fellow who could create a story now for now, even if something didn't happen to him like that, possibly that must have led to his later ability to write.

For instance, if two little boys had a little fight outside, which was a common thing in those days, then he would bring the information, he wouldn't bring it like the ordinary fellow, you know, he highly dramatised the issue and make it look bigger than it was big, so that immediately you have to take action because, you see, the report that you get is kind of critical. But generally, other than that, he wasn't a mischievous fellow. To say he'd go and make fight with nobody, no, not that I know of. When he left Trinidad I don't know, 'cause I left in '65, so after that, what he did I wouldn't know, but up to the time I knew him in school, he was a nice fellow, friendly, good friend with everybody, except that the family had to live under the very strict rules of the father. He was an extraordinary disciplinarian, you see, and I personally believe, and I used to tell him also, that he was a little tightfisted on the children. I don't think the father did give them much freedom.

*CL:* So as far as you know Harold was Sonny's natural son. He wasn't adopted?

*RP:* No, no, no. There's no two ways, that's his son. Now I can't say we'd do a DNA test, …but looking at mother and father, there's no two ways about it.

*CL:* But there were no rumours or anything going around that he was adopted or anything?

RP: I never knew of that, never did.

I pressed Ramsoondar Parasram on this last point, because of something Peter Such had mentioned in an interview:

> He told me the story of being raised in an orphanage. I said, "Well, so was I," because I was raised in an orphanage too. And so there was this kind of instant recognition of what we'd been through.[8]

It seems that teacher Parasram had Harold's number, when he described him as "a fellow who could create a story now for now, even if something didn't happen to him like that."

Ranjit Ragoonanan, a school friend of Harold's, remembers him this way:[9]

> *RR:* We attended primary school together. He was most of the times a loner, but at certain times we got together. As a matter of fact, we planted those palm trees that you see in front of that school there, because we were the first batch of students that came into the school. But Harold was on kind of distant terms with his father, who was a very strict disciplinarian, 'cause he concentrated mainly on his produce and whatever.
>
> *CL:* But he was a first-rate farmer, eh?
>
> *RR:* He was the best in the village.
>
> *CL:* What was Harold like, a regular sort of fellow?
>
> *RR:* No, no, no, no. Harold would go into his shell every now and then, even in primary school. He was not violent or disruptive, but sometimes he would just get into his moods and then we and the other classmates would continue with our hi-jinks.

In the Trinidad education system at the time, students began their primary education in the first form ("kindergarten" in other systems), and then progressed through five "standards" or grades. In the Fifth Standard, normally at age 11 or 12, pupils sat for the School Leaving Certificate. Success would not only confirm their graduation from primary school, but would put them on track to be trained as teachers' assistants and school monitors, as well as assisting them in securing other jobs.

Those who failed could repeat the exam if they remained at school. And successful students could stay on too. With no secondary school in the area, many pupils chose to remain at primary school until age 15. Those who did, entered what were called "post-primary" classes, which had curricula similar to those in the first and second forms of secondary school.

There is no record of when Harold completed primary school. But from what another friend, Sarjoo 'Chanlal' Ramsumair, told me,[10] and given Sonny Ladoo's support for his son's education and the lack of a local secondary school, there is every reason to believe that Harold stayed on at McBean Hindu Primary School until age fifteen. It was within walking distance of home, the education was free, and he would cover the syllabus for the first two years of secondary school.

But like most people in his community, Harold understood that education was his only way out of a life in the small agricultural settlement. He knew he had to pursue further schooling. So, in 1960, at age fifteen, he enrolled at a private secondary school, St. Andrew's Academy in Chaguanas, a large town ten miles north of McBean. To attend St. Andrew's, he (or his father) would have had to pay school fees.[11]

Private secondary schools were concerned with only one thing: preparing students for the Cambridge School Certificate exams. "It was literally the sole business of Private Secondary Schools to provide Cambridge Certificates."[12] There were two such certificates in the 1960s: the "School Certificate" or "O (Ordinary) level," usually attempted around age 16 or 17; and then the "Higher School Certificate" or "A (Advanced) level," two or three years later. The latter diploma was the prize, because it fulfilled the entrance requirements for North American, British, and European universities.

Harold and his friend Chanlal went to St. Andrew's Academy in 1960. They had to commute daily, a drive of about 20 minutes by route taxi, which cost 6 cents (3c US) in those days. St. Andrew's no longer exists, so it is difficult to pin down exactly how long Harold stayed at the school. But we do know he stayed on longer than his friend, Chanlal, who dropped out after two terms; "Harold was brighter than me."[13]

Another friend of Harold's, Puran Ramlogan, went to McBean Hindu with Harold. He told me that Harold did not stay long at St. Andrews, leaving "after a year or two without his parents' permission" to transfer to another private school, Chaguanas High School (no longer in existence), for a few months, before transferring yet again to Kenley's College in San Fernando (another private school that no longer exists). There he sat London University School Certificate[14] exams in history ("Caribbean, African, American, European and Ancient histories") and literature. Puran says that Harold "had a photographic memory, and could read 6 books at a time and tell you what page he had left off reading in each one."

Puran says Harold got a number of 'O' Level certificates, in history and literature, from London University, and two 'A' level certificates in the same subjects.[15] Here is his sister-in-law, Phyllis:

*PS*: Well, I knew that he got his 'O' Levels[16], but I don't know how many. Yes, because I know he would study all night and sleep during the day because he always passed here to go to the shop there to get things to eat and he would always say, "You know I didn't go to bed yet, I'm now going to have some breakfast and go to bed," and he would sleep all day and wake all night studying.[17] That I know for a fact.

*CL*: What sort of subjects was he studying?

*PS*: Oh! [sighs] I don't know.

*CL*: You can't remember?

*PS*: No. All what I know he was always reading, reading, reading, reading, you know, he and some other guys together, they always studied together.[18]

This story of a group of friends who studied together is picked up by another of his friends, the attorney and political activist, Lennox Sankersingh:

I recall that Kenneth Valley, former minister in the PNM government, was a close associate of his when they lived in McBean and there is a story that people talk about that Kenneth Valley and Harold and a few others didn't get through their exams. They started school late and when they reached their late teens they took up studying very very seriously and they would study night and day and try to pass their O levels and their A levels. They didn't have a proper school education but they tutored themselves and eventually passed their subjects.[19]

Puran Ramlogan was a member of the group, and he tells how "they used to meet each night at Joseph and Kenneth Valley's mother's home in Calcutta Road #3 and work, sometimes till 3.00 am." Puran was in awe of Harold's mind. With his photographic memory, Puran says, Harold could recite huge chunks of Shakespeare by heart.

Harold had a very good friend "Scotty" (Hanif Mohammed), who worked at the sugar company and ran a small shop in McBean. Puran remembers that Scotty and his wife (who was very interested in political and cultural issues) would occasionally drive the group to public lectures at the Port of Spain City Hall and Public Library. These would have been adventures for young people (mainly young men) from central Trinidad in those days; they indicate the serious nature of the study group's activities.

Other villagers remember the group as well. In a typically macabre Ladoo touch, a cousin remembers the boys going to study in the McBean Cemetery. And from what Phyllis, Lennox, Puran and Meena report, Harold eventually passed his school certificate examinations at both levels.

This would later help him in gaining admission to the undergraduate programme at Erindale College in the University of Toronto, where he would meet up again with Lennox Sankersingh and Ken Valley.

What did Harold do with himself in these years, apart from studying with the group and sitting his School Certificate examinations?

In the normal course of events, his family would have had first call on his time. His father's agricultural enterprise required constant and intense work. So when he was not in school, he might have been expected to spend long hours planting and weeding and harvesting. Puran Ramlogan (who lived next door to the Ladoos) told me that Harold did no work in the fields. He attended school, and he studied independently, and that was his job.[20] His younger brother Toy and his older half-brother Cholo didn't escape fieldwork, and Puran too was enlisted to work for Sonny. (He was paid $3.00 a day – about $1.75 US.) This suggests that Sonny recognised his son's intellectual ability and supported his education as a means of improving his employment prospects and his future as potential heir to Sonny's estate. This (and Sonny's later assistance in financing Harold's emigration) would have placed a serious obligation on Harold, one that he rebelled against even as he knew he couldn't avoid it. The young Harold's uneasy relationship with his powerful and successful father would continue to be a significant and telling element in the years to come.

What opportunities for entertainment and fun did young people in McBean have in the 1960s? Chanlal told me that after Harold had received the obligatory permission from his father, he would go to Harold's home, where they would wrestle and lift weights under the house.[21] According to Chanlal, Harold was thin but strong. He particularly loved movies featuring "strongmen" like Steve Reeves,[22] often "breaking biche" or playing truant from school to do so.

Teacher Parasram told me there was not much in the way of organised activities for young people at that time, other than the cricket offered by the McBean Sports Club where teams from different streets in McBean would play against each other. But, again, Puran was adamant that Harold played no sports, though as boys they would ride bicycles around the area, even as far as Chaguanas or Couva. Beyond that, the elders were very cautious about allowing their young people to go outside the community on beach or river excursions, but the McBean Hindu Primary School did organise tours to places of national interest. Still, according to Chanlal, he, Harold and their friends would walk or bicycle to the nearby Carli Bay beach or to Couva River, over five miles from McBean.

*Carli Bay, Couva 2019*

Another factor affected leisure activities. At that time, the political landscape and social structure of Trinidad & Tobago were undergoing rapid changes. The People's National Movement, which came to power in 1956, had its base mainly among the population of African descent, leading the country to full independence in 1962. Indian Trinidadians, feeling marginalised and somewhat besieged, looked inward for their entertainment. This included singing and dancing at social and religious events, pujas at the mandir,[23] occasional recitals of traditional devotional songs.[24] Harold would also have been familiar with some of the Indian classics such as the *Ramayana* and the *Bhagavad Gita*, as these texts were well known among the Hindus in Trinidad (often in English translation), where they were chanted at pujas[25] and dramatized in the annual 'Leelas'[26] in some villages. Harold's friend, Chanlal, also told me that Harold liked to attend lectures (in English) by visiting Indian swamis.

And, probably most frequently, there were trips to the cinema, which was increasingly programming Indian movies subtitled in English, as the aging population that could understand Hindi dwindled.

Harold went to the movies fairly often. There were two cinemas in Couva, the Metro and the Carib, as well as the Jubilee in Chaguanas. San Fernando (18 miles to the south) boasted at least eight cinemas. According to Chanlal, apart from Harold's penchant for strongman and legendary-hero movies, like Steve Reeves, they mainly went to see westerns. And of course there were the serials designed by Hollywood for juvenile audiences, which V.S. Naipaul describes disparagingly as "one of the staples of adult entertainment"[27] in Trinidad. Though television had been inaugurated on Independence Day (1962), few homes in McBean had TV in the 1960s.

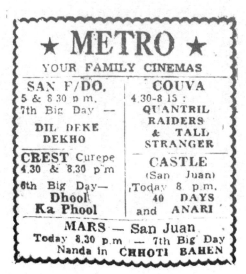

*Newspaper advertisement in the 1960s for the Metro chain of cinemas showing Indian movies, and the one in Couva showing a Western double feature.*

Chanlal describes Harold as a loner, quiet, always having a book or comic book with him. This would have marked him out in McBean. Trinidad at that time had perhaps two shops devoted to selling literature other than school texts, and these were in Port of Spain and San Fernando. In a society not known for its reading habits, to grow up as a reader sets you apart. But as we hear from his sister-in-law Phyllis, Harold was a reading evangelist: "He was always reading, always encouraging us to read too." The swaggering image Harold presented is nicely captured by Chanlal: "He always had a book or a comic in his back pocket." This image also suggests the type of books Harold was carrying around, books that could be crammed into a pocket. These would have been "dime-store" novels of crime, romance, and westerns with paper covers.

Being a solitary and voracious reader can foster lively internal fantasies. Harold was fascinated by the worlds of swashbuckling and gun-toting heroes and villains. But in the process of absorbing those stories from books and at the movies, he evidently developed a clear appreciation for the techniques of storytelling on the page and screen, resulting in writing that told its stories predominantly through action.

He had to read more serious books for his School Certificate exams. One subject would have been English literature, which required reading set poetry, novels and plays. In the 1960s, teachers in the Trinidadian school system preferred to select nineteenth-century literature.[28] Thus Harold would have been familiar with poetry by Wordsworth, Coleridge, Keats, Tennyson and Walter de la Mare; novels by Austen, the Brontes, Dickens, George Eliot; and of course, plays by Shakespeare, often *Macbeth* or *Julius*

*Caesar*. These texts could have been purchased from bookstores, most of which depended on filling school booklists to be sustainable. Since bookstores were very limited in what they offered and with financial resources limited, Harold did not buy many books but haunted the available libraries. One library he and his study-group friends frequented was the American Library in Port of Spain (part of the US Information Service, attached to the embassy). It provided a quiet, air-conditioned space, which also had information on educational opportunities in North America.

There were small branch libraries, first in Couva (a one-room library with few books), and later in Chaguanas. Chanlal told me Harold used the library in Chaguanas. And Meena and Puran told me he also went to the Carnegie Free Library in San Fernando, where he was attending school. Comic books featuring superheroes like Batman and Superman could be purchased from most booksellers and even grocery stores, as could popular novels like those by Mickey Spillane and Louis L'Amour, and other lurid thrillers and westerns.

Caribbean literature would have been hard to find in central Trinidad in the 1960s, but V.S. Naipaul, being Trinidadian, was better known. Harold would almost certainly have read one or more of his books – especially since Naipaul's best-known novel, *A House for Mr. Biswas* (1961), is largely set in nearby Chaguanas.

A bright, self-motivated, well-read young man who lived in a world of books, comic books and action-hero movies, who felt trapped in a rural community in the middle of a small island, and was determined to make a name for himself in the wider world: this is not an unusual circumstance in the history of literature.

Since the 1950s, when Caribbean literature began to flourish, aspiring writers had journeyed to the metropoles – whether England, France or Spain – in order to become established: to learn their craft, and make their mark. Not only to be published, but also to escape what they saw as the cloying, insular and claustrophobic life in the colonies.

At that time, there was only one short-lived Caribbean publishing house in Jamaica (Pioneer Press) and four significant "little" literary magazines: *Kyk-over-Al* in British Guiana, *Bim* in Barbados and more occasionally *Focus* in Jamaica and Clifford Sealey's *Voices* in Trinidad (1964-1966). For anglophone writers such as V. S. Naipaul, George Lamming, Sam Selvon, Michael Anthony, Edgar Mittelholzer, Wilson Harris, Andrew Salkey, E.R. Braithwaite, and many others, this meant moving to the UK – usually London – in order to have access to publishers and to the fees that the BBC *Caribbean Voices* paid for scripts and for reading.[29]

As Shiva Naipaul (the novelist younger brother of V. S. Naipaul) said in an interview with the BBC shortly before his untimely death in 1985:

Escape; that had always been the goal, and academic success offered the only hope of its fulfilment. Education under these circumstances became a barely controlled frenzy. ... A popular theme of local folklore centred on those unfortunate to have failed by a mere mark or two to win a scholarship and then gone mad or bad. ... However, let me not be misunderstood, I did not hate the island, my life there was not intolerable, it was just that its constrictions, its complicity, offered me no vision of myself beyond a certain point. One grew out of it as one grew out of one's clothes. If I constantly dreamt of escape it was not because I was especially perverse or especially wilful, it was because there genuinely seemed to be no alternative. I wanted to be neither mad nor bad.[30]

Or as V. S. Naipaul wrote in *The Enigma of Arrival* (1987):

My real life, my literary life, was to be elsewhere. In the meantime, at home, I lived imaginatively in the cinema, a foretaste of that life abroad. ... it was painful, after the dark cinema and the remote realms where one had been living for three hours or so, to come out into the very bright colours of one's own world.[31]

In the late 1960s, the debate about having to leave the island to become a writer in the international market was well under way. The novelist Earl Lovelace and the poet Derek Walcott (later to win the Nobel Prize for Literature) were adamant that they would stay on-island and make it as writers; but both had already been published in the UK and the US. Harold, isolated in rural Trinidad, would not have been aware of this debate, but might well have been aware of the exodus in the 1950s.

As he would later declare in a letter (already quoted in the Introduction) to Dennis Lee, on 20 November 1971:

I had no formal schooling, I had no money or encouragement, but I had the capacity to endure. I began to work when I was eight years old and I knew that one day I was going to leave the rice-fields and go out into a greater world. It was that thought that kept me alive.[32]

This statement is critical in answering the question, "Why was Harold so focused on leaving McBean?" The image of him working in the fields from the age of eight is typically over-dramatic, and another example of Harold's conjuring alternate histories for himself, since he did attend school (and his father planted very little rice, mainly for the family's use). Nevertheless, it holds the kernel of his motivation.

For Harold, with an older sister in Toronto who could sponsor him as a landed immigrant to Canada, the UK was not the first option.[33] But he had a suitcase full of writing. The outside world awaited the emergence of a new writer. He was intent on escape from McBean. Very intent.

But first he wanted to get married.

# Endnotes

1. 85% of indentured labourers were Hindu and 14% Muslim.
2. "He could carry a sugar bag [450 lbs] on his back, and in competitions he was known to lift a sack of rice [162 lbs] with his teeth." Interview with Puran Ramlogan by Christopher Laird, 2021.
3. "Trace" – a path or track.
4. Harold's self re-invention will be examined in Chapter 10, "Who Was Harold Sonny Ladoo?"
5. Harold's friend and mentor in Toronto, Peter Such (in an interview with Christopher Laird in 2003), says he saw Harold's birth certificate, and it stated he was 'illegitimate,' which Peter thought supported Harold's contention that he was adopted. But an "illegitimate" status on birth certificates when Harold was born would have been common, because it wasn't until after 1945 that the colonial administration recognised Hindu marriages.
6. "Whilst many parents are not willing to have their children baptized, yet they are desirous of having them attend the Mission school1": Miss Kirkpatrick, a missionary, to the *Presbyterian Record* in 1891.
7. Normally the Second Standard (Grade Two) would admit students of about 7-8 years old, but Ramsoondar Parasram says it was not unusual in those days for students to be older, since they started school much later.
8. Interview with Peter Such by Christopher Laird, 2003.
9. Interview with Ranjit Ragoonanan by Christopher Laird, July 2003.
10. Interview with Sarjoo 'Chanlal' Ramsumair by Christopher Laird, 2019.
11. Private secondary-school fees varied from $.50 to $5.00 a month (worth 0.30c and $3.00 in $US at that time).
12. See Brinsley Samaroo, "The Presbyterian Canadian Mission as an Agent of Integration in Trinidad During the Nineteenth and Early Twentieth Centuries", *Caribbean Studies*, Vol. 14, no. 441.
13. Interview with Sarjoo 'Chanlal' Ramsumair by Christopher Laird, 2019.
14. Though the national education system prepared students for the Cambridge School Certificates, the equivalent certificates from London University, London University School Certificates, were available to students sitting privately or through the Extra-Mural classes of the University of the West Indies.
15. His university transcript later records that he presented Ordinary Level ('O' Level) G.C.E. Certificates in English Literature, English Language, History of the British Commonwealth, Religious Knowledge, and Advanced Level ('A' Level) certificates in History and the British Constitution.

16. The Cambridge School Certificate and Higher School Certificate were later superseded by the General Certificate of Education O level and A level, both of them run by Cambridge (in the state or assisted schools) or London Universities (for the private and University of the West Indies Extra-Mural schools).

17. Harold's penchant for working/studying by night became his routine for writing his fiction in night-long 'binges' in later years.

18. Interview with Phyllis Siewdass by Christopher Laird, 2003.

19. Interview with Lennox Sankersingh by Christopher Laird, 2019.

20. "Harold never worked." Interview with Puran Ramlogan by Christopher Laird, 2021.

21. Most houses in the area were traditionally built on tall stilts, and the open space under the house – the bottom-house – would be used for relaxation in a hammock, informal gatherings and other activities which did not require access to the living quarters.

22. Stephen Lester Reeves was an American professional bodybuilder, actor, and philanthropist. He was famous in the mid-1950s as a movie star in Italian-made peplum films, playing mythic characters such as Hercules, Goliath, and Karim, in *The Thief of Baghdad*.

23. Hindu prayer ceremonies and rituals at the temple.

24. A neighbour, Hugh Ramdeen, told me (interview 2019) that Harold "liked to talk philosophy, knew a lot about Hinduism and liked to attend lectures – mostly by visiting Hindu Swamis."

25. Hindu religious ceremonies

26. 'Leela' or 'Lila' – a 'divine play'. A play based on classic Hindu religious texts often performed by and for the community in open spaces.

27. V.S. Naipaul, *The Middle Passage: Impressions of Five Colonial Societies* (London: Andre Deutch, 1962), 59.

28. According to people I interviewed who were teachers in the area at the time, like Pundit Ramsoondar Parasram, St. Andrews Academy would have had few qualified teachers; many of them may have been school leavers themselves. The syllabus they chose to teach would have been influenced by what they themselves had studied.

29. See Glyne A. Griffith, *The BBC and the Development of Anglophone Caribbean Literature, 1943-1958* (London: Palgrave, 2016)

30. Shiva Naipaul, *Beyond the Dragon's Mouth*, BBC television, 1984

31. *The Enigma of Arrival* (London: Viking, 1987), 108

32. Letter to Dennis Lee, 20 November, 1971.

33. "The arrival of the Canadian Presbyterian Missionaries on the Caribbean islands during the colonial period laid the foundations of the migration of the Indo-Caribbean people to Canada. The Indo-Caribbean people were encouraged by the Canadian Missionaries

to pursue higher education in Canada by offering them scholarships. The history of migration of Indo-Caribbean people in Canada can be traced to the early nineteenth century but it was only after the introduction of the 'Point System' in 1967 that the Indo-Caribbean people began to arrive in Canada in significant numbers." *Canadian Diaspora: Surviving Through Double Migration And Dis(Re)Placement,* Ramchandra Joshi and Urvashi Kaushal. *Journal of Indo- Caribbean Research* in Vol. 8, No. 1, 2013.

## CHAPTER TWO
## LEAVING MCBEAN – IMAGINING TOLA

"He say if I don't married to him, when I walking down the bridge
somewhere there, the corner of the road, he'll take a gun and shoot
me."
— Rachel Ladoo

Harold set his sights on a young widow, Rachel Singh. She was a year
older than him, and lived close by in McBean. Her background was striking.
Her father, Ramkaran Singh, was tall and fair, a cricketer and a tailor to
the prime minister. He had children by two sisters at the same time, pairs
of children of the same age. One was Amin Khan, Rachel's mother.

In 1957, when she was 13, Rachel married Jewan Singh, who had a
reputation as a mouth-organ player. They had three sons, followed by a
daughter, Deborah. They separated in 1961. Her second partner was Absal
Mohammed, with whom she had a son. In 1963, however, Absal was killed
in a hit-and-run on the Southern Main Road.[1]

Rachel was now a widow at 19, with five children.

In a 2002 interview with Ramabai Espinet (the novelist and colleague of
the author's), Rachel recalls how she married Harold in 1968, despite an
impediment to the marriage:

*Rachel Ladoo (2002)*

*RL*: Like he used to come over at our place every evening and one day he said he liked me and I said, "No, I don't like you because we're family and I can't have feelings like we like each other, I like you as family, I must be in love with you to get married."

He said, he don't care he has to get married to me. I said, "No."

And then my mother went to see a movie and I and him alone was home with my little daughter Debbie. I was rocking her in the hammock and he came and sit down next to me and he said how he's in love with me, and I said no, I don't and he start kissing me, and I said no, I don't like what you're doing there, to leave and go, I told him to go home. He said no, he's not going. I said when my mother come home I'll tell her I don't want you to come back here anymore. He said you say what you want to say but I will still come back and I can't stop him coming there. So, then he used to come by every day, so he say he have to get married to me, and I say I don't want to, he say if I don't married to him when I walking down the bridge somewhere there, the corner of the road, he'll take a gun and shoot me if I don't get married to him. So, I say I don't care; you can do what you want to do, and after he came and tell me the same story over and over, he went and tell his mother he was getting married to me and then the father get to hear about it and the father did not agree because we were relatives.

*RE*: How were you all related?

*RL*: My grandfather and his grandfather were brothers and that's why they didn't want us to get married. Then the father called a pundit, a priest, and people around to talk to him not to get married, 'cause the relationship we had was like family, close related family.

   Then when the Pundit and everybody came across and he see them come, and he came down from upstairs, he tell his father if they don't leave in five minutes time he will chop up everybody, and they did leave. And so, he went to Chaguanas and put up the notice for us to get married, and he said, "We going to get married," and I said, "I didn't go Chaguanas, I didn't agree to it, why'd you do it?" He said he don't care, but I have to married to him and so I agreed to married him and that's how we get married.

*RE*: You didn't think that you could do anything else? Did you try to go somewhere else?

*RL*: I went away by some family, I tried to hide, but he get to know where I was and he came looking for me and he said, "Come home," because I think he will do what he said if I don't married to him, so I just married to him after, and that's how we got married.

*RE*: So, did you like him?

*RL*: Not at the beginning really, but after we get married and we came to Canada, I guess I get to like him a little, but not really wholeheartedly.

*RE*: Tell us about where you got the money from to come to Canada?

*RL*: His father had land and we plant bhagi [spinach] and we sell bhagi and we get the money to come to Canada.

Since their maternal grandfathers were brothers, Harold and Rachel were second cousins. In an interview in 2003, Rachel's older sister Phyllis remembers their discussions about marrying Harold:

*Phyllis Siewdas (2003)*

*Phyllis Siewdas*: She was living across the street from here and he would pass to go to the shop to get things to eat, and they would talk because you know, as I said, we grew up from small together and everything. I don't know, I just knew that it wasn't even a long friendship or anything and the next thing you know they got married and they went to Canada and that's all I know about the relationship really.

*Christopher Laird:* Rachel says that she didn't want to marry him but he forced her to marry him and threatened her and that you advised her what to do. Tell me about that.

*PS*: Well the only thing I know about that one... since her husband had died and it was a good escape to go to Canada, why not do it you know, better than staying here, when you could go to Canada and do something for yourself and your life should be better off than here, you know.

*CL*: But she didn't want to marry him?

*PS*: I know at the beginning, no. She never even loved him before. [Chuckles.] To be honest with you she didn't really, because as I said we were like distant relatives, second cousins, and she really looked at him in that way, you know, like a distant cousin and she didn't really want to get married to him, and I used to say, "Well girl, it's a good thing for you to get married and just go to Canada and see what you could do from there. If things doesn't work out, well..."

It's clear that when it came to achieving the goals he set himself, the pleasant, friendly boy described by teacher Parasram drew on a different side of his personality. We get more glimpses of Harold's "dark side" as his story progresses. And in this case, he achieved his goal. After their abrupt courtship, Harold and Rachel were married in August 1968, and emigrated to Canada a few days later. Rachel left her children behind; her sons remained with her first husband and his new wife, and her daughter Debbie stayed with Rachel's mother and her sister Phyllis. (Rachel would later bring Debbie to Toronto.) Her son with the deceased Absal stayed with his father's family.

And though Harold's father opposed the marriage, he helped them financially. According to Harold's sister Meena, "My brother planted a few crops and stuff like that, and I think [our father] gave him money. He wouldn't let him go without doing his part."

Waiting for their flight in Port of Spain, Harold and Rachel were poised between their familiar past in McBean and the unknown future in Toronto. And it was an open question: would Harold achieve his goal of becoming a writer there? For that matter, is there any evidence that he had started to write in McBean? If so, it was a completely private pursuit; none of his contemporaries made any mention of it. But as one indication, we have Rachel's recollection of him settling directly into writing when they reached Toronto: "He say he will get a job but then he started writing the scripts in his book and those things."[2] And in a larger perspective, if Harold took refuge in writing after this massive uprooting, it was a characteristic impulse. Writing as a consolation in difficult times, a way to reinforce his sense of worth when everything around him looked dire, was a reflex he would rely on increasingly. It may have been a reflex he had already learned in McBean.

There is his draft of a short story from 1972, "The Agony", in which an aspiring Indo-Caribbean poet tells his lover, "I showed you the stacks of paper that I carried in an old briefcase." Later she asks him, "Where is the briefcase with the poems?" And, indeed, Harold did have a "small brown suitcase" full of manuscripts, nearly all of them poetry.

Did the compulsion to write begin only at 23, when he got to Toronto? It's possible. But it seems much more likely that it started in McBean – with Harold composing soulful verse, like many young people, based on the only models he knew: the Romantic and Victorian poets he read for the School Certificate exams. It's even conceivable that the briefcase or suitcase that keeps cropping up was originally a secret, treasured repository for his writing in Trinidad.

What is known for certain is that none of this early writing has survived. Whether it included juvenilia from McBean, or consisted solely of writing from the first two years in Toronto, it all went down a garbage chute in the fall of 1970. The torrent of fiction that ensued – the only writing of his that has survived – was composed in a single three-year span, 1970-1973.

Several stories from that period offer a parallel to Harold's experience in moving to Canada. There is often no way of knowing whether a given detail is autobiographical or invented. But in either case, the stories show his imagination engaging with the challenge of leaving McBean.

One such story is narrated by a character called Sohan Singh, who lives in a village called Tola.[3]

[…] At that time I was a labourer on Coolie Trace Sugar Estate. In preparation for Canada I had made two grey suits, because my brother in law had so advised, because grey can be worn for business, funerals or parties. There were good reasons for alarm. People in the village knew I was about to migrate to the whiteman's land. Worse yet, I had already given up rum. Sometimes in the rumshops peasants went mad with envy when I ordered whiskey instead of rum, and ate sandwiches instead of curried chicken and roti. Instead of listening to calypsos or East Indian music, I bought myself a stereo and spent hours listening to classical music. Dialect was below me, only proper English was used. Confident that I would be a Canadian soon, I stopped talking to most people in the village.

So when I couldn't get a letter from Canada I felt terrible. One day I went to Tolaville Post Office to inquire whether they had any letters for me. I was doing this because the postman who brought letters to Tola was in the habit of stealing letters. The postman lived in Rajput Road and once he tried to get into Canada but failed to make an impression on the Canadian officials as a desirable alien. Since that happened he became a strong threat to potential Canadians from the Tola district. Visas, letter of invitation, almost anything that came into his hands were destroyed. Aware of the maladministration on the island, nobody cared a damn about what the nut was doing. So one morning I walked to the post office to inquire. A burly Negress, racism written on her face, said, "Wot you want?"

"I wonder if you have any letters for me. My name is Sohan Singh."

"It have no letters for you here."

"Can you still check?"

"Why?" And there was a stare in her face that suggested ultimate bigotry, hatred, insanity – all in one.

"Because you are a government worker."

"You must be tink de govament care a blasted ting about Indians, nuh. Look boy, is niggers who have de govament in power, yeh. But who you tink you is, comin here and talkin to me like dat."

"Coolie," a slender negress murmured from somewhere in the prison-like post office.

"Niggers!" I shouted, running out of the post office almost in tears.[4]

Since I had already left the work on the sugar plantation, I decided to try something. Taking a taxi, I went to Spanish City to send a cable to Canada. The taxi driver drove like the other motorists – madly.

On the way to the city I had glimpses of people walking barefooted; neighbours fighting; government workers in charge of road projects and electricity playing cards under the trees; dead dogs being ripped by vultures on the roadside.

An hour later I was in Spanish City, the capital of the island. Quickly I walked to the Cable and Wireless Office. There were clerks of many ethnic origins, but Negroes formed the majority. Judging from what I had planned to put in the telegram, I chose a clerk of East Indian descent. She gave me a form and I worded the telex carefully. It read:

"*Send plane ticket immediately before I commit suicide. Ma and Pa threatening to marry me to a nigger girl.*"

When I handed the Indian clerk the message she was speechless. I paid her and rushed out of the building.

For two days I didn't venture out of my room. People were making fun of me. Our neighbour was in the habit of saying to my mother, "Wot about you Canadian son, like he gone Canada aready."

On the third day there was a miracle. A cable came that read: *Collect ticket in Air Canada office. Fly Saturday morning at 9.15 am. We'll be waiting at airport. Good luck. Sawak.*

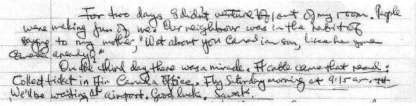

*The last two paragraphs of Sohan's story, in Harold's manuscript.*

Welcome to Harold Sonny Ladoo the writer.

Here I am using Harold's writing to tell his story – or at least, to give a fictional parallel to it. In the absence of a diary, journal, or any other direct account of his experience, I've turned to his surviving manuscripts. But this raises a tangle of questions. At what points in the stories was Ladoo depicting his own life? And when was he simply telling a good yarn, perhaps with a few autobiographical elements? It's often impossible to know – as it is with any fiction writer. But there's a separate question as well, having to do with the manuscripts themselves. When Ladoo died, he left unpublished drafts of a number of stories and novels or novel fragments. What biographical clues did these contain? Furthermore, many of the surviving pieces appear to be first drafts, and there's no way of knowing whether, or how, Harold would have revised them. So, we're left guessing at his final intentions.

Even so, the story featuring Sohan Singh has several features worth exploring. One is Ladoo's distinctive way with narrative. He often presents the action in cinematic terms, as if it was unfolding in the medium of film.

Consider the trip to Spanish City. Harold doesn't spend time on elaborate descriptions of the scenes Sohan encounters, as the 19th-century novel and its inheritors would have done. Instead, in the space of one short paragraph, he gives us a picture of the entire journey – or rather "pictures" of the journey, like a series of still frames, a montage:

> On the way to the city I had glimpses of people walking barefooted; neighbours fighting; government workers in charge of road projects and electricity playing cards under the trees; dead dogs being ripped by vultures on the roadside.

There's a similar cinematic montage effect in the opening paragraph, where Sohan caroms from tailor to rumshop, to a store to buy a stereo, to the confrontation at the post office. Also worth noting is that, although Ladoo is writing about experiences he may have shared with Sohan Singh, Sohan is not idealised; his negative characteristics are not glossed over. I am tempted to suggest that, writing some five years after his own departure from McBean, Harold was looking back and recognising what an unsympathetic character he was. The sulky, pretentious Sohan is not an attractive figure. But in his frenzy to get out of Tola, his hyperactive trajectory, he keeps us fascinated. Ladoo's ability, in his fiction, to look at his own faults objectively, even critically, is a mark of his commitment to serious writing. It's a quality that emerges often in his fictional treatment of characters that may be based on Rachel and his relationship to her.

Another feature of the story is its depiction of Harold's home turf. Once he recognized that he was a storyteller rather than a poet, he set out to create an entire mythic history and landscape, based on the places where he grew up. We can see the outlines of this invented geography in the Sohan story. McBean becomes Tola (or sometimes Curry Tola).[5] The area around McBean is Tola District (later Karan Settlement). Couva becomes Tolaville, Port of Spain is Spanish City, Trinidad is Carib Island. And this is not just a matter of changing the place-names. In Ladoo's vision "Tola" becomes something wilder, more intense, more primal than the village of McBean. When he left Trinidad in August 1968, he brought McBean with him – later to reinvent it in the mythic guise of "Tola". It was the same impulse that led to Faulkner's Yoknapatawpha County, and García Márquez's Macondo.

To continue with Harold's fictional account of leaving McBean, consider another novel fragment.[6] There are some changes of detail; the young man leaving for Canada is now called Sawak, and he has a wife and children who see him off at the airport. But the basic story-line is the same, so that this fragment is the closest thing we have to a "Portrait of the Artist as a Young Immigrant" that must be emotionally congruent with Ladoo's experience, if not a literal account.

Walking across the Tarmac towards the plane, Sawak enters a traveller's limbo. As he climbs the steps to the plane he pauses at the top, turns, and looks back at the distant figures waiting to see the plane depart:

Standing on the platform he looked back at the raggedness of the landscape, and felt somehow that the island was going to be incomplete without him. Frantic he gazed at the restless crowd jumping and chattering like monkeys behind the wire-netting fence. Realising that he had forgotten or perhaps neglected to say goodbye to his wife, he gazed at the crowd. Here and there he saw a hand. Once he thought he saw her, but it was not her. Sucking in his breath he groaned aloud. Wishing to have no more to do with that jeering crowd, he turned and entered into the aircraft. As the first time on an airplane, he was nervous. Sweat and coconut oil were forming a lump around his neck. A tall full breasted Canadian blonde who spoke English with a French accent looked at his ticket. "Go right to the end of the plane, Sir."

Her voice was full of music; it sounded [...].[7] Looking at her breasts, he muttered, "Thank you."

With a broad smile on his face, he journeyed to the last seat. Sitting down he took out his kerchief and wiped his face. The Negro girl sitting next to him put on a sour face, and Sawak wondered if he was smelling bad.

Once the plane was in the air, it was easy. Opening his briefcase, he fished out a copy of the Bhagavad Gita. It was a gift from the Pundit of Las Salinas. The Gita was the word of God, yet he was afraid to read it. In fact he was more embarrassed than afraid. Putting back the Gita into the brown brief[case] he gazed at the clouds; disrupting the scrutiny of space only when one of the white hostesses drifted carelessly to the tail-end of the plane.

— "New Novel" or "1st Canadian Novel", 1973.

As raw as this initial draft may be, it captures a combination of insecurity and insubordinate self-awareness that feels characteristic of Ladoo's writing. And it prompts questions. Sawak has the Hindu holy book in his briefcase, though he's embarrassed to be seen reading it. Did Harold have the *Gita*, or even his own poetry, in *his* case? And is there a hint of irony in the "Thank you" and the "broad smile" Sawak gives the hostess? Is it relief and joy at being virtually in Canada, or is he irked that she sends him to the last seat on the plane?

Sawak encounters this foreign world on a more official level when, on arriving at the Toronto airport, he faces an immigration officer:

The immigration officer was white, tall, partly grey, and he had reddish, catlike whiskers. A cap sat on his head comfortably and the emblems on his jacket looked expensive. His gait proclaimed his importance. "Follow me"

Sawak followed.

He was delivered into the hands of a short fat officer. The fat one had an office for himself. Taking his passport he said, "Welcome to Canada Mr. Sawaywak."

"Thank you sir."

The officer waddled torturously and shut the door. Sitting on a chair, he said, "There are some formalities Mr. Sak. Medical examination for instance. Did you submit medical reports?"

"Yes Sir. I had received my visa only because my medical report had been satisfactory."

"Well... Wot is your name again?"

"Mr. Sawak."

"Well, Mr. Sakak, you will have to be re-examined."

"How long would it take Sir?"

"About three to four hours Mr. Sakytak."

Exhausted and sick, Sawak took out a bottle of rum and placed it on the well-polished desk. With unbelievable swiftness the fat white hand swept the bottle off the table, and hid it inside a drawer.

"All right Mr. Bak. Your passport please."

LANDED IMMIGRANT was stamped firmly.

— "1st Canadian Novel", 1973.

This scene is like a cartoon in its crude, satirical comment on corruption and the mistreatment of a helpless immigrant. Since it is from a draft manuscript, there's no way of knowing how Harold would have adjusted it in the final work. But we may take it as an expression of resentment at the treatment he may well have received or knew of. Harold Ladoo was a recognisable and known figure in his own now far away village. But when Sawak presents himself to the foreign (white) power, embodied in the immigration officer, he realises that his status has drastically altered. He is now an outsider, existing only at the discretion of Canadian officialdom. Ladoo's treatment of Sawak's encounter with the immigration officer resembles his treatment of Sohan's encounter with the postmistress, exercising her bureaucratic power to discriminate against him.

So in August 1968, just a few days after getting married, Harold and his new bride escaped what he saw as his fate: the petty, oppressive and ultimately vicious world of McBean. Harold was single-minded in his determination to escape and make something of himself. But while he was able to physically escape McBean, no matter what fortune had in store for him in Canada, he carried the place with him in the mythic form of Tola. And he could not escape the fate he feared.

Some inkling of this was not lost on Sawak's wife. In a scene just before Sawak walks across the Tarmac to the plane, his wife senses the existential change he is undergoing as he ignores her, and moves through Departures. She turns to a bystander, and their conversation evokes the primal, larger-than-life reality that Harold was longing to escape, yet aching to depict – the curse of Tola.

"Like me husband feel he white," she said to the woman standing behind her.

"It look so gal," the woman said. Then she asked, "Which part all you from?"

"I from Clarkson Road. But me husban from Curry Tola."

"Well you have plenty trobble to see gal," the talkative woman prophesied.

"How?"

"De wost people on dis island is from Curry Tola. De riceland could never come from dem. Nastiness is in dey heart and dey soul. Believe me chile."

— "1st Canadian Novel", 1973.

Endnotes

1.  A bypass around the McBean section of the Main Road was built in the late 1940s, and became infamous as the "McBean Stretch", the only straight section of the road. This encouraged speeding, and consequently fatal accidents. As Harold wrote in his second novel, *Yesterdays,* "Twenty people had been killed on one spot within 15 years." This is where Rachel's second husband was killed and where Harold's body would be found on the morning of August 17, 1973.

2.  Rachel Ladoo, in an interview with Ramabai Espinet and the author in 2002.

3.  This story comes from a fragment of a proposed novel, titled "New Novel". The manuscript is a handwritten draft of three pages, undated but written in the early 1970s.

4.  In Trinidad, the terms "nigger" and "coolie" carry an historical charge that is unique to the territories that instituted Indian indentureship. After white plantation owners could no longer use Afro-Trinidadians as slaves, they began importing East Indians as indentured labour. These two oppressed groups vented their resentment and rage by maligning each other as "niggers" and "coolies". Harold depicts their trash-talk as an everyday fact of life. In the narrative voice, by contrast, he uses the terms "Negro" and "Negress."

5.  "The Hindi 'tola' means 'quarter' or 'section' of a larger whole. Giving the entire district the name Tola thus indicates the minority status of the villagers in the society." Jassodra Vijay Maharaj, *A Caribbean Katha Revisioning the 'Indo-Caribbean' 'Crisis of Being and Belonging' Through the Literary Imagination.* PhD dissertation, University of the West Indies 2011. This quotation is taken from a longer discussion of Harold's work:

    The villages of central Trinidad grew out of indenture. Their locations derive from estates, and the barracks in which labourers were housed." And while many of Harold's characters may be based on McBean citizens he knew, they live their literary lives in all their existential starkness as vessels of history and indentureship.

6.  The following excerpts come from a 15-page handwritten manuscript, with the notes: *"1st Canadian Novel" to be worked later"* and *"This novel to be worked later 3.3.73."* The notes are dated 3.3.73, but the manuscript itself was most likely written earlier.

7.  Word indecipherable in Harold's handwriting.

# CHAPTER THREE
## TORONTO: MAGNIFICENT CAPTIVITY

"Man, in Toronto a man have to move he tail and look for someting to do."[1]

So far I've refrained from conjectures about what Harold "would have thought" about this, or what he "must have felt" about that. But it isn't hard to imagine his first response to seeing Toronto, in August 1968. As their plane crossed Lake Ontario and began the descent to what was then Toronto International Airport, he and Rachel would have devoured their first glimpse of the city. It was a daunting, yet exhilarating prospect.

In Harold's fictional account of the descent, his *alter ego* Sawak declares, "At 16,000 feet, Toronto and the suburbs blossomed. [...] What could be more pleasant than to look down on the city [I] had dreamed?"[2] But as Harold and Rachel descended further, the vista would have become less idyllic. There were so many buildings, strangely similar, laid out in right-angled grids that stretched for miles till they reached the skyscrapers downtown. People like ants all jammed together, piled on top of each other – so unlike the village they'd left that morning. How could anyone live this way? They were about to find out.

Harold's eldest sister Sylvia and her husband Maniram Sookram had moved to Canada some years before; Sylvia worked in a bank, and Maniram was an engineer. They were sponsoring Harold and Rachel as landed immigrants. The couples met at the airport and taxied together into downtown Toronto – passing sights that, till then, Harold had seen only in movies: cars driving on the wrong side of the road,[3] throngs of white people bustling along the sidewalks.

Toronto at ground level was nowhere near as inviting as it was at 16,000 feet. At least not at 15 Belshaw Place, the dilapidated high-rise where Harold and Rachel would live during their first year in the city. They were crammed into an apartment with Sylvia, Maniram and their five children.

Their new home was a 14-storey tower in Regent Park, a huge public housing project. It occupied 69 acres in the eastern part of Old Toronto, replacing a large portion of a blighted area known as Cabbagetown.

*15 Belshaw Place, where Harold and Rachel lived with Harold's sister Sylvia. (Now demolished.)*

*Regent Park, looking southwest to downtown Toronto and Lake Ontario. 15 Belshaw Place is in the middle ground – the tower furthest to the right.*

Historically one of the poorest neighbourhoods in the city, Cabbagetown had been settled in the 19th century by Irish immigrants (who prompted the area's nickname by planting vegetables in their front yards). After World War I, the district became even more depressed, succumbing to squalor and crime. After World War II, the City decided to "clear the slums", bulldoze a sizable part of Cabbagetown and build a "Garden City" in its place, with pastoral green spaces, and pathways for residents to stroll. Housing was reserved for low-income tenants, with a mix of high-rise apartments and walk-up townhouses. There was no provision for stores,

restaurants, or recreational facilities within the project. In 1948, construction on Regent Park began, but by the late 1960s, when Harold and Rachel
arrived, it had become one of the most notorious slums in the country,
reproducing the very problems it was meant to solve:

> By the mid-1960s, for example, there were complaints about the housing
> projects falling into a state of disrepair. [...] Immigrants from the Caribbean,
> China and Southeast Asia settled in Regent Park in the 1960s and 1970s,
> changing the ethnic and racial composition of the neighbourhood.
> Meanwhile, the area continued to have a reputation for crime.[4]

A more graphic description appeared in *Maclean's* magazine in 1989.
Though twenty years after Harold and Rachel lived there, the lurid details
had changed little:

> A white Plymouth Caravelle [...] pulls into Belshaw Place, which cuts
> an arc through the dingy towers of Regent Park. [...] The driver is Constable
> Bruce Kane, 31, a dark-haired, 10-year veteran of the force. Kane admits
> that the squalor of his beat is depressing. He talks about finding putrefying
> corpses in flophouses, about 15-year-old prostitutes victimized by pimps,
> about drug addicts, drunks, purse-snatchers and parks littered with
> unconscious winos.[5]

Without realising it, Harold and Rachel had signed on for a crash course
in down-and-out Toronto.

There is no first-hand account of Harold and Rachel's time in this part
of Toronto. But there is "1st Canadian Novel", the 15-page fragment from
1973, unpublished till now, where Harold recast and probably heightened
his own experience as a new immigrant through the character of his
protagonist and *alter ego*, Sawak. Unlike Harold, Sawak travels to Toronto
alone, and stays with a friend from the island, Sally Khan, who lives in a
squalid rooming-house with his wife. In this excerpt, Sawak awakens on his
first morning in Toronto to face a series of culture shocks. Here Sally Khan
is preparing eggs and slicing bread:

> Putting the fried eggs on two old plates he went to the rug on which
> Sawak was sitting, "Eat dis egg and dis bread. We had a toaster, but
> it not workin."
> Sawak was surprised. He had expected a heavy meal; rice and
> roti. As he ate the egg he missed home, especially his wife Indra.
> She had always fed him good. The egg tasted lousy.
> Khan said, "You have to get accustom to dis kinda food. Only
> people who have money could eat good in Toronto."
> "But you have some ketchup or something to put on de egg?"
> "Wot I go tell you boy Sawak? It hardly have anything to eat in

de house. Me wife workin in dat factory for just a little ting. She on dat factory job two months now. But de odder day somebody report she to immigration. People is some son of a bitches, boy Sawak. Just imagine, after ten years me wife have to hide from immigration! I can't work in peace no place. I always have to fraid."

"You will get ahead," Sawak said; "you just have to live wid a plan. Vishnu of Tola had a plan, you see how well tings moving wid him."

"Dat is different man. Vishnu of Tola come here as a landed immigrant. He had a good brain. He is a professor. But if he had to hide from immigration, you tink he coulda make anything?"

"Perhaps not," Sawak admitted.

After they were finished, Khan carried the plates and put them in the sink.

Walking back to the rug with two pieces of board, he said, "Help me kill some cockroach nuh boy."

They began by removing the rug. The floor had the odour of rotting vegetables. A few cockroaches were swatted with the flat boards. While they were still hunting down the cockroaches, the Italian landlord came up the steps. Without knocking or even calling, he walked right into the hall. A red glow on his face made him look formidable. He said, "Me want no noise! Oright! I spika before about noise! No spika again! You have one people stayin den you pay twenty-five dollar more. Pay tomorrow or get out"

Khan tried to explain about the cockroaches in the house. But the landlord said, "Dis is my house. You no like, den go. You pay one hundred five dollar or go. Me no spika again."

This was not a terrible scene for Khan. In his magnificent captivity he had met with more arrogance. Long ago he had learnt to exercise considerable patience in such situations.[6]

Harold's writing is replete with such cinematic images: comic, bizarre, but also serious and existential: two men, each holding a piece of board, squatting on the floor with the rug rolled back and swatting cockroaches (accompanied by loud bangs), with an Italian man standing over them, berating and threatening them. Their lives caught between the landlord and the cockroaches: lose-lose either way.

How was Harold to avoid Sally's "magnificent captivity"? Did he, like Vishnu of Tola, have a plan? Was he smart enough? First, he had to get work. Here's Sawak again, taking his first ride on a streetcar, as Sally Khan guides him to the employment office. It is Sawak's introduction to multicultural Toronto.

Ear-splitting sounds rose up in the streetcar: Italian accents here; Portuguese gruntings there; Greek yakking here and there, and now and then a faint English voice came as the sound from a dying man. For Sawak this chattering sounded strange and wild. He had been accustomed to people speaking on buses back on the island but he understood what they said. For the first time he felt as if the city was conspiring against him.

"Dis is Parliament Street," Khan said. And a little later, "Yonge Street comin up. We have to get out to get de [subway] train."

Since Khan was at the other side of the seat he got out first. Sawak followed. A shrunken man with a consumptive face pushed Sawak. Turning back he heard the man muttering in a strange language. Once he came out of the streetcar, he felt free again.

"You have to walk fast in Toronto, the foreigners trample you," Khan informed him.[7]

It was Rachel, however, who quickly landed a job – as a waitress at a Howard Johnson's restaurant at Yonge and Dundas Streets. To get there from the apartment, she took the same route as Sawak and Sally Khan. Catching a westbound streetcar along Dundas, within five minutes she was at Yonge.[8]

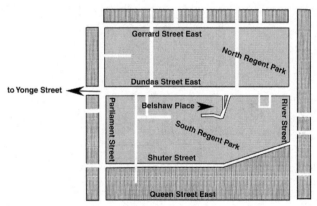

*Regent Park in 1968*

Rachel's hours at the restaurant were gruelling. She worked a double shift, from five in the afternoon till seven the next morning; she then returned to Belshaw Place and slept for part of the day. This would be her regular schedule for years to come. And so, shortly after their wedding, Rachel became the primary breadwinner in the family.

Finding a job was a lower priority for Harold, but he knew he had no choice. It's impossible to retrace all his attempts, but we learn of his eventual success from his youngest sister, Meena. She had come to Toronto before Harold and Rachel did, and it was she who found work for him – albeit in a lowly, part-time position – some time in 1968 or 1969.

*Christopher Laird:* So what was Harold doing in Canada at the time that you met him?

*Meena Ladoo*: Well, he had the desire to go to university. He was trying really hard to be able to do that, but in so doing I think he was meeting a lot of stumbling blocks because he was a very small [i.e. very thin] person, small built at the time. He had a hard time getting a job, a very hard time; as a matter of fact, when I met him he told me he was delivering handbills, trying to make ends meet. And I used to work in a restaurant at the time, a decent place, and I talked to the manager and asked her if she would give him a try but she was very sceptical – because he was so thin. Automatically when they saw him, they said, "Are you from India?" That would be the first response – Are you from India?

*CL:* And did they give him a try?

*ML:* Yes.

*CL:* So what restaurant was that again?

*ML:* Fran's.[9]

*CL:* What was he doing there at Fran's?

*ML:* Well when he first got the job like I said they were sceptical. He said, "Anything, give me anything to do and I'll do it; it's survival." So they said, "Okay, we need somebody to do the dishes, clear the tables and stuff like that." He started from there and I think by the time he leave them he was a cook.[10]

Rachel confirmed this story in an interview in 2003:

*Ramabai Espinet:* What was his plan to come to Canada? What did he want to do when he came to Canada?

*Rachel Ladoo*: He didn't talk about any plans, he just say he will get a job but then he started writing the scripts in his book and those things, and so he started writing.

*RE:* Was he writing at home?

*RL:* I haven't got any idea.

*RE:* Okay, tell us about the work. You were working a double shift?

*RL:* Yes, I worked from five [p.m.] to seven in the morning at Howard Johnson's [...].

*RE:* And he was working too?

*RL:* I don't think he was working at that time. After, he was working like dishwashing, a short order cook, but not for long.

*RE:* Where?

*RL*: At Fran's restaurant, part-time I think [...].

*RE*: And the rest of the time what did he do, write?

*RL*: He write and I think [later] he was going to school, but I don't know when exactly he started school.[11]

If Rachel's memory serves, in this and other interviews, Harold worked three or four-hour shifts, up to five days a week as a part-time busboy, dishwasher, and eventually short-order cook. And that, along with his previous odd jobs, appears to exhaust his work history in Toronto. There's no doubt that Harold had a ferocious work ethic but he applied it only selectively to earning a living. Once Rachel had a full-time job, and he had these sporadic shifts at Fran's, his interest in gainful employment seems to have faded.

Meena referred to his desire to go to university, and that's entirely credible. But when she spoke of him "trying really hard to be able to do that", she was talking about his attempts to find a job – which would help pay for university. But there's no evidence that Harold actively pursued that goal; it's as if he was in a passive holding pattern – waiting for some external agent to make his dream of going to university happen.

A more active concern for him was writing and reading. He had come to a city rich in bookstores, with a strong public library system. New writers and publishers were emerging. And while lack of money was an obstacle to buying books, his obsession with reading made it likely that he tapped into these new resources one way or another, but there is no direct evidence of that, nor of what specific directions his reading in Toronto took.

As for writing, we know from Rachel's tart comments that it was Harold's activity of choice. And at this stage, "writing" meant writing poetry. Two years later he would show his new friend, Peter Such, a large batch of work, most of which was verse. And his first submission to a publisher would be a poetry manuscript.

But that lay in the future. From 1968 to 1970, there's no sign he had found anyone to give him feedback on his work – let alone anyone who was also trying to write. He was on his own. Such isolation isn't unusual for an apprentice writer, but it was definitely part of Harold's experience. Meanwhile, a more clandestine apprenticeship was occupying his attention.

When the city's planners laid out the future Regent Park, it wasn't designed to replace the whole of Cabbagetown (which in any case had blurry borders). To the north, Regent Park ended at Gerrard Street – leaving intact the then tawdry neighbourhood running further north. And to the west along Dundas, the nine-block strip between Parliament and Jarvis remained a slum as well. The main streets in this latter section were a jumble of bargain stores, pawnshops, taverns, strip joints and by-the-hour hotels, with narrow, decaying rowhouses on the sidestreets.

  This part of the older slum played a vital role in Harold's imagination –
not to mention in his daily and nightly outings. It is true that his actual
dwelling was in the badlands of Regent Park. But that was a sterile, socially-
engineered milieu, with no restaurants or bars to hang out in. He would
write some powerful stories set in Toronto, but none of them takes place
in Regent Park. What fired him up was a different cityscape: the unplanned,
sleazy, pulsating, sometimes dangerous turf he could reach by walking the
few steps to Dundas, turning left, and heading west to Parliament Street.
Beyond that lay a world that a seething twenty-three-year-old, already
prone to imagining extremes and just released from a rigidly-disciplined
family in a faraway village, had only dreamed of till now.
  He took to it like a longtime denizen.

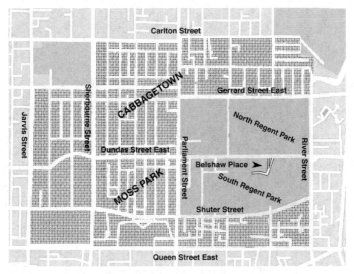

*Regent Park, with the remnants of South Cabbagetown, in 1968*

  In that first year, in a lowly part-time job with plenty of time on his
hands, Harold must have felt the need to get out of the apartment since
Rachel, working nights, slept during the day. So, when not doing his part-
time job at Fran's, we assume that he either wrote or walked the streets and
hung out with new-found friends and acquaintances, many of them fellow
Trinidadians and West Indians, also hustling to find their way in the big
city. His sister Sylvia had sponsored Harold and Rachel's landed-immi-
grant applications, so they were in Canada legally, but some of the West
Indians in the area were illegals, overstaying on a temporary visa – as was
the fictional Sawak. They lived in fear of immigration officials:

> There were thousands of West Indians like him; people living under
> the dreadful eyes of Immigration and informers; people who were
> determined to stay alive in Bathurst Street and Parliament Street and

meet now and then in some dilapidated tenement and sip a beer to feel alive.[12]

It's not hard to imagine Harold wandering the mean streets day and night, an anonymous loner exploring the seedy environment to the west with its strip clubs and hookers, taverns and bargain stores, peopled with immigrants like him.[13] Fascinated though he was by the dynamics of this new "village," however, he must have wondered how he was going escape the dead end he found himself in his "magnificent captivity." Magnificent, in that he was in the huge modern city he'd dreamed of, which, if not paved with gold, at least offered him tantalizing possibilities that would never have come his way in the traces of McBean. But captivity, in that he was stuck at the bottom of the heap, with no obvious way to clamber out.

Harold had arrived in Toronto in summertime, but by the second winter, walking the icy, colourless city as a biting wind mercilessly probed his vulnerability, thousands of miles from Carli Bay, the question must have bubbled up almost without bidding, "What the hell am I doing here?"

A couple of years later, he would attempt to recapture his earlier state of mind in a draft short story, albeit in prose of the deepest purple:

For days, I drowned the city in wine and watched the night dreaming of blood. Sitting on the grey concrete steps of the flat I eavesdropped the conversation of walkers. At times I re-smoked the cigarette butts, stupefied by the past. Bleeding and blinded by wine I felt the night dying to the echoes of my dreams and with shouts and drunken regrets I used to lift my fists to the sky.[14]

Endnotes

1. "New Novel" or "1st Canadian Novel," January 1973.
2. Ibid.
3. Traffic in most formerly British colonies, including Trinidad & Tobago, drives on the left.
4. The problems were so acute that, starting in 2006, Regent Park would be demolished and rebuilt once again. In the process, 15 Belshaw Place and Belshaw Place itself would disappear. Because Cabbagetown is not an official district or ward, there has never been agreement on where its boundaries lie. Here I follow the rough consensus that prevailed in the 1960s (leaving the northern border undecided). For Harold, of course, the matter was of no concern.
5. "Patrolling the Night," *Maclean's*, 9 January 1989.
6. "New Novel" or "1st Canadian Novel" January 1973.
7. Ibid.
8. Yonge Street (pronounced, "Young Street") runs north from Lake Ontario. First laid out in the 1790s, it serves as a central artery in the Old City, with a subway line running beneath.
9. Fran's was a 24-hour eatery on College Street, just west of Yonge. College was the first subway stop north of Dundas. Both Howard Johnson's and Fran's had several restaurants in Toronto, and Rachel and Meena have conflicting memories as to which Howard Johnson's Rachel worked at (and likewise with Harold and Fran's). On balance, it seems most credible that Rachel's long-term job was at the downtown Howard Johnson's (at Yonge and Dundas), and Harold's at the Fran's at Yonge and College.
10. Interview with Meena Ladoo/Jagroop by Christopher Laird, 2003
11. Interview with Rachel Ladoo by Ramabai Espinet, April 2003
12. "New Novel" or "1st Canadian Novel" January 1973.
13. The area of Regent Park and Cabbagetown became Harold's adopted 'hood'. Not only did he live there for fourteen months with his sister and family, but his half-brother Cholo later opened a grocery store nearby.
14. "The Agony", short story June 1972

## CHAPTER FOUR
## TWO FROM THE HOOD

"He would have created a haunting city: gritty and unforgiving and unforgettable."
— Rabindranath Maharaj

Despite the suggestion of operatic despair in some of the unpublished Toronto fiction, Harold clearly relished this neighbourhood of immigrants and hustlers, con-men and hookers. It became his new village, offering anonymity and the chance to live by his wits – a far cry from the suffocating embrace of McBean, and the ironclad rules of his father.[1]

The novelist Rabindranath Maharaj conjures a potent image of Harold on his new turf:

> One imagines him prowling along the dark corners of Regent Park and Parkdale and St. Jamestown in the evenings, gazing at the grindhouse theatres and massage parlours on Yonge Street and the row houses on Queen and Sherbourne; writing his observations late into the night at the Edgewater or Elm Grove taverns. He would have created a haunting city: gritty and unforgiving and unforgettable.[2]

I have discovered no writing by Harold from the period 1968-1970 (for reasons that will become clear in Chapter Seven). But during those years he was soaking up background and atmosphere, which he would put to use when he moved from poetry to fiction. And among the unpublished manuscripts from 1970-1973 that have survived, there's a group of six stories and a novel fragment which do "create a haunting city".[3] It's the low-life Toronto he'd landed in, with its immigrants and prostitutes, its taverns and rooming houses and loneliness – lit up by the characters' creole, which ripples and skitters through the often squalid action, creating a nimble, vibrant counterpoint.

Two of these stories were written in dialect (unlike the other four) and are set on the familiar turf of the Cabbagetown slums, just west of Regent Park. In the first story, "Lying Munroe", the unnamed narrator is mainly an observer, and only tangentially a direct participant in the action.

## LYING MONROE

From the time I living in Toronto I see a lot of things. It have a young East Indian fellow from Guyana call Monroe. Well I get to know Monroe through my Guyanese friend call Joseph. Monroe was a nice looking boy when he first came to Toronto, but now he tail in real trouble with the syphilis he get from Laura. It really hard to see how that boy life finishing just like that in this city. But Monroe is not the kind of person to feel sorry for. Look man, Monroe come from a real classy family in Georgetown. Back in Guyana the boy had a good start. Plenty times he make the Guyanese cricket team when they came to play Carib Island. He was an all-rounder; he coulda bowl and bat good. One time it had a rumour that he was going to get pick on the West Indies team to play Test cricket against England. Perhaps he woulda make the side, because a good batsman like Kanhai come outta Guyana. But Indian parents kinda funny especially when it come to sports. Monroe parents had some good cash in Guyana. Instead of encouraging the boy to play good cricket, they put him in a plane and send him up to Toronto with the hope that in a few years he woulda make a doctor or a lawyer. There is where they make their first big mistake.

Joseph say when Monroe first came to Toronto, he start living in hotels and thing. Well after some time, he money run out. Then he write to Guyana for some money. He didn't get a cent from he family, because like they figure out that he was just playing the fool in Canada. Suddenly a period of catch arse getta hold of Monroe. It was then he start looking for West Indians; all the time he didn't even think a little bit about the darker races. So he inquired and thing until he reach in Parliament Street home by Joseph and them. Well you know how West Indians heart kinda soft. Instead of letting Monroe drift in Toronto, they give him free board and lodging till he coulda get a work or something.

Every morning Monroe used to get up early and walk through the cold looking for work. Well you know how Toronto is a funny place to look for work in Canada, especially when you see the ice start coming down heavy in the winter. For weeks Monroe beating the cold looking for job. Anywhere he went they just make him full out forms, telling him they don't want nobody, but if they want somebody they going to contact him. Soon as Monroe reach in the house, he sitting down by the telephone, hoping to God some white bossman could phone and give him a job. Then a time reach so that it looked as if he woulda never get a work. But man does born with their own luck. Suddenly Monroe luck strike, and strike real big too. Some white people really good yes. One day a white fellow phone up Monroe and call him in a metal company. Just like that the whiteman take a liking to the boy, and give him a work as a welder. Well Monroe didn't know from he arse to he elbow in welding, but he start off welding. Eventually he learn to weld good. From there miracles start working; not too long after Monroe come a foreman in the place. Well when Monroe start making good money he leave Parliament Street. Not one day Monroe ever take it in he head to give Joseph a ring. Just like that a rumour start; West Indians saying how Monroe is a big shot; he buy big house in Toronto and married some rich arse white girl.

One Saturday night me and Joseph was sitting down in Abattoir Hotel in Parliament Street drinking some drafts. Joseph start telling me how this Monroe is a real ungrateful man. Just as he was talking Monroe walk in the hotel with this white chick. For shame sake, Monroe come by the table and talk a little bit. He introduce she as a Jew girl. But I find something looking funny with the girl. It was the black purse she had around she shoulder and the way she eyes was moving sharp all over the place. Then again she was blond. Well I make up me mind; after all me and Monroe was no good friend, I just happen to know him because of Joseph. So I ask Monroe if the girl he with was not Laura, the girl who make Hanso from Carib Island nearly make a jail in Toronto. My Jesus Christ, soon as I say that, I sorry like hell. Monroe get in a high horse. He want to fight, telling me how I like bacchanal, and getting he girl mix up with some other hooker. Joseph, he want to keep everything quiet, so he stop we from getting on with each other.

Some people really boldface yes. Monroe sit down on the chair and watching we in we face he start lying. He say how he married this Jew girl out in Rexdale, but he like this blond girl he with. Then Laura start lying too, saying how she like Monroe and she have she Bachelors Degree from the University, and how she going to get she PhD and thing. But every now and then Laura getting up to go in the washroom and on she way back she talking to the men and them who having they drafts. Some of the guys running their hands around she waist and thing. Soon as Monroe figure out that me and Joseph taking a note of what going on, he start lying in another direction. Sipping he beer he say how Laura was writing a book, I think he say a novel or some kinda nonsense like that. To tell the truth he get me and Joseph like two arses believing him about this book and thing. Right away we start feeling glad: so long we was in Toronto and we never lucky to meet somebody with good education and writing a book too besides. By the time Monroe and Laura leave the hotel they was kinda drunk.

Same night me and Joseph decide to trail them. We follow them down Parliament Street, then Dundas Street till they reach Ontario Street. They head up Ontario Street and gone inside one of them old house. Since it was night and we couldn't buzz no doorbell and thing, we gone back in Parliament Street. As it was a Saturday night, I decide to stay over by Joseph and have a few beers with him, and play a few games of card.

Well a little after daybreak on Sunday morning, me and Joseph gone down Ontario Street and buzz the doorbell. A fattish looking middle age Polish woman come outta the house, asking we what we want. We tell she how we have a coloured friend from Guyana living over at she. She ask how he name and we tell she he name. So we gone up the steps and knock on the door. Who woulda open the door but Mr. Monroe in person. From the time he see we, he face get small; he start stammering. Surprise write in big on he face, but just for the shameness he invite we in. To tell the truth the room was stinking; I don't think it have another West Indian in Toronto to keep a place nasty like Monroe. Dirty sheets on the bed; the pillowcases and them like they never see washing for years. In spite of the shame Monroe ask we if we want a beer. Before I coulda say yes, Joseph say he don't want no beer. So me and Joseph sit down on the bed; Monroe sit down on a old arse chair. All the time Monroe sitting down, he keeping he face on the floor, trying to hide he shame and work out excuses. To get a conversation rolling, I ask him where Laura gone. He say the girl he was with last night didn't name Laura. He say she name was Mitzi and she was German. Playing more vex than the law allow, he ask we in a rough voice how we find him in the house. Joseph tell him that we see him moving in the room from the road, so we come inside to see if was he in truth. Without any shame, the man start lying again. He say how he have this big job and he rich wife, but he does keep the little room, because some time he does want to make a little outside screw. According to him, he Jew wife was living a respectable kinda life in Rexdale, so he didn't want to do anything too much in the public to make she shame and thing. He say how she planning to give him a divorce and some money for settlement, so when he get he divorce, he going to marry Laura. Well I get vex right away, because in Toronto a West Indian not suppose to lie to another West Indian. Immediately I tell him that it was Laura who make Hanso loss he work the first night he even start working at the Manhunt Hotel. Who tell me to say a thing like that? Monroe get in a high horse and all that Joseph try to get him down he wouldn't come down. Like a gamecock he start he cursing and swearing and challenging me to fight. If I was back home, I woulda throw good lix in he tail, but Toronto is a place in which you have to play it cool. So I just hold down me temper and sit down.

Well these Europeans here with houses don't make no joke with coloured tenants. Stamping up the steps, the landlady come and say that we disturbing the peace, and she going to phone the police. Back on the island no landlord or blasted landlady can't talk so, not after a man paying rent to live in a place. But me and Joseph didn't want to talk to no policeman that Sunday morning, so we get outta the place quick as hell.

Not even a week later the news come out in the open. In the first place, Monroe never get no frigging job in no welding company. He didn't have no damn wife either. He was working as a security guard somewhere down in Rexdale and paying a little rent in Berkerley Street. Well these days with the syphilis eating him out, he does come by Joseph and them to play some cards. He seeing a East Indian doctor from Carib Island who have a little office in Bloor Street. The doctor is a nice fellow and he promise to cure Monroe crotch sickness, but even the doctor say that only a Obeah woman could stop Monroe from lying.[4]

"Lying Monroe" depicts a world of immigrants sharing accommodation, looking for work and trying to find their feet in a strange city. In this it echoes the Trinidadian Samuel Selvon's *The Lonely Londoners* (1956), which fifteen years earlier had done the same thing with postwar Caribbean immigrants in London.[5] One cannot read "Lying Monroe" without sensing the influence of both Selvon and V. S. Naipaul, who in their early work told stories of the colourful characters around them and the gap between their reality and how they presented themselves.[6] But Harold's "haunting city" was not populated solely by charming, idiosyncratic characters and fabulists. For him, the immigrant's life might be amusing, but it was also ruthless, duplicitous and sad.

Despite that difference, Harold was experimenting with the loose and playful storytelling he found in Selvon. Consider a typical passage from *Lonely Londoners*:

There was a fellar name Captain. Captain was Nigerian. His father send him to London to study law, but Captain went stupid when he arrive in the big city. He start to spend money wild on woman and cigarette (he not fussy about drink) and before long the old man stop sending allowance. Cap had a greenstripe suit and a pair of suede shoes, and he live in them for some years. He used to wash the clothes every night before he go to sleep, and when he get up press them, so that though he wearing the same things they always fairly clean. If he have money, he would get up in the morning. If not, he would sleep all day, for to get up would mean hustling a meal. So all day long he stay there in bed, not really sleeping but closing his eyes in a kind of squint. Come evening, Cap get up, go in the bathroom and look to see if anybody leave a end of soap for him to bath with. Come back, press the clothes and put them on, comb hair, blow the nose in the sink and gargle loud, watch himself in the mirror, and then come down the stairs to the dining room, wiping his face with a clean white handkerchief.[7]

Selvon showed that you could compose a whole novel from these, in the main, good-natured sketches. But his influence on other Caribbean writers went beyond that because he had pioneered a striking new narrative technique as well. When he started writing *Lonely Londoners*, he used an omniscient, third-person narrator to tell the story. At first, he had written the narration in standard English, using creole only for the dialogue of the West Indian characters. He was dissatisfied with the results, so he recast the narrative voice in modified creole too – and with that the book took off, both in the writing and in the reception it received.

I think I can say without a trace of modesty that I was the first Caribbean writer to explore and employ dialect in a full-length novel where it was used in both narrative and dialogue.[8]

In "Lying Monroe", Harold picks up on Selvon's innovation – using the rhythms and syntax of Trinidadian dialect in the narration, along with standard English vocabulary laced with creole slang. Elsewhere, he would go even further, giving the narrator a more raw and undiluted creole, in the confident and accomplished way that distinguishes his writing, and is more in tune with the post-1970 acceptance of creole in Caribbean literature.

At the same time, "Lying Monroe" doesn't go all the way with Selvon's innovation. It's true that the narrator writes in dialect. But that's because he's a West Indian himself – a minor character in the story, who witnesses Monroe's disgrace and describes it, first-person, in his natural idiom. It wasn't until *No Pain Like This Body* – his first novel – that Harold would adopt an omniscient, third-person narrator who writes in creole.

The intricate dance of influence and independence from earlier writers continues in the second Toronto story written in dialect, "Jametin Laura!"[9] Here we see Harold revelling in his own virtuosity with creole speech and his Trinidadian limer's humour. "Jametin Laura!" is a story about a prostitute. "Jametin" is obviously a reference to her being a prostitute, as in "jam it in," and the creole word for prostitute, "jamette".[10]

## JAMETIN LAURA!

My good God, Laura is too much of a wretch. A nice nice girl like she have crotch sickness. Dey say wen a man don't have too much education dat is a good ting, because ignorance is bliss or some kinda nonsense like dat. Well I leff de island good good and come to Toronto to better meself. From de time I reach, I start lookin for a good job, but good work hard like hell to get. Wen I couldn't do better I take dat work in Manhunt Hotel in Jarvis Street. Pappayuh, I know from back in de island dat hotel work is a commess kinda work, but wen you unlucky, you must catch you tail in one way or de odder. Me landlady in Berkeley Street nearly drive me crazy for dat three weeks rent I de owin' she. Man, in Toronto a man have to move he tail and look for someting to do. Here is not like back home where you coud jus go and tell somebody you hungry and dey go give you some food. Dat day I say lemme buy a papers and see how work lookin again. Just like dat I see a vacancy for a desk clerk. Well I didn't know me ass to me elbow in desk clerkin, but I decide to give it a try. To ask de landlady to use she phone wouda land me right in trobble, because de woman was cross too bad. So I gone in a phone booth and phone up de hotel. A man answer de phone. Right away he ask if I have experience. To say de truth I was a country bookie back home, but I tell de man I used to work in a hotel and ting back home. Surprising enuff, de manager tell me to come to work de same night. Glad like hell I gone home and whistlin and ting in me room. De landlady hear de whistlin and ting, so she ask wot happen to make me feel so nice. So I tell she about de work I get.

Right away she get in a high horse, saying how fust ting I have to do is to come up wid de rent. Since I know I had a work in hand, I bust a few cuss in she ass. Later in de evening I put on suit and ting and gone down de road. De manager was some kinda Jew man. Playin gentleman, he shake me hand and ting. While I talkin to him, I watchin in de road to see if I see any West Indian passin and ting, so dey coud see dat little me coud talk man to man wid a big manager. Well, I smoke a few cigars, just standin dere and searchin out de place. After a while, I take up duties at Manhunt Hotel. First night on de work, so I feelin good. De manager givin me bibbil, telling me how de work is decent and ting, and I believin de man. Den he say how it good for a coloured man to have a good work, because people does want to run dey mout on coloured people too blasted much. Yet I siddin down behine de desk wid someting on me mind. Just like dat me mind tell me to leff de work and go to hell outta de place. Man look, I console me mind dat I have a work and I not goin to leff de damn ting. But same night I get trobble in me tail.

De clerk on de afternoon shift sign off at 11.55 p.m. He even write a note dat say: *Quiet afternoon. No unnecessary occurrences, except two whores thrown out. Elevator out of order. One cook fired from the kitchen for stealing salmon steaks.* Five minutes after de clerk leff, I take up duties. From de time I see dat ting about jamets trown outta de place, I get kinda friken. But de manager tell me is notten to worry about. Since it was a Monday night it was really kinda quiet and nice. Man, see me sittin down behine de desk and turnin pages in de ledger like a big boy. Den again me ass start cuttin nail. In one page I read: *August 10th, Night shift. The police had been trailing a pusher from Buffalo. He had registered two days ago in this hotel as Mr Chris Robson. Police identified him as Mr John Anthony of Buffalo, ex-con. Bridie, stripper downstairs was his girlfriend. Police arrested both of them at four a.m.* Dis get me friken. Well I close de book and fold me arms. Shuttin everyting outta me head, I decide to work, because none of dat nonsense in de ledger didn't concern me anyways.

But curiosity is a funny ting. Makin up me mind, I open de damn ledger again. It read dis time: *Page 45, Night shift. Tonight two men came into the hotel and booked room 31, Later a caller from another room said that there was a fight in room 31. The police was called in. One of the men had tried to castrate the other with a broken bottle. They made an arrest.* Well I shut de book one time. Nearly twelve o clock in de night dis nice lookin gal walk up to de second floor. Man de music was blastin downstairs and dis chick come by de desk. De coat she had on was expensive like hell. Puttin on me best smile, I say, "May I help you, Miss?" Soon as I say it, I realise I make a mistake, because she had on a diamond weddin ring in she finger. Well I make a quick apology and ask she wot she want. She say she from New York and she want to book a room for de night. I put de ledger in front she and she sign: Mrs Laura S.A. Den I give she de key to room 30. She walk up de steps and gone in de room, because de elevator was outta order.

Now if I had experience I wouda go to show she de room, and ting, but I didn't know one ting about dat. Bacchanal start not too long after dat. A few minutes after midnight, a yong East Indian fella walk in de lobby. De way I see he face lookin soft, I say he eidder from India or Pakistan. But wen I talk to him, he say he from South Africa. Den he say he name Santosh Anand, and he is Laura husban. De son of a gun had on a fat weddin ring. Man I decide not to take too much chances. Right away I begin inquirin for de manager. A waiter say I can't see de manager, because de manager downstairs in de back room where de strippers and dem does change and ting. Bein as de manager was around and was de fust night I workin, I tell Santosh dat he wife in room 30.

Well he gone to look for she. About 1 a.m. Laura phone from upstairs, askin for a bottle of brandy, ten beers and a corned beef sandwich. Well I write down de order and start lookin for de night watchman, an old Yugoslavian guy. Macoman dat he was, I coudnt find him no place. Man I dash downstairs and I give de bartender de order me self. Settlin down by de desk I book a few more couples for de night, most of dem kinda drunk. Sometime later, Laura come down by de desk in a see-through nightgown, wid she tits and she reddish hairs showin. Befo I coud take in front, she take in front. Right away she ask about de tings she order. Kinda friken to lose de work, I tell she it was me fust night on de job and ting. Right away she get de upperhand on me. She say de manager is she oncle. Assness in me, I start beggin she to stay quiet. Soon, I get she to go upstairs and wait in de room. Downstairs everyting was quiet, and de bar was close up and de people gone. Well I lookin for de manager, and a bellboy say he sleepin wid a stripper in some room or de odder.

As I sit down again figurin out wot to do, two white fellas wid suit and ting come by de desk and ask wot room Laura in. I tell dem. To me surprise de fellas start walkin upstairs. Dotishness in me tail, I mark down in de ledger de tings Laura de order befo, and takin a spare key from de draw, I go and open de bar. Well I take de drinks upstairs and hand dem it by de door. Wen I reach downstairs dere was de Yugoslavian guy watchin me kinda funny. Right away I tell him how I was waiting for him all de time. To me face, de man start sayin how I tief drinks from de bar, and carry de drinks for a whore in room 30. Cut me no blood now. While I still trying to tell de night watchman wot happen, de manager reach. He face was blue. De manager and me gone upstairs and he open de room wid de spare key.

Well fust time I see dat. Laura stretch out on de floor naked, and dem three fellas feastin on de jamet. Man, de manager phone de police. To me good surprise, dey put me in de squad too. Pappayuh, in Tola I never put me ass inside a police car, so I was cuttin nail. De rest of de night pass me in jail. Next day de Magistrate in City Hall put me on bail and tell me to get a lawyer. Only a month I was in Toronto and I had to spend de rest of dat night in jail. Praise God for Legal Aid. Man, I hold a crackpot lawyer, wid Q.C. and dis kinda shit behine he name. Case call two times and de lawyer argue like a real pro. I get off widdout a conviction, but de Magistrate warn me good.

Dese days Laura still in Toronto jametin as usual. Now I is a dishwasher in Yonge Street in a little hamburger place. No more ambition to get good work wid me again. Even dese days wen I pass Jarvis Street and see de Manhunt Hotel me ass does cut nail. Laura is a bitch any how I tink about it.

Harold was experimenting with narrative personae, and in "Jametin Laura!" he settled on a stance he would utilise in his other Canadian stories. Gone is the arm's-length, amused observer of "Lying Monroe"; instead we hear the desperate and subversive protagonist, trying to finesse his way ahead but discovering that he is powerless against the entrenched interests that rule the world around him.

Through this beleaguered first-person narrator, Harold brings the outlook and textures of *noir* to the urban underworld his naive hero stumbles into. The *noir* genre in film and literature is characterised by its dark lighting, its seediness, its sense there is no exit. Characters are vulnerable individuals living in private desperation, small cogs in a corrupt, dangerous and greedy hustle of a world layered with lies.

I don't know if Harold had read such authors as Dashiell Hammett and Raymond Chandler who pioneered 'noir' in their writing or had seen the films that their fiction inspired, films like *The Big Sleep* and *The Maltese Falcon*. But the parallels are unmistakable. In his "gritty and unforgiving" world, his characters are never in control of the hostile forces around them. And that perception becomes a defining feature of his writing – not just in the mean streets of Toronto, but equally in the oppressive world of Tola. Such a grim world-view is in marked contrast to the "triumphant hero" movies and comics he devoured in McBean. Now his typical protagonist is often, as Raymond Chandler put it, "A dirty little man in a dirty little world."[11] Even in their moments of drollery (which he chronicles with zest), his Toronto stories portray a city drenched in *noir*.

These stories show Ladoo testing himself against some of the leading lights in Caribbean fiction – adopting their concerns and techniques but modifying them as his own instincts dictated. Until the publication of this book, however, this stage of his development has been invisible; none of the Toronto stories were published either during his lifetime, nor since his death. Critical engagement with his work has focused almost exclusively on the two published novels. These hitherto unknown writings expand the canvas on which to assess his growth and achievement.

At the same time, we have no idea how Harold viewed the Toronto stories. Did he consider them as separate and apart from the vast epic of

Tola and Carib Island which he seems to have envisaged as his life's work? Were they to play some part in the latter stages of the saga? Or was he uncertain of where, or whether, these stories would fit into the planned epic?

We do know from the fragments that remain that he intended at least one "Toronto novel". As in Selvon's *Lonely Londoners,* the same characters recur in his stories. And the creation of a novel from stories is something that Harold, a natural storyteller, would latch onto in his writing, as we shall see.

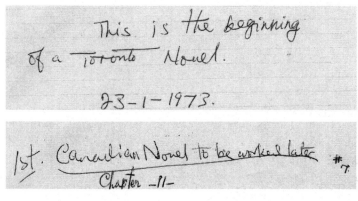

*Notes scribbled on surviving manuscripts of Toronto novel & Canadian novel*

At the very least, the Toronto stories – along with the other surviving material – give us a glimpse of the eruption that followed his turn to fiction. It's time to investigate what triggered that turn.

Endnotes

1. Of the five Toronto neighbourhoods Harold lived in, it was only the seedy Cabbagetown district that kindled his imagination. None of his later, more respectable residencies appear in his surviving fiction.
2. "Dark Imaginings – Harold Sonny Ladoo's *No Pain Like This Body.*" Rabindranath Maharaj, *Canadian Notes & Queries,* 50th Anniversary issue (# 103, Fall 2018).
3. The stories are titled "Lying Monroe", "Spadina Boardinghouse", "Jametin Laura!", "A Short Story", "The Teacher's Wife", and "The Agony". The novel fragment is "1st Canadian Novel". None have appeared in print till now.
4. "Lying Monroe" survives in a four-page typescript, dated 1 April 1973. (This may be the date it was typed up.)
5. It's likely that Harold was also influenced by the Barbadian/Canadian author Austin Clarke, with whom he corresponded. Clarke's collection of stories about Caribbean immigrants in Toronto, *When He Was Free and Young and He Used to Wear Silks,* was published in 1971 by the House of Anansi Press.
6. V. S. Naipaul's *Miguel Street* (1959), his most popular book in Trinidad, was a collection of stories about the characters who lived on the street where he grew up in Port of Spain.
7. *The Lonely Londoners* (London: Wingate, 1956),
8. *Tiger's Triumph: Celebrating Sam Selvon*, edited by Rutherford and Nasta (Hebden Bridge: Dangeroo Press, 1995).
9. "Jametin Laura!" survives in a five-page typescript, dated 1 May 1973.
10. One must not forget that Trinidadian "limer's" humour is never far from the surface with Harold.
11. Raymond Chandler, *Farewell My Lovely* (1940).

## CHAPTER FIVE
## AN HISTORIC ENCOUNTER

"So I said to him, 'Oh! I see you're a writer,' and he said,
'Well, I'm kind of trying to be.'"
— Peter Such, March 2003

After a year in Toronto, dependent on Rachel's earnings, his own part-time job and any other hustle he could initiate, Harold still hadn't found a path forward. He was no closer than before to continuing his education, let alone becoming a celebrated writer. And things were about to get more difficult.

By the summer of 1969, it was clear that Rachel was pregnant. Staying on at Belshaw Place, crowded in with Sylvia, Maniram and their children, was not an option, and in October they moved to an multistorey apartment building on Grandravine Drive in North York. It was an unlikely area to choose; North York was a sprawling suburb, and their new home was more than ten miles from Yonge and Dundas, where Rachel would return to work after her three-month maternity leave. Their son Jeoffery was born there on the 7th of January, 1970. Rachel went back to work at Howard Johnson's, probably in April, on the same double shift as before, and Harold was tasked with babysitting Jeoffery at night. But that didn't go well. Rachel describes her daily routine, and Harold's contribution to the baby's care:

*Rachel Ladoo*: Yeah, it was kinda hard for me.

*Ramabai Espinet*: Tell us about it, what was it like every day?

*RL*: Every day you had to go to work, come home in the morning, hustle, go back to work, a big responsibility for myself.

*RE*: You took on the responsibility.

*RL*: I had to, yeah [...].

*RE*: Did you talk about it?

*RL*: No, I never really, because I just never said anything. I just go to work and come home and that was it. We never really discuss it.

*RE*: But when the baby was born, how did you all deal with that?

*RL*: Who, Jeoffery? (sighs) Well, that's a big story by itself because I used to go work and I used to leave [Harold] to see Jeoffery at home, but he never stayed home and see him [i.e. look after him]. He used to leave him alone in the crib. When I come home in the morning Jeoffery was all messed up and his mouth was so dry and he was alone.

RE: Where did Harold go?

RL: I don't know where he used to go, I never used to be home. When I come home, he never home and Jeoffery was alone in the crib rocking himself to sleep, and he was thirsty, he was all in the dark, because I leave in the evening time, no lights on at that time.[1]

It's clear from this appalling account that Harold was completely unready for fatherhood, and had no intention of changing. Freed from the confines of a small rural village, he had barely begun to claim his independence from his own father, and sow his wild oats in Toronto. Now one guesses that he saw Rachel and the baby as trying to take that chance away from him – and he wasn't going to knuckle under. Ramabai asked Rachel, "Where did Harold go?" And we can surmise that he was with his new-found fellow villagers in Cabbagetown's taverns and strip joints, observing and writing, and spending the rest of each night in whatever sleeping arrangement presented itself.

Whether this occurred every night or more sporadically, it was an impossible situation and in the September of 1970, Rachel took drastic steps. She flew to Trinidad with Jeoffery to bring Debbie, her 8-year-old daughter, back to Toronto to help look after Jeoffery. They missed the return flight, however – and that accident would change Harold's life, and the history of Canadian/Caribbean literature.

★

The novelist Peter Such was born in England, and orphaned during the war. He came to Canada in 1953, at age fourteen, and his first novel was published in 1969 by the House of Anansi Press. Here he recalls his first encounter with Harold, sometime in the early fall of 1970:

I was writer in residence at the University of Toronto, Erindale College, and Erindale College is quite a ways out on the west side of the city. The subway is now extended much further, but in those days it stopped at Islington Avenue, and then they jumped on a bus, those kinds of express buses that went back and forth to the campus. So I'm there waiting for the bus along with tons of students, and sitting on a bench is Harold.[2]

Peter's memorial essay, "The Short Life and Sudden Death of Harold Sonny Ladoo",[3] gives a fuller account of coming upon Harold in the station. It includes the most graphic physical description of Harold that we have:

He was huddled in a cheap coat too large for him: black hair, thin dark face, small moustache, large dark eyes staring straight ahead, looking at somewhere else completely. I noticed he was jotting words down on the back of a TTC transfer. It could have been a shopping list he was writing, an address, anything. But I had a strange and certain feeling I knew what it was. I'd done exactly the same thing myself.[4]

Harold was coming home from the airport, where he'd discovered that Rachel, Jeoffery and Debbie were not on the Toronto flight. Now he was waiting to catch the bus back into the city – and, characteristically, writing obsessively on the first scrap of paper available. Peter takes up the story in the 2003 interview:

I was feeling like I needed to sit down, and so I sat down next to him. And Harold had this little brown suitcase on his lap and was writing and I assumed he was a student at first. And I looked over and I realised he was writing poetry, and being the writer in residence, you know, I wanted to encourage students to be writers and so I said to him, "Oh! I see you're a writer," and he said, "Well, I'm kind of trying to be."

I'm trying to remember what exactly he said because you know in my mind I've dramatised all this (laughs), and I then started talking to him about how I was writer in residence at Erindale College. I assumed he was a student and I said, "Well, you must drop into my office and bring your stuff and I'll have a look at it and we can talk about writing." Then he told me he wasn't a student but that he was very interested in being a scholar and a writer and that he had just come down from the airport where he had been waiting to meet his family and they hadn't arrived, and so he was going back [home] on the subway.

I said, "Oh!" and I kept talking to him about all this and I talked about Trinidad a little bit and so on. And I said, "Well, what are you doing? How are you working?" and he said, "Oh well, I got this crappy job," and I said, "You're obviously a literary person. Do you feel like you might want to go to university some day?" and that kind of thing. He said, "Oh, I'd love to go to university, but I can't afford it," and then he said, "I was a very good student in a United Church Mission School in Trinidad." And I said to him, "Well, if you're at loose ends, I'm just going out to Erindale College where I'm writer in residence," and that got things started. And I said, "Why don't you come out and I'll take you to the Faculty Club and we'll have lunch, and you can see what the university is like, etcetera."

So we went on the bus and I chatted on the bus with him and he opens his suitcase up and it's full of writing (laughs). And he asked what a writer in residence did, and I explained to him that I encourage people to write and he said, "Will you look at some of my stuff?" and I said, "Yeah, sure."

Anyway, we got there and we had some lunch and during the lunch along came Linda Webber, who at that point was the chief assistant at the registrar's office, and I introduced her to Harold and talked about Harold, and Harold was very literate, very charming. And in those days, it was a possibility for getting grants for students and Linda just said,

"Well, if I could get you a grant, maybe you'd like to be a student here,"
and within the next few days she gave him a lot of forms and things
and I suppose he filled them out, I wasn't there exactly, but a few days
later there he was and he was a student, and had got a grant (chuckles),
and started to get his B.A. Well, the rest is history (laughs).[5]

With this chance encounter, Harold's whole life changed. One minute
he was a part-time short-order cook with unrealistic dreams; an hour later
he was about to start university, and conceivably find his place in a vibrant
new literary milieu. It was almost too good to be true.


Endnotes

1. Interview with Rachel Ladoo by Ramabai Espinet, September 2002.
2. Interview with Peter Such by Christopher Laird, March 2003.
3. Peter Such, "The Short Life and Sudden Death of Harold Sonny
   Ladoo." *Saturday Night* (Toronto), 89, 5, 1974.
4. Interview with Peter Such by Christopher Laird, March 2003.
5. Ibid.

CHAPTER SIX
HAROLD AT UNIVERSITY

Harold was an adult among teenagers, an outsider who kept to himself,
his bearing mysterious and aloof.
— Randall McLeod, professor at Erindale College[1]

In September 1970, Harold Ladoo entered Erindale College as a mature
student, preparing to earn a three-year Bachelor of Arts degree, with a
major in English literature. Compared to the stalled energies of his first
two years in Toronto, these three years would come on like a hurricane;
so many developments took place at once that it's hard to keep up. This
chapter focuses on one element in the mix, his career as a university
undergraduate, but the extent of his growth becomes more visible in the
following chapter, which looks at his writing. What is quite astonishing is
that in addition to the degree and part-time work, Harold Ladoo wrote
the two published novels, at least a dozen short stories and fragments of
unpublished novels during this period.

Erindale College was a 'satellite campus' of the University of Toronto,
established only three years previously. Situated on 150 acres of farmland
along the Credit River, west of the city, it was a dynamic young institution,
which would be rebranded as the University of Toronto Mississauga in 1998.

As the transcript of his sojourn there shows,[2] Harold took six courses in
the first year (1970-71), and five courses per year after that. Concentration
on literature began in the second year.

Peter Such tells us that Harold was somewhat intimidated initially.
"Like many people who don't have 'college' as an accepted axiom of family
life, he had a very inflated view of the knowledge factory, and felt uneasy
about it at first."[3] He seems to have kept his head down that first year, played
by the rules, and performed more than acceptably. Here are the transcripts
from his first year:

```
LADOO  HAROLD SONNY                        703113665
               1 YEAR    1970-71
            FINAL AVERAGE       B
      ENG152   ENG CANADIAN LIT       B        75
      ENG218   MAJOR AMER AUTHORS     B        78
      HIS100   EUROPE & WLD 1789-96   C        64
      POL101   INTRO POL SCI          D        55
      REL230F  ROLES OF REL           A        85
      REL250S  TEILHARD DE CHARDIN    A        81

      PASSED
```

Harold got B's in his Literature courses, but did not do well in 18th-century History or in Political Science. The courses he did best in, Roles of Religion and Teilhard de Chardin, were essentially looking at existential, philosophical and religious questions.

Douglas Hill taught Harold on the American Literature course that first year. According to Hill, Harold was "an intense man with a strong commitment to his writing." He remembers Harold visiting him in his office while they were studying Faulkner. Harold told him, "Faulkner's pretty good, man, but I'm going to be better." Hill found this both amusing and exciting. He did not have many students who were so focused and determined.[4]

Overall, Harold's final average in first year was a "B."

Sometime in the fall of 1970, the Ladoos, with Rachel's daughter Debbie, moved from Grandravine to a second-floor apartment at 21 Roseneath Gardens. This was a semi-detached house in a middle-class neighbourhood, much closer to the centre of town (and to Erindale), which eased Harold's and Rachel's commuting.

*21 Roseneath Gardens (2021), where the Ladoos lived from fall 1970 to fall 1971*

With more convenient accommodation, and now settled into Erindale, Harold shone in his second year:

```
LADOO HAROLD SONNY                          703113665
      SECOND    YEAR    1971-72
            FINAL AVERAGE    A

   ENG212  SHAKESPEARE                    B       72
   ENG324  FICTION 1832-1900              B       75
   ENG328  MODERN NOVEL                   A       85
   ENG348  MODERN POETRY                  B       75
   ENG369  SEM IN WRITING                 A       91

PASSED
```

*Harold's grades year 2*

All five of his courses were now literary, and he did particularly well in the Modern Novel and the Writing Seminar. He scored a final average of "A". His trepidation about entering the halls of academe was a thing of the past. Even in his first year, Peter tells us, "he began to realise he was probably brighter and better read than anyone in his classes, including, in some cases, his professors." He made no effort to conceal the breadth of his reading. "By the second year, the more insecure of his professors began to think he was putting them on, because he'd make references to all kinds of work outside their narrow speciality."[5]

Randall McLeod, who taught the Shakespeare course, remembers him in a related but slightly different light. He speaks of Harold as "an adult among teenagers, an outsider who kept to himself, his bearing mysterious and aloof, very bright but not personable."[6]

The curriculum dictated some of his reading. The courses in 20th-Century Literature and the Modern Novel filled gaps in his knowledge of the modern British and American canon. But he ranged more widely. His letters refer to Sartre, Camus, Conrad, Henry Miller, John Barth, Cervantes, Thomas Carlyle, Samuel Johnson – and there were clearly many others he never mentions. He was also familiar with Asian writers such as Yasunari Kawabata and R. K. Narayan. According to Peter Such:

> The things he'd been set to read in his courses began to fill up the spaces in his vast undirected reading of English and American literature. On his own he was reading Canadian literature too. He'd also learned literary Hindi, and had access to great Eastern works as well.[7]

Dennis Lee remembers Harold "slurping up all the Caribbean literature he could find – discovering what he could make his own, *aka* steal, and determined to write all these rivals into the ground."[8] He would have "slurped up" Selvon (as another Indian from Trinidad), possibly Mittelholzer (he would have enjoyed the lurid family drama of the *Kaywana* trilogy (1952-1958), and maybe *Corentyne Thunder* (1941), which had been republished in 1970, an acute portrayal of the rural Indo-Guyanese world).

There is one Caribbean/Canadian writer Harold definitely read: the Barbadian Austin Clarke, who emigrated to Canada in 1955 at age 21, and broke ground as a Caribbean and a Black writer in Toronto. As Michael Enright wrote: Clarke was "the author of African descent in English, in Canada, that anyone who was interested in being a writer would have to be aware of, to challenge as well."[9]

Harold read Clarke's books closely, and there is an effusive letter to Clarke from March 1973, declaring that he has read all the senior writer's published work, including Clarke's collection of stories about West Indians in Toronto, *When He Was Free and Young and He Used to Wear Silks* (1971),[10] also published by House of Anansi and edited by Dennis Lee.

During this second year, Harold's life outside the classroom was a jumble of highs and lows. His formidable father Sonny had died in August 1971, just before the school year began. Harold had endured a traumatic visit home for the funeral, and the aftershock was still with him.

> My mother was so taken up with grief that she took to the bottle – she was drunk for days. My sisters in Trinidad as well as neighbours were quarrelling and fighting for property etc. My youngest brother who had been hospitalised for one year as a result of injuries suffered in a car accident (he got a broken leg and a fractured skull) was released from his confinement in the hospital. He came home to attend and take part in the funeral ceremonies. One week after the cremation, he went insane. I took him to the city and at the present time, he is still in a lunatic asylum. I was desperately short of cash: the five hundred dollars which I received from the Canada Council did not take me very far considering the fact that my passage to Trinidad was three hundred dollars.[11]

And that same summer, Peter Such's writer-in-residency at Erindale ended. While he would remain a close friend, there was now no one on campus whom Harold could trust and confide in.

Yet at the same time, he was on a roll. A publisher, House of Anansi had accepted his first novel, *No Pain Like This Body*, and Harold worked closely with the editor, Dennis Lee, who was to play a significant role in Ladoo's literary life, all through this school year. Taking that in tandem with his classes, his late-night shifts at Fran's, his forays to Cabbagetown, and his fraught home life, it made for an intense year.

Harold's final year at Erindale (1972-73) took a different turn again. By now he had a somewhat caustic view of higher education, or at least his own. As he wrote to Dennis Lee:

> The third year is really rugged. I have a racist professor who is teaching me some Victorian bullshit so I am very busy with class work. Erindale is like a fucking tumour. Daily the campus annoys me. Those American pricks are crossing the border more and more. Anyhow soon I am going to be out of the mill. Soon as I get out I am prepared to do a book on my years in hell.[12]

And his state of mind was reflected in his marks.

```
LADOO HAROLD SONNY                              703113665
        THIRD    YEAR     1972-73
                 FINAL AVERAGE    C

        ENG306   ENG POETRY PROSE DRA    C         66
        ENG364   CANADIAN POETRY         B         74
        ENG368   VICTORIAN PROSE         D         56
        ENG377   POL NOVEL-20TH CENT     C         67
        ENG469   SENIOR ESSAY            D         51

     PASSED    BACHELOR OF ARTS THREE YEAR

               CONFERRED JUNE 1973
```

*Harold's grades year 3*

While he got a 'B' in Canadian Poetry, he scored 'C's and 'D's in Victorian Prose, 18th Century English Literature, and the 20th Century Political Novel. Particularly surprising is the dismal 51% on his Senior Essay, where one would have expected him to excel; the reason can only be conjectured.

Even though Harold squeaked by with a final average of 'C' in third year, he did in fact pass. And in June 1973, he graduated with a Bachelor of Arts degree.

He had two months to live.

★

Around the university, Harold had begun carrying himself differently. By coincidence, some of his "study-group" friends from McBean, who had swotted together to get their O and A level GCE Certificates, ended up at Erindale at the same time as him. There the Caribbean students commandeered their own meeting place, the "Caribbean Table" in the cafeteria. One of those students was a Trinidadian, Ian Jeffers. According to Ian, who became Harold's closest friend at Erindale, Harold and he were the only Caribbean students who enrolled in a Philosophy Course run by a Professor Smiley. Harold was fascinated by philosophy and by Smiley, who, acording to Ian "was also an advisor to the then Canadian prime minister, Pierre Trudeau", and he and Ian would have interminable discussions after classes about the philosophical issues raised by Smiley. That, and Harold's argumentative nature led Ian to name Harold "Plato", the name by which he became known at the Caribbean table.

Lennox Sankersingh (nicknamed "Chorros", after his family's roti shop in Couva), Israel Khan (another Trinidadian friend at Erindale), and the future poet and novelist Dionne Brand recall an argument which obviously created a lasting impression. Here is Dionne's account, in her introduction to a later edition of *No Pain Like This Body*:

One particular fight was over V.S. Naipaul. Plato argued that he was a better writer than Naipaul, and Chorros, being a logician, asked him how he had come to that conclusion and could he measure it scientifically. Plato exploded, grabbing hold of Chorros, at which point our room in the cafeteria went uncharacteristically silent. Suddenly, referring to Chorros's broken down car, Plato said, "Hey Chorros how the Volkswagen going?" The violence of the moment diffused.[13]

Meanwhile, the simultaneous highs and lows in Harold's life continued throughout his third year. In the fall of 1972, *No Pain Like This Body* had appeared – to generally enthusiastic reviews. But he was now pressing a series of manuscripts on his publisher, with a second publication in mind – and none of them was deemed satisfactory. At home, the family was on the financial brink, almost totally dependent on Rachel's income, and there was another child on the way. This left her understandably bitter; of one of their fights, she said, "[Harold] even told me he married me for me to give him [ie pay for him to receive] an education. That's it. That's what he needed me for."[14]

While Erindale offered Harold intellectual stimulation of sorts, and the prospect of realising his literary dream, Peter Such highlights another key function of the College – as a physical refuge, at least in Harold's first year.

*Peter Such:* I think one of the things about Harold was that he had to journey quite a long way to get out here to Erindale College. ... Suddenly you're out here in this pastoral paradise, away from the city and all that noise and bustle and striving for a living and so on. [...]

So I think Harold had these two worlds that he navigated between, you know, the bustling city and then the Erindale campus, particularly this woods and the bridge. ...[15]

*Peter Such at Erindale 2003*

Here in the grounds of the principal's house is this lovely forest space. ... This was a favourite spot for us. And I would often say to Harold, "I'll meet you at the bridge," you know, because it was removed from the rest of the campus and we could stand on this lovely bridge and look down, and in those days, the principal had some koi in the pond here that lived there all through the year. This little bridge just seemed to represent something for us, where we could stand and talk about writing and talk about art, sometimes just eat our lunch with our feet dangling over the edge and watch the fish in the water and watch the ducks and be in this beautiful woods.

*"The Bridge" at Erindale (2003)*

*CL:* And what would Harold talk about?

*PS:* Oh, I guess he would talk about his writing and his ambitions and some of the problems he was having with some of his classes, some of the people, and sometimes he would talk about Trinidad, and I guess it must have seemed to him that this was very, very different from Trinidad. This is a very Canadian kind of place really. For me this is a very special spot. I kind of remember Harold here and remember the things...[16]

The significance of Harold's meeting with Peter Such in September 1970 went far beyond getting the chance to go to university. Peter was to become a close and enduring friend and mentor – at a time when Harold was trying to survive simultaneously as an undergraduate, an apprentice writer, a husband, a new father, and a short-order cook. The stakes – and the pressure – could hardly have been higher.

Endnotes

1. Randall McLeod in conversation with the author, April 2021.
2. See Appendix Nine.
3. Peter Such, "The Short Life and Sudden Death of Harold Sonny Ladoo." *Saturday Night* (Toronto) 89, 5 1974, and *BIM* Volume 16 No 63, 1978.
4. Douglas Hill in conversation with the author, April 2021.
5. Peter Such, *The Short Life and Sudden Death of Harold Sonny Ladoo*.
6. Randall McLeod in conversation with the author, April 2021. In fact, according to his transcript, Harold passed Randall's *Shakespeare* course with a B grade (72%) though according to Randall: "That is a low grade for someone of his intelligence. He may not have submitted all the assignments."
7. Peter Such, ibid. Rachel and Meena claim that Harold read Eastern literature in the original, having taught himself Sanskrit. But since no one else in the family of his generation could read Sanskrit, or even speak Hindi beyond a few common words and expressions, this is impossible to verify. We have only his word for it.
     In an interview with the author in 2019, Harold's sister Meena said that when Harold visited her in the days before his death:
   *Meena*: "He told me, 'Girl, I can speak Hindi now.' You know, he learnt the language because he had this desire to go to India and he was offered [a chance] to go and turned it down, and his reason was he couldn't speak the language – and 'I trust no one so I'm not going to go.' So he was very proud of the fact that he could speak Hindi now, very, very good, just like English, he said, 'I can do Hindi now just like English.' I say, 'That's great, that's wonderful.'"
   *CL:* So he learnt that in Canada?
   *ML:* Yes." (Interview with Meena Ladoo, September 2019)
8. Letter to Dennis Lee 20 November 1971.
9. Michael Enright (February 17, 2019). *Revisiting Austin Clarke's novel about memory, migration and a chance encounter* https://www.cbc.ca/radio/thesundayedition/the-sunday-edition-for-february-17-2019-1.5017616/revisiting-austin-clarke-s-novel-about-memory-migration-and-a-chance-encounter-1.5020914 (Radio program). CBC.
10. Letter to Austin C. Clarke, 26 March 1973, among Peter Such's papers at McMaster Library.
11. "I felt young and free knowing that any day now, I would be wearing silks. (Can you imagine a niger wearing silk outside of New Orleans?)" Letter to Dennis Lee, 25 September 1972.
12. Letter to Dennis Lee 14 November 1972.
13. Dionne Brand, introduction to the Anansi 2003 edition of *No Pain Like This Body*.

14. Interview with Rachel Ladoo by Christopher Laird and Ramabai Espinet, September 2002.
15. Peter Such's position as Writer in Residence came to an end in the summer of 1971.
16. In this extended quotation, Peter's words have been lightly edited to reduce repetitions.

## CHAPTER SEVEN
## WRITE WHAT YOU KNOW

"I took the suitcase full of writing that I had and I tipped it down the
garbage chute in my apartment building."
— Harold Ladoo, quoted by Peter Such

As noted in the last chapter, Harold Ladoo never stopped writing during
his studies. The two published novels, the surviving stories and fragments,
the missing manuscripts – all were written during his three years at Erindale.
In fact, his time there became less about getting a degree than about learning
his craft as a fiction writer, and getting published. How he accomplished
that is a testament both to his extraordinary work ethic, to the support
provided by Rachel, and to his good fortune in having Peter Such and
later Dennis Lee beside him. Later chapters look in detail at the two published
novels; this retraces, as far as possible, Harold's growth as a writer during
the Erindale years.

   In September or October 1970, shortly after arriving in Erindale, Harold
brought Peter a small brown suitcase full of poetry. Peter recalls his
reaction:

   I read his stuff and it was all very nineteenth-century-Tennysonian-poetry
   kind of thing, and there was one poem which I liked out of the whole
   lot [chuckles], I hate to say, and I said to him very gently, "I like this
   poem because it's authentic, it's about Trinidad, it's about your voice,"
   and so on. "And the other stuff – you've got skill, there's no doubt about
   it, but you're really writing about something foreign…"[1]

Harold was undeterred by the criticism. What he had shown Peter
possibly incorporated half a decade of intense and solitary work, and a great
deal of ambitious dreaming. He wasn't about to turn his back on it. Peter
continues the story: "I'd spoken a bit about Dennis Lee and Lee's publishing company, the House of Anansi, and he thought he might send his work
over to them." And so, despite Peter's caution, Harold submitted a poetry
manuscript to Anansi that fall.

   The House of Anansi was a small literary press in Toronto, founded in
1967 by the poet Dennis Lee and the fiction writer Dave Godfrey, both in
their late twenties. They expected to publish a few titles a year, mostly
poetry. But almost at once, submissions started pouring in from all across

Canada. And Lee, who would direct the press by himself from 1968 on, saw a pattern: many of the most intriguing manuscripts were first novels that pushed the boundaries of conventional realism. In choosing what to publish, he favoured this palpable, risky energy. And within a few years Anansi had become the rallying point for a vibrant group of young, talented and hungry Canadian writers. They included Margaret Atwood (who would edit for the press), Michael Ondaatje, Graeme Gibson, Marian Engel, Matt Cohen, Austin Clarke, Paulette Jiles, Roch Carrier and Lee himself, along with dozens of others.

Anansi's first big success was *Five Legs*, a stream-of-consciousness novel by Graeme Gibson, published in 1969. Despite its difficulty, the first printing sold out in two weeks. And with a kind of eerie symmetry, Gibson's estranged wife Shirley would become the office manager at Anansi (and later the managing editor), while Atwood's estranged husband Jim Polk would succeed Lee as editor when he stepped down in 1972.

To keep up with the flood of new fiction, Lee initiated the "Spiderline" series of first novels. And in the fall of 1969, Anansi released five first novels on the same day – one of them being Peter Such's *Fallout*. It was no doubt through Peter Such's relationship with Anansi that Harold set his sights on this enterprising publishing house.

But it didn't take long for his manuscript to bounce back. In Peter's words:

> The whole pile came back with a long letter from Dennis, who had himself gone through the same kind of exercises years earlier. The key phrase in the letter was, "Write about the things you know."[2]

Harold was furious at the rejection. But Peter reinforced Dennis's advice:

> *PS:* I said to him, "Well, you know what you maybe want to do is write about Trinidad, the real Trinidad, not the official Trinidad but the unofficial Trinidad, which you know all about." So he went home, and a week later he came in and he had this short story, which was actually the beginning of some stuff in *No Pain Like This Body*.

> *CL:* What was it that caught you about the writing?

> *PS:* It was the language, you know, the cleanness of it, not being pretentious … It was just straight from the heart. Like, I have had several hundred students, and a lot of them can be very competent and skilled, but it's only once in a blue moon that you get this feeling that – boy! This guy is a writer! 'Cause there's more to writing than just words, there's a lot of stuff to it.
>   So when he came in I said, "This is really great stuff," etc. and he said, "Well, I hope it is, because I took the suitcase full of writing that I had and I tipped it down the garbage chute in my apartment building,"

[laughs] "and this is the only thing I have in my suitcase now," [laughs] and I thought – Wow! I said, "I didn't mean to have that much influence on you, Harold." But it was that kind of gesture, you see, he just made up his mind he was going to be a great writer and that was it, that was it.[3]

There's no copy of this story, but it marks the beginning of Harold's most authentic writing. In the fall of 1970, at age twenty-five, he had found his subject matter and voice – discovered his calling. He was a fiction writer, a storyteller. With this discovery came a particular way of working. And the dam was ready to burst. As Peter Such recalled:

Well, more and more after he began to get published, he wrote in what I called "binge style", and he would say something like "I'm going home now and I'm going to write", and he would disappear for two days and then he would phone me up and he would say, and he would always have this funny voice, he would say, "Mister Such," and I'd say, "Yes," and he said, "I've just finished another novel" [laughs]. "I've been up for thirty-six hours," and I would say, "Oh, okay, great!" and he'd say, "I'm going to bring it to you," and he would come in looking completely haggard and throw this manuscript at me and after this happened a few times I said, "You know Harold, the first six hours is pretty good, this is really good, but the next thirty hours need some work." [laughs]

And I think a lot of it was to do with his domestic situation too, that he tried to find these blocks of time and sometimes they were just two days and he felt that he had to do everything in those two days, he had to write this whole big novel. It was funny on one level and kind of tragic on another, you know, and when he wasn't in the binge mood, he kind of laughed about it himself a bit, 'cause he did recognise what he was doing, but I think it was necessary for him to do it.[4]

Rachel gives a similar account:

*Ramabai Espinet*: So how did Harold write, when he was writing, tell us...

*Rachel Ladoo*: How he write? When he would travel to go university, he would write on the subway, scripts and those things, that's how I remember it, and when he come home he used to write again and do it on typewriter and those things, that's all I remember about that.[5]

*RE:* He used to lock himself up?

*RL:* Yeah, in the [bed]room.

*CL:* Explain what he used to do?

*RL:* When he come from university or wherever he come from, he used to go in the room and lock himself up and start writing or typing and that's it. He never used to sleep, he wake all night, then he go back to school again, and he come back and he eat something and he go and shower whatever and go and write again. That's what he used to do.[6]

*RE*: That was his room, or that was…

*RL*: Our room.

*RE*: But you weren't home when he was writing?

*RL*: I was in the living room most of the time because you can't be around when he's writing, he need his privacy to write.

    Most nights I used to sleep in the living room, because he used to be writing and well, I have to go to work and I have to get my sleep too. And then we have an extra room and I would sleep there with the children sometimes.[6]

After Peter gave the stamp of approval to that first story, Harold evidently went into a frenzy of new writing. But despite the early morning calls trumpeting the completion of yet "another novel", the latter claim is misleading. While the possibility of multitudes of novels in manuscript can never be disproved conclusively, what has survived gives a different picture. There are many fragments, ranging from one page to thirty-two pages, often annotated by Harold in 1973: "To be worked on at a later date." He was more likely writing what were essentially short stories, some of which would later serve as building blocks for novels. Because some files disappeared, there is no way of knowing how many such pieces he wrote.

    For instance, his first appearance in print, in a single-issue magazine, *Thirst*, published in April 1971, by an Erindale student, Patricia Gilhooly, was entitled "an excerpt from his new novel, as yet untitled". It was a few pages featuring some of the characters and situations that would later appear (totally rewritten) in his second novel, *Yesterdays*.

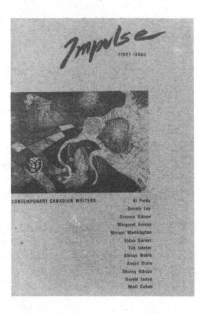

To compound the ongoing confusion of the titles Harold would use, another story, which was published by Peter Such in the summer of 1971, in the first issue of his journal *IMPULSE*, was titled: "An excerpt from a new novel, *Yesterdays*",[7] but was in fact later rewritten into the opening portion of *No Pain Like This Body*.[8] Harold was in classy company at *Impulse,* appearing alongside such established luminaries as Al Purdy and Dennis Lee.

And in November of that year, *The Erindalian*, the college's student newspaper, published what it billed as an excerpt from his "new novel," purportedly a 400-page manuscript called "Rage".

*Image of Rage review*

So in 1971, Harold was writing stories that would be repurposed for the novels he would publish a year or two later. As Peter says:

> Those short stories of his proved to be quick exploration passes over the material for his first novel, which he began almost immediately. This habit of getting into novels through his short stories was one he kept through his brief writing career. I didn't realise this at first and wanted to do some work with him on tightening them up as stories. But the canvas was really too small for the vastness of his conceptions, and the long creative input a novel demands was more to his liking.[9]

There was one early exception to this pattern of churning out stories and labelling them novels. Harold submitted what was apparently a manuscript of novel length (titled *All Our Yesterdays,* and of perhaps 100-150 pages) to Dennis Lee at Anansi. He submitted it in May 1971 – meaning that he must have written it, along with the stories, during his first year at Erindale. No copy of the manuscript survives.

Dennis responded in a long letter on 31 May, where he praised what Harold had accomplished:

> First off, you are a natural writer! Sections of the novel come on like a house on fire. You obviously have a beautifully firm sense of the reality of what you are writing about. I kept getting a sense of excitement, from time to time, at realising that this was someone writing who probably had a really fine body of work ahead of him – I think you are going to write some excellent, moving books.

Dennis's praise was unstinting, but his critique was unsparing:

> At the stylistic level, I found the clipped and simplistic style working very well over short periods, especially where the material was quite painful and the laconic understatement threw that into high relief. But as a medium for the whole book, I eventually found it chopped up everything into discrete little units which came at me with a flat relentlessness, and which levelled out all the highs and lows of the book into something that began to approach tedium.

There was no avoiding the ultimate verdict:

> Harold, I can't step up & offer to publish YESTERDAYS as it stands...I'd very much hope, though, that you'll pat yourself on the back for having accomplished far more in your first book than the great majority of writers do, and then either go back at it or grow past it in the new books (I must say, I hope you can eventually bring it off, whether right now or later – there's a splendid book here). And if you are inclined this way, I'd like you to let Anansi see further drafts or new mss.[10]

A disappointment? Yes. A setback? No. Harold showed his mettle as a writer. If he didn't rise to this challenge, he wouldn't have what it took to be a writer. Not the writer he wanted to be. By the fall of 1971 Harold had rewritten and re-submitted his manuscript.

Endnotes

1.  Peter Such, "The Short Life and Sudden Death of Harold Sonny Ladoo." *Saturday Night* (Toronto), 89, 5, 1974.
2.  Peter Such, Ibid.
3.  Interview with Peter Such by Christopher Laird, March 2003
4.  Ibid.
5.  According to Harold, writing conditions were terrible at home. He typed under the bed. '"Under the bed?" Jim Polk asked. 'Yes, under the bed,' Harold affirmed." Note from interview with Jim Polk 2002).
6.  Interview with Rachel Ladoo by Ramabai Espinet and Christopher Laird April 2003.
7.  Published in the first issue of *IMPULSE*, a literary journal edited by Peter Such and published out of Erindale College of the University of Toronto in the summer of 1971.
8.  The working title for *No Pain* was *All Our Yesterdays* or *Yesterdays* but this later became the title of his second novel published posthumously in 1974.
9.  Peter Such, "The Short Life and Sudden Death of Harold Sonny Ladoo." *Saturday Night* (Toronto), 89, 5, 1974.
10. All three quotes are from a letter to Harold Ladoo from Dennis Lee, 31 May 1971.

CHAPTER EIGHT
NO PAIN LIKE THIS BODY

Nana[1] and meh nani they
went to tie a goat
Meh nana make a mistake
and cut meh nani throat
Sundar Popo, *Nani And Nana* (1971)[2]

In the winter of 1971 Harold submitted a new draft of the novel Dennis
Lee had rejected. This still carried the title, "All Our Yesterdays", and was
referred to in letters as "Yesterdays"; this was later changed to "No Pain
Like This Body". This time it was accepted by House of Anansi Press,
and Dennis Lee assumed editorship. The bhaji planter from McBean,
the short order cook from Fran's in Toronto, had suddenly gained entry
to the world he had dreamed about.

Dennis Lee brought a poet's meticulous sensitivity for the right word,
the telling phrase and structure, and he also brought a generosity and
openness to different ways of seeing. It was a master class. Dennis records
his first impressions of his meeting with Harold in his poem, The *Death of
Harold Ladoo:*

> remember how we met? We sat drinking
> outside at the Lion, sun lathering us, the transport-trailers
> belting along on Jarvis, your manuscript
> between us on the table and
> what did I see?
> A skinny brown man in a suit – voice tense, eyes shifting, absurdly
> respectful ... and none of it connected:
> that raucous, raging thing I'd read, and this
> deferential man.
> [...]
> then it hit, the
> whirling saga
> the table going away, the
> drinks, the traffic     those liquid
> eyes unhooding, a current like jolts of
> pain in the air – I'd
> never seen the need to write so
> badly founded; nor so quiet, deadly, and convincing –
> and I was at home, relaxed.[3]

In a 2002 interview with me, Lee expanded on this:

I guess I'd heard about him from someone else, from Peter Such, who knew him at Erindale College and had seen some of Harold's work, I think maybe in literary magazines. But it was a manuscript of *No Pain Like This Body* and at this distance, you know, I can't remember whether it was submitted first or whether he brought it in, but the memory I have is of sitting with this man called Harold Ladoo about whom I knew effectively nothing. I didn't really know about the make-up of Trinidad; I didn't have any context for understanding that from Trinidad came someone who was clearly East Indian. He had a suit on, he was very understated, very deferential, skinny as a rake, although he got skinnier and skinnier over the next few years, and I wasn't sure if I was going to be able to get any conversation out of this man whatsoever. I must have seen something because I knew that there was a spark here...

The time began to stretch out and those layers of deferentiality and 'Yes sir, Mr. White Editor', peeled away one by one, and I realised I'd been sitting ten, twenty minutes at a time as he went deeper and deeper into what his plans were, all his dreams and I kept getting glimpses of Harold's childhood and upbringing, which I never did manage to fit together in the several years I knew him because they kept changing, but it was this incandescent intensity that I remember.

...

So, I can't remember now what the first draft of *No Pain Like This Body* actually looked like, but I am sure it was pretty choppy and jumping around and sometimes getting into just one vein for twenty pages at a time and then a very staccato mix up of things. So we did quite a bit of work. That was the one thing that I think maybe I had to offer as editor. It wasn't a matter of grabbing a pen out of his hand and saying "This is how we're going to do it", but it was a matter of pushing him and saying "Will you take chapter two back home now and see if you can get it shaped in a way that tells the story a lot more excitingly and satisfyingly". And even though there's no way anybody was going to tell Harold how to write his books, he did find a new source of new energy and he grew just enormously in the course of that editing. I can't remember now whether that lasted two months or six months or whatever, but it was very intensive.

It was a pretty thorough rewrite of the manuscript and, as I said, it was very much a matter of Harold coming into his own as a craftsman and if he had lived I think with all the different kinds of material he had, 'cause the second book, the shape of it is very different, it called for a different kind of craft. He would have gone on growing, he might have been five or ten years really mastering the kind of craft that the breadth of his vision called for, but it was just awe-inspiring really to see the speed with which he was growing.

And he would go off and read three books, five books, ten books just to see what somebody else had done and slurped them in. Now, Eliot said "Weak poets borrow, strong poets steal"; you don't just carry something around like a kind of patina, you actually make it your own, it becomes your property and you discard what isn't right for you. That was very much how Harold was working, so whenever he saw something that just clicked with the way he was trying to write, that became his property.[4]

★

*No Pain Like This Body* is set in 1905, 12 years before the end of Indian Indentureship in Trinidad. The family of Pa, Ma and four children live on the riceland they farm. It rains throughout the first half of the novel. Pa comes home one day and vents his rage on Ma and his children. One of his children dies because of his violence and, eventually, Ma goes mad despite the efforts of her parents, Nanny and Nanna, who, as ex-indentured labourers, born in India, live close to their traditional Hindu deities and bring with them a sense of order and compassion.[5]

Victor Questel wrote the first (and still the only) in-depth Caribbean review of *No Pain Like This Body* in 1974:

> Ladoo's first novel *No Pain*, adds a new dimension to the West Indian novel. It is the kind of dimension that complements Michael Anthony's exploration of the world of the child and the adolescent as seen in *The Year In San Fernando* (1965) and *Green Days By The River* (1967). *No Pain* is also very instructive for any reader coming from a sitting with a novel like Shiva Naipaul's *The Chip-Chip Gatherers* (1973). *No Pain* explores a fragment of the world of the Trinidadian East Indian which has not been previously done. (Samuel) Selvon has skirted around the area but never really got into it. I am referring to life for the first and second generation Trinidadian East Indian practising subsistence farming here, while their gods fall around them and the middle-aged and the young move around without meaningful points of reference and standards. Ladoo shows us that such a world is really a world of anarchy in which one has three choices; patient suffering or madness or an early death.[6]

In his review Questel called Pa, "the most violent father in West Indian fiction". It's possible that Harold's portrayal of the father was influenced by his own, strict, father, but Pa in *No Pain Like This Body* is more than just a deeply flawed individual; he represents a generation that the cultural destruction wrought by indentureship and separation from India had stripped of traditional Hindu gods and left loose in a chaotic and godless world, or rather, a world the gods witness but in which they do not intervene.

> "Balraj, come outa dat wadder!" Pa shouted.
> "I fraid you beat me."
> "Boy com outa dat wadder!"
> Balraj was afraid. He knew Pa was going to beet him real bad. *Crax crax cratax doom doomm doomed!* the thunder rolled. Balraj looked at the sky; it was blacker than a dream of snakes and evil spirits. Pa bent down and picked up dirt from the riceland bank. He started to pelt Balraj. Balraj was moving from side to side trying hard to get away from the dirt. Pa couldn't hit him. Pa was in a rage; he was pelting as a madman. Then Pa shouted, "Now come outa dat wadder boy! I goin to pelt inside dem snake holes."

Balraj made no effort to come out of the riceland. Pa kept pelting dirt into the deep holes. The water was bubbling and bubbling and bubbling; bubbling and bubbling as if it was boiling over with rage; it was boiling and bubbling as when a ricepot bubbles over a fireside, but Balraj just stood there and looked at Pa.

"You feel you is a big man?" Pa asked him.

"No."

"Den come outa dat wadder!"

"I fraid you beat me."

"Den you is a big man?"

"No, I is a little little chile. Little little."

"Well I goin to make a snake bite you ass!"

It was August, the middle of the rainy season. The rain was falling and falling and falling as if the sky was leaking or something. Sunaree, Rama and Panday were still by the rainwater barrel. Sunaree was holding the enamel dipper, but it slipped from her hand and fell in the yard. The dipper was dirty; full of mud all over. Rama and Panday were still naked. Trembling.

"I feeling cold."

"Hush else Pa go bust you liver wid a kick," Rama said.

"Pa stupid," Panday declared.

"Pa stupid like God."

"Now God have big eyes and he seein wot all you doin," Sunaree said.

"Somebody shoulda hit god one kick and bust he eye!" Rama shouted.[8]

The late Arnold Itwaru, Director of Caribbean Studies at the University of Toronto, in a 2002 interview said:

The one that really touched me with a kind of a poetic profundity, as well as, you know, really emotional honesty is *No Pain Like This Body*. I think that *No Pain Like This Body* is unlike anything else that has come out of Trinidad so far, and I'm going to make a big kind of a wide statement here, (chuckles), but I think *No Pain Like This Body* is one of the best literary works to have come out of Trinidad. And you know, it's too bad that it hasn't been widely read.

When I read *No Pain Like This Body* I thought – this man understands and he's asking questions and he's posing a dilemma that is happening here. And within it all, he engages in a kind of critique of, you know, people like pundits and so on, who come and they're not what they're supposed to be. But he does that unlike Naipaul, you know, like *Mystic Masseur*, in Naipaul's case, the pundit is totally hollow and he's nothing, he's nothing, he's a sham. But, Sonny Ladoo's pundit, he's not like that, you could see the human being in him still and the other critique is there.

His treatments of women's suffering, you know, during the storm and that sort of thing, the role which they play, the strength of the women, the fear of women. …And I thought the work contains it all and it's succinct, it's small and to the point. I particularly like writing like that.[8]

As Arnold Itwaru points out, Ladoo's treatment of women is significant. Three generations of women provide the fixed structure of the novel. The grandmother, Nanny, beating her drum and marshalling the family to take practical action; the mother, Ma, beaten down by Pa, adrift and burdened by motherhood; and Sunaree, her daughter, who is the wise elder sister, who seems to be the witness of the novel and wonders, "Is there a future for her generation?"

Maybe here is where we need to begin to raise the contradictions between Harold's privileging of women in his literary world and the unpleasant way he treated the women in his immediate family. Rachel tells of his violent treatment of her and her daughter, Debbie.[9] Yet it is instructive to note that in Harold's novels it is female figures who own their world, who seem to be the points of reference, of nurturing, of comfort, for the children (and the men).[10] The men, on the other hand, are free to indulge and impose their emotions and their power.

One cannot ignore other influences at play, especially Harold's Hindu upbringing. Is his portrayal of women in the novels an expression of the Hindu veneration of womanhood, as in Rama's consort, Sita, and Mother Lakshmi? But then, *The Ramayana*'s narrative also points to male insecurity. After Rama kills her abductor, the evil king, Rawan, and rescues Sita, his insecurities lead her to literally have to walk through fire to prove she was not defiled by Rawan.[11] Sometimes men are not happy unless their women can be tainted with impurity, thus providing a rationale for violence.

In *No Pain Like This Body*, the first images of Ma portray her as a sort of Mother Earth. Here, she is making a poultice from some young guava leaves she asks Balraj to bring her to dress the cut on her forehead, a result of Pa's violence:

> Ma held the leaves in her right palm. She spat on them. Then she crushed them between her slender palms. A greenish juice leaked out from her palms and fell on the ground. The juice smelt as something to eat. Ma looked at her right palm; the leaves were ground enough; it looked as if moss was growing in her palms. She gathered the green spots together with her left index fingers; she joined the spots up and made something like a green worm, then she lifted up her hand slowly as if the crushed leaves were heavier than a stone. *Slap!* She slapped the green stuff on her forehead.[12] [...]
>
> Ma faced the wind and the rain as a thin living stump, but she was using her brain. Rama and Panday couldn't hear her brain working, because it worked as a seed growing. Ma stood with her hands over her face as if she was trying to see behind her red eyeballs. Then she removed her hands and told them, "I go carry you all in dat cane field."[13]

This is the woman (Ma) whose brain is working like 'a seed growing' but who, by the end of the novel, is eating dirt and wandering into the forest in a state of madness. This is the result of her husband's insecurity, anger and impotence. The conflict embedded in this Hindu cultural space of motherhood is what Shalini Khan focuses on in her essay:

> Indeed, Rama's death forces Ma out of the mythological womb and into what Ladoo calls the void – that space beyond the safety and predictability of mythology where the individual recognises a startling incongruity between myth and lived reality. Not surprisingly, Ma's realisation of this incongruity is accompanied by a cessation of regular behaviour and her performance of acts that are inappropriate in the community and culture, such as eating dirt and defecating on the floor: the rituals of the prior world – cooking, bathing, taking care of the family – are no longer meaningful to her. By ending the narrative on the brink of the Tola forest, the place where wild, dangerous animals are said to live, Ladoo ends with a *Heart of Darkness* image, the uncharted savage territory of the unconscious, an appropriate destination for those expelled from mythology's womb and who come to embody the terrible truth.[14]

In general, though, the five women featured as main protagonists in Ladoo's two novels are strong and very clear about their role as carers and guardians of their children, who they would do anything to see survive and grow, and it is only Ma who eventually succumbs. What beats her down directly is Pa, but Ladoo is clear that ultimately what sends her mad is experience of the system of indentureship that the characters in the novel have passed through and then been abandoned by, the situation that creates the anger and impotence of men.

Ladoo, aided by the map in the frontispiece to the book, makes clear the state of physical and psychological limbo in which Pa and his family are trapped. They are no longer part of the "bound coolie estate", the barracks of the sugar estate with its hierarchy of manager, overseers, drivers and bound labourers – a repressive and often squalid existence that was responsible for stripping the bound labourers of their cultural identity, but one where managers had a responsibility to pay and provide health care and where there was an agent of immigrants ultimately responsible to the British colonial secretary for the operation of the system.

Some ex-indentured Indians lived in relatively flourishing villages, beginning from the 1870s onwards, where there had been a partial restoration of Indian village life with the patriarchy of panchayats and caste hierarchy. Perhaps this kind of settlement is what is labelled "Indian estate" in the map. Contemporary observers and later historians have drawn attention to the relatively free economic space some women fought for as wage earners on the sugar estates and even of the phenomena of women seeking out more prosperous partners, whilst in the "free" Indian settlements and villages there was an observable effort to restore patriarchy and subordinate women, frequently with violence and a spate of "wife-murders".[15] This, perhaps, is part of Pa's motivation for his violence towards Ma.

There is also an area labelled "Jangli Tola" on the map, literally a jungle or wild space, from which the aggressive character Jadoo emerges at the wake with his tale of violent cutlassings. Quite possibly this was an area at the bottom of or even outside the caste system, possibly a reference to the non-caste tribals who were an early part of the indenture system. In his research from the late 1950s, Morton Klass records many of the inhabitants of Jangli Tola as "crab-catchers", for caste Hindus a term of abuse, like "chamar".[16]

Nanna and Nanny live in neighbouring Karan settlement, but where Ma and Pa live has no name and is simply between Lima and Rajput roads. Places like Indian Estate were gradually becoming part of Trinidad; everything in the description of where Ma and Pa live stresses their isolation and abandonment, their inbetweenness, no longer rootedly Indian and not yet in any sense Trinidadian. Such a reading of depths below the naturalistic surface of *No Pain* is supported by what Peter Such had to say:

> He (Harold) really wanted to go into some philosophical depth, to really try and plumb this whole notion of the postcolonial inheritance, the violence and the social disruption, which carries down to a sort of personal abuse between people and their relationships with each other."[17]

As Shalini Khan points out:

> Ladoo's characterization of Ma is similar to other depictions of mad/ mentally disturbed females in Caribbean literature, including Antoinette in Jean Rhys' *Wide Sargasso Sea* (1966) and Annie in Jamaica Kincaid's *Annie John (1985),* both of whom are out of sync with those around them and who come to embody the "terrible truth" about life in the Caribbean.[18]

In writing this novel set in 1905, it is clear that Harold was familiar with the *Ramayana*, the epic story of Prince Rama's victory over the evil king Ravana, and with the history of Indian settlement in Trinidad, but he was also very clear about the dysfunction of contemporary life in McBean, drawing on his own experiences there and asking questions about how that disfunction arose. In particular, the stories he was hearing about his mother wandering the streets like a vagrant after his father's death in August 1971 must have been a factor in his depiction of Ma's madness at the end of the novel, with its haunting description of Nanny and Sunaree, beating drum and playing flute, following the demented Ma into the forest.

Victor Questel concludes his review of *No Pain Like This Body*:

> One of the questions not answered is what kind of belief must one have

to survive in a hostile environment in which standards are nonexistent, but in which one must create new standards so that the next generation can survive?

The strength of *No Pain* is its directness. It is a novel stripped to the bone of pain. Ladoo by looking back steadily at Tola Trace has made it the earth's centre, and that is a success that few first novels can boast.[19]

But not all the women in *No Pain Like This Body* fulfil a positive role. In the wake scene it is the village women who curry favour with Pa by keeping Ma drunk and unable to oppose his desperate rage against the world. The wake scene shows a spectrum of villagers still mired in the exploitive and merciless world of indenture though no longer themselves indentured: the pundit, the whore, the cripple, the stickfighter, centred on the figure of Pa who stands like a tree blackened by lightning strike in a cage of rage. As appalled as we are by Pa's behaviour as he plays the hypocritical role of the caring father burdened by a drunken wife, Ladoo somehow still conjures pity for him as we understand his rage against the history that has robbed him of his manhood and cast him adrift without the certainties of religion in a land without gods. Ladoo's ability to make us care for his characters, even those benighted by ignorance, greed, anger and malice is an attribute that lifts his writing beyond the ordinary and is a feature that he develops and learns to exploit as his work matures.

★

There were some reports after Harold's death that he had complained about the cutting of parts of the wake scene in *No Pain Like This Body*. I asked Dennis Lee about this:

*Christopher Laird*: Tell me about the wake scene, which obviously is a chunk in the middle of the novel that plays different functions, but it's also a scene that could take off on its own if you're not careful. So I wonder if you remember anything around those issues.

*Dennis Lee*: The wake scene, I would say when I reread *No Pain* in this last week, it really knocked me out, the absolute tautness and economy. You know what it reminded me of, particularly, was some of Synge's plays, John Millington Synge, like *Riders to the Sea*, that wonderful heartbroken elegy for people who die at sea and their families at home. You wouldn't quite say that it's a beloved Greek tragedy but it comes in that neighbourhood and the economy of it. I thought the wake scene, which I remember our working on a great deal because there's so much going on and just the question of how you hold it all together without suddenly getting a narrative voice that's completely outside of things. It's got to have the same first-handedness and immediacy of the rest of the book, but suddenly you've got about twenty-five different points of focus. Technically it was a big challenge.

I thought it worked in the economy of the whole book just beautifully because the wake does open out into how many pages, it is twenty pages or something, you get this mixture of goofiness and horrific stuff, the horribleness in some of the people, the depths of caring and the grandparents, their hearts breaking for Ma as she's being brutalised the way she is, to keep it dancing along like that.

Much of what is affirmative in the book is in the dance of the book itself. It seems to me that gives you something to resonate with, it's moving so sure-footedly and taking us through these often horrendous scenes, and it's like listening to music that is somewhere out beyond the ordinary range of what we hear. So for me the opening out, the amplitude that that wake scene creates, I thought worked beautifully. I am not taking credit for these things, I was just part of the editing process, but it was catalysing at best and if it played any part it was to make the book more fully Harold's own book and it wasn't me saying – this is how to write the book. I am not a fiction writer. I learn from every novelist I work with.[20]

Harold's friend and mentor, Peter Such, ever caring and insightful when it comes to Harold, in a review of *No Pain Like This Body,* wrote:

Unlike Naipaul, Lamming, Mittelholzer and the others, it scorns the polished Oxford descriptive mode entirely. It takes instead a poetic scuba-dive into the richness and terror that characterize the mythological deeps of a castaway colonial society.

The last half of the book consists of the wake held for Rama. This event brings together these ragtag bits and pieces of Indian, African and Christian cultures that make up Tola's highly flexible codes of personal, social and religious behaviour. It's in this section that we get hints of Tola's colonial beginnings, glimpses into sources of its impotence and some notion of the causes of its ignorance and brutality. But Ladoo isn't taking the easy fashionable way out and laying the blame entirely on a colonial past. We're into a much deeper conception of existence than that one.

Ladoo's perspective encompasses a view of man's relation to God that could come from Thomas Hardy, and a view of the mysteriousness of Nature that suggests Faulkner. But then there's something else all Ladoo's own which the reader will discover like violets in the shadows of his style's poetic and symbolic levels. The dialogue is earthy and brilliant, true to the natural speech rhythms and complicated puns of a truly oral, storytelling society. (Zany stories are told by characters within the novel itself.) These oral patterns slough over into the rest of the diction and create a unique language – exotic yet at the same time simple and very telling.[21]

We must remember that Harold in early 1971[22] had started writing scenes which later appeared in *No Pain Like This Body* and had submitted the first draft of a novel (titled "All Our Yesterdays") to Dennis Lee and Anansi by May 1971. This was rejected. By the time Harold re-submitted the manuscript, in late 1971, Harold's father, Sonny, had died and his mentor, Peter Such, had left Erindale. It is interesting to consider how this combination of loss and the unexpected burden of being forced to assume the role of son and heir to the Ladoo clan affected his revised treatment of *No Pain*. I think this was the beginning of a reassessment of his responsibilities and filial duties that would eventually influence his later writing, but in *No Pain* it manifests both in anger at Pa and his enablers in the village, and in taking refuge in the comfort of the women of the family. On cannot help but speculate how much Harold's experience at his father's funeral in August influenced his rewrite of what was to become *No Pain Like this Body*, for example, his mother's drunkenness that he reported in his letter to Dennis. What part did that play in his portrayal of the village plying Ma with rum during the wake in *No Pain*?

One of the abiding feelings one has as one reads *No Pain Like This Body*, especially the wake scene, is the desire to see Pa get his comeuppance. It never happens. The nearest it comes to that is when Benwa, the stick fighter,[23] slaps him verbally and Pa is too cowardly to respond:

Ma, drunk from the rum poured down her throat by the other village women, accuses Pa of the death of their son, Rama:

> "De man runnin de chile in dat rain. De moderass man drinkin rum…"
> Pa ran inside the kitchen. "Shut you kiss me ass mout! You drunkard bitch! You son in de house and befo you try to do someting, you drinkin rum. I go hit you one kick and break you kiss me ass back! You chamar modderass you!"
> And Ma: "Now you want to kill me! O God de man want to kill me. He kill me son and now he want to kill me…"
> Benwa came into the kitchen. He said to Pa, "Babwah leff de woman alone!"
> "I go beat she ass! Pa shouted.
> And stick-fighter Benwa got mad. His face became red. "Now Babwah if you beat dat woman I go put so much lix in you ass! If you want to fight, den fight me!"[25]

*No Pain Like This Body* thus not only gives us clues as to how Harold saw women but also his idea of a male hero. Benwa, the stickfighter, who appears in a few of his short stories is the nearest we come to male hero in his work.[26] Perhaps this figure of the stickfighter conforms to Ladoo's fascination with the Hero figure, with his comic book heroes and his Steve Reeves film action hero in movies. It possibly informed his fatal decision to return home to right the wrongs being done to his mother and claim his inheritance.

The novelist, Graeme Gibson, one of the early House of Anansi Press authors, reflected on how *No Pain Like this Body* was received at the time, a time when Canada itself was experiencing a counter-cultural upsurge, beginning to reflect on its colonial past and its multicultural future:

It was so hugely refreshing in its apparent simplicity, in its intensity. Ambition we were accustomed to, because we all had it, it's all we had at that point. The voice of it. I come back again to the ferocious simplicity of it and the fatedness of it, it was hugely refreshing, it was exciting.

It was hard at the time to disassociate the book from Ladoo because he in many ways had similar characteristics as his book that he wrote with such intensity and stared and glared at you while talking about it and about what he was doing or at least physically what he was doing.

The whole thing was hugely exciting, it added immeasurably to the sense of where we were in Canada at that time, and at Anansi at that time, that everything was possible. Here he appeared from nowhere. Peter Such, of course, led him or brought him and, that he wasn't like the rest of us, and it sort of opened up the world for us all in a way, that he came from another culture and he wrote about it with such passion. It was exciting, it was important.[27]

Gibson's response exemplifies the views of a radical elite of writers, but there is evidence of a more grassroots response, too, as told to me in an interview in 2002 by the Canadian artist, Jamelie Hassan. She came to Trinidad in 2001 to work as an artist in residence at the Caribbean Contemporary Arts. She dedicated her project to Harold Sonny Ladoo and visited his sister and mother. She had never met Harold. She reported:

We had, myself and Marwan (*Jamelie's brother, a novelist*) and Ron (*Jamelie's partner, an artist*), in the early seventies, had all, like Ladoo, worked in restaurants and that was the way that we were surviving as people who were wanting to have a life in the arts. So the fact that this book came out in '72, *No Pain Like This Body*, you know, it really inspired us in a particular kind of way and we were like – Oh great! You know, this is possible, you can slug it out here in the kitchen doing this, bang around with the dishes and stir up crepes or whatever we were doing, you know.

...But it was really the drama around what did it mean to become an artist, a serious working artist in Canada in the early seventies. And I was 25 and here was this young writer who had the book published and we passed it around, literally, we passed it around from kitchen staff to kitchen staff, from shift to shift and we read it, we talked about it.[28]

What an image! Restaurant kitchen staff passing Harold's book from hand to hand, reading it, discussing it. Harold's work left an indelible mark in the lives of so many, even those who had never met him.

I, who grew up in the optimism and the heady dream of West Indies Federation (1958-May 1962) and Independence (August 1962), would, like most Trinidadians, reject the jaundiced views of V.S. Naipaul whose often dismissive comments about Trinidad and the Caribbean in *The Middle Passage* (1962)[27], the *Suffrage of Elvira* (1969) and other works offended us caught up in our desire to build a new nation, a new way of seeing ourselves and our possibilities in the world. But Harold Ladoo didn't have the distance of the brahmin Naipaul, he couldn't just leave and put us behind him. The earth was between the toes of this boy from McBean. The violence of the darkest side of life in Trinidad was part of his experience. If Naipaul in the "Pastoral" chapter of *A House for Mr Biswas* portrays a world where Biswas's childhood is "unnecessary and unaccommodated", a childhood of sores and the malnutrition that stunts his growth, it is a period that is swiftly passed over in a novel which chronicles at much greater length the emotional torture suffered at the hands of his father's in-laws; by contrast, Ladoo portrays the assault physically, with the sharp edge of a cutlass.

In *No Pain Like This Body* it isn't just the violence that hits you when you read it, it is the incredible economy, the deft control of dialogue and characterisation, the vivid visualisation and the maelstrom of emotions, the idiosyncratic perspectives, and the hostile environment orchestrated with the surest of instincts. Peter Such records that:

> He was terrified that as he grew into technique and achieved a literary objectivity he would begin to lose the unique poetic density and essentially oral structure of his ideas. I felt he was already at what Joyce calls the dramatic stage in writing, the place where people and events are presented rather than described, where things are felt rather than recounted. If he lost it, this natural talent, it might take him years to get it back.[30]

*No Pain Like This Body*'s 'post-indentureship' characters are adrift; bewildered by a repressive social system and an environment that answers no appeals to a higher power. But those who stand outside Pa's godless universe can call on tradition to centre them. Nanny and Nanna, as arrivals from India, are still supported and informed by the religious beliefs they came with, and while Benwa is, like Pa, of the first generation born in Trinidad, he is secure in his position as a village stickfighter, the champion and defender of his community ruled by a strict tradition of morality and courage.[31]

The rest of the community struggles with the disconnect between applying apparently anachronistic cultural myths in a strange land and facing daily the 'terrible truth' of the 'lived reality' of what indentureship has done to them.

Here is novelist Rabindranath Maharaj in his review of *No Pain Like This Body*:

> Throughout the novel, Ladoo seems to be saying: This is the way this will play out. These people are doomed because they have been separated from all that is familiar and yoked into submission. And so they must turn against themselves, villager against villager, husband against wife, parents against children.
> Even the landscape presents an adversarial visage. The lagoon is teeming with snakes and scorpions and pariah dogs, and regular thunderstorms

inundate the village with mud.

    … There have been a couple of books, like Ismith Khan's *The Jumbie Bird* and David Dabydeen's *The Counting House*, that reference the effects of Indian indentureship in the Caribbean, but none has delved so deep; none has managed to throw up the utter savagery of its victims, even those a generation removed.[32]

Dionne Brand, the poet and novelist, expresses it clearly in her introduction to the 2003 republication of the novel:

"Better than a thousand verses, comprising useless words, is one beneficial single line, by hearing which one attains peace."
    These words uttered by the Buddha possibly describe Harold Ladoo's contribution to both Caribbean and Canadian literature. How can I say this of a novel so unrelentingly brutal, because *No Pain Like This Body* is a novel that strips its reader of sentimentality of any kind – pity or superiority. It is a novel unconcerned with anything but truth-telling. And because peace is nothing without truth, I suspect for Ladoo this was obvious. So much of his life had been spent in truth's bald presence that he was able to capture it in his brief time.[33]

Here I cannot resist inserting an intriguing curiosity. On 6 December 1972, a review of *No Pain* was published in the *Erindalian*,[34] the college's student newspaper. It is uncredited, (which was unusual for the *Erindalian*) and covers issues that only someone close to the writer could have known. It mentions the debts to *As I Lay Dying* by Faulkner and *La Guerre, Yes Sir!* by Roch Carrier that Dennis Lee cites in both his review of the draft of "All Our Yesterdays" in May 1971[35] and his notes on the accepted draft.[36] It also raises Ladoo's grouse (mentioned above in discussion of the 'wake scene') about the editing of the manuscript which in the writer's view sacrificed cultural authenticity.[37] Going out on a limb of speculation, I think it is reasonable to conjecture that this review was in fact written by Harold himself.

    It is still amazing that this ground-breaking novel continues to be ignored in some sections of the Caribbean literary establishment, dismissed cynically as a 'one hit wonder'. As Professor Emeritus Frank Birbalsingh, a pioneer of Indo-Caribbean Studies, explains:

You know, it's really just the one book *No Pain Like This Body*. The volume of work is not there. I mean *Yesterdays* is an inferior book, and doesn't have the weight that *No Pain Like This Body* has. So I think part of the reason why he has not established a place in the canon, as it were, would be because of the smallness of the volume of his work. It's a little unfair, because sometimes, you know, volume alone is not all and that is a very powerful book.[38]

Quite apart from its reception by academics and critics, this is a novel that galvanised its readers and lodged itself in their lives in memorable fashion. I quote here three views of the book that express a characteristic relationship with the book that Harold seems to inspire in his readers.

First the novelist Monique Roffey:

> … to anyone who knows Caribbean literature, his novel is infamous [sic], and Ladoo is seen as one of the region's great literary stars. I have read the book several times and it is my favourite novel written by a Trinidadian novelist hands down. It deserves to be known and read by anyone who wants to know more about the small complex republic of Trinidad and Tobago.[39]

And a review of the French editions of the novels from Michaëla Danjé of Cases Rebelles:

> Ladoo's first novel, *No Pain Like This Body*, … his first masterpiece totally enveloped in the anger at the unleashed elements and the destructive fury of a domestic tyrant, father and husband. The breathtaking poetic picture of a dangerous environment, made even more threatening by poverty and destitution.
>
> Living beings, men, scorpions and snakes that kill without distinction or pity. The weakest who live in fear of being crushed, split, snapped up, eaten. Infant fears saturated with superstitions, men changing into dogs and horses. Lucid fears born of violence without respite. The living crush the living; no harmony, no shelter. In the same way that Panday, one of the children, will crush the crab and the little crabs in his belly, the storm, the scorpions and Pa will crush Rama. Above all there is only an indifferent god, "dead or rotten in the sky" in which nobody believes anymore except the grandparents Nanny and Nanna, the positive characters of the novel.
>
> … It is also about showing how the history that the powerful tell is false, how it can drive you crazy. Here it is Pa, personifying abject patriarchy, who imposes his version of the death of his son.[40]

I give the last words to David Chariandy:

> Set in 1905 in the Tola district of the fictional "Carib Island," *No Pain Like This Body* offers a horrific glimpse into South Asian indentured labour in the Caribbean. The environment is not idyllic and sunshine drenched, but overcast, cruel, and quite literally poisonous. The transplanted Hindu community is comprised neither of happy labourers nor heroic resisters of oppression, but of individuals consumed by fear, self-hatred, and madness – casualties of the voyage over the *Kala Pani* or "the Black Waters." In this respect, Ladoo's novel is uncompromisingly bitter. Yet we continue to read precisely because of Ladoo's extraordinary talent in leavening such grim circumstances with the ironic, bacchanalian, and occasionally even poignant voices of those who live in Tola. As the narrator himself reminds us, "there was life in Tola." And it is precisely this life, "quiet, deadly, and convincing" (as Dennis Lee reminds us) which remains Ladoo's enduring accomplishment.[41]

Endnotes

1. *'Nana' and 'Nani' (or Nanna and Nanny) Hindi for 'Granpa and Granny'.*
2. Sundar Popo the singer and musician was a contemporary of Harold's, also from central Trinidad. *Nani and Nanna* was his first nationwide hit and single-handedly ushered in a new genre of Trinidadian popular music, Chutney.
3. Dennis Lee, "The Death of Harold Ladoo". *Heart Residence. Collected Poems 1967-2017* (Toronto: Anansi, 2017), pp. 86-87.
4. Dennis Lee mentions Faulkner's influence in his first letter to Harold after first seeing the manuscript for *All Our Yesterdays* in May 1971 (before he was officially editor) – see Appendix One. It was my colleague, writer and academic Ramabai Espinet, however, who pointed out to me that there is so much in Faulkner's *As I Lay Dying* (1930) that echoes again in *No Pain Like This Body*: the coffin being built in the yard, the children's perspective on death, all sorts of things were appropriated for *No Pain* including some of the syntax and phrasing. The wake scene, with its drinking and carousing is also reminiscent of the wake scene in Roch Carrier's *La Guerre, Yes Sir!* (1970) (see Dennis Lee's comments in Appendix Two).
5. Interview with Dennis Lee by Christopher Laird 2002.
6. *When Gods Have Fallen*, Victor Questel, *Kairi* 1/1974. Dr. Questel's whole review can be read in Appendix Six.
7. *No Pain Like This Body*, pp. 18-19.
8. Interview with Arnold Itwaru by Christopher Laird, 2002.
9. *"He used to want to hit me a lot, slap me up all for nothing"*. Interview with Rachel, 2003. See also Chapter Thirteen: WHO WAS HAROLD SONNY LADOO? Jeoffrey Ladoo, however, said that the description of Pa's abuse of Ma was influenced by a couple living next door to the Ladoo home in McBean.
10. As noted in Chapter Four, in Harold's Toronto stories the women are strippers and whores. In his Tola stories the women are more often victims of the prevailing social and economic structure, acted on rather than actors.
11. A few years later, pregnant with Rama's twin boys, Sita goes into self-exile as Rama's subjects are not convinced of her purity and she doesn't want Rama to be embarrassed. Rama's battle with Rawan can be seen as due more to a male power contest than marital devotion.
12. "Mythopoesis and the Fevered Body in Harold Ladoo's *No Pain Like This Body*", Shalini Khan, *Wasafiri* (26 March 2013).
13. *No Pain*, p. 27.
14. *No Pain*, pp. 29-30.
15. Not only were Indian-Caribbean men and women often the victims

of violence from white and black people in Trinidad but, during the time of indenture, domestic abuse – including wife murders – was alarmingly common in the Indian community in Trinidad. As historian, Bridget Brereton, has explained, 'Between 1872 and 1900, there were 87 murders of Indian women, of which 65 were "wife-murders"'. Although the first female Indian indentured workers enjoyed comparative freedom in their new Caribbean location, as Paula Morgan and Valerie Youssef note, 'Pivotal to the subsequent attempt at Indian cultural reconstruction was the task of harnessing these women in accordance with traditional patriarchal strictures. Violence was a major plank of this process'. "Place, Language, and Body in the Caribbean Experience and the example of Harold Sonny Ladoo's *No Pain Like this Body Literature's Sensuous Geographies (2015)* by S.P. Moslund.

16. See Morton Klass, *East Indians in Trinidad: A Study of Cultural Persistence* (New York: Columbia University Press, 1961), pp. 36-37, 43-44.
17. Interview with Peter Such by Christopher Laird, 2002.
18. Shalini Khan, "Mythopoesis and the Fevered Body in Harold Ladoo's *No Pain Like This Body*", *Wasafiri* (26 March 2013). Shalini Khan also points out: 'New World' Rama, for example, is a boy of eight. Both Lord Rama and the child Rama… undergo trials in their period of exile. The prince, demonstrating his skill in war and his favour among the gods, successfully vanquishes demons and other evildoers and, at the same time, proves his worthiness as a warrior and future King. The child Rama is also tried in exile. His adversaries are invoked as wind, rain and even scorpions, as well as the father who initiates the child's self-inflicted exile. Unlike his epic namesake, however, the child is not victorious; he becomes ill and later dies. "Harold Sonny Ladoo's *No Pain Like This Body*: The Ramayana and Indo-Caribbean Experience", *Wasafiri* Vol. 28, No. 2, June 2013.
19. Victor Questel, "When Gods Have Fallen", *Kairi* 1/1974.
20. Dennis Lee's notes to Harold in Appendix Two gives great detail on how the wake scene and other aspects of the novel were approached.
21. Typescript among Peter Such's papers in the McMaster Library.
22. A scene from *No Pain Like This Body* (subsequently reworked with Dennis Lee) appears in the first issue of Peter Such's *Impulse*.
23. Some in McBean believe that the characters in *No Pain* are modelled after people Harold knew in the community and in his family e.g. Ma modelled after Harold's mother, Hamidhan. A cousin, Lily Jogie, believes that Benwa was modelled after Harold's deceased younger brother, Ramesh or Toy.
24. *No Pain Like This Body*, pp. 100-101.
25. In fact, there exists among the surviving manuscripts, a fragment

of a proposed novel called "The Death of Victor Benwa".

26. "In times before when you have stick fighters in a village. People used to look up to them. They were considered to be men who were sort of upstanding. People would go to them for advice at times. If there was contention among the people, the stick fighter in the village would be the sort of peacemaker. The stick fighter would play a part in bringing them together or settling it. Sometimes they would settle it with a stickfight or talking – dialogue." Christopher Laird's 2011 interview with Mother Marie-Anne Cummings, Warrior village mother, herbalist, healer, counsellor. Steeped in the Moruga Orisha (African traditional religion) tradition.

27. Graeme Gibson, interview with the author.

28. Interview with Jamelie Hassan.

29. "History is built around achievement and creation; and nothing was created in the West Indies," V.S. Naipaul, *The Middle Passage* (1962), p. 29.

30. Peter Such, "The Short Life and Sudden Death of Harold Sonny Ladoo."

31. "God could kiss my ass!" shouts Pa in *No Pain Like This Body*.

32. Rabindranath Maharaj, "Dark Imaginings – Harold Sonny Ladoo's *No Pain Like this Body*", *Canadian Notes & Queries*. 50th Anniversary issue (# 103, Fall 2018).

33. Dionne Brand, Introduction, 2003 edition of *No Pain*, pp. xiii-xiv.

34. "Ladoo obviously has the stuff in him to write a more extensive novel, and I personally would rather have seen the Hindu rituals and prayers of the villagers presented rather than summarized but *No Pain Like this Body* is a novel of which anyone could be proud." Review. *Erindalian*, 6 December 1972.

35. Dennis Lee, appendix 4.

36. Appendix 1.

37. Appendix 2.

38. Interview with Frank Birbalsingh by Christopher Laird 2002.

39. Monique Roffey, *The Independent,* 10 July 2014.

40. Michaëla Danjé, "Harold Sonny Ladoo, filant dans nos nuits indo-caribéennes" (Harold Sonny Ladoo, Spinning in our Indo-Caribbean nights) Review of *Yesterdays* and *No Pain Like This Body*", *Cases Rebelles,* April 2006.

41. Review of *No Pain Like This Body*, David Chariandy, *Canadian Literature* Number 1887, 2006.

## CHAPTER NINE
## THE PHOTOGRAPH

Harold "moving, ducking and weaving and defending".

With *No Pain Like This Body* on the verge of being published Harold Ladoo was about to become known to the public. He was in the early stages of re-inventing himself, presenting intriguing personas for his Canadian friends. While he was increasingly adept at this in personal, everyday encounters, he was instinctively cautious about his image in the media; he knew he needed to keep control of it.

House of Anansi Press needed a photograph of Harold for his book cover. It was Graeme Gibson, a novelist and one of the House of Anansi Press founding authors, who was tasked with photographing Harold for his book cover.

> *Peter Such*: One of the things about Harold was that though he was a very handsome looking guy, and I think he knew it, was that he was very camera shy and I think I understood this. I studied with Marshall McLuhan, and he talked about how certain societies are what he called "oral acoustic" and so they hate having their photos taken because it steals the soul. And I remember talking to Harold on this subject because he told me he really didn't like having a picture, and I had to really persuade him to let Graeme take some pictures of him – Graeme Gibson that is – for his first novel on the cover.[1]

I spoke with Graeme Gibson:

> *Christopher Laird*: Tell me about photographing him [Harold] and what you were looking for and what you were happy to find when you got that famous photograph?

> *GG*: Okay. It was sort of like photographing a flyweight boxer who was always moving, ducking and weaving and defending. I haven't looked at the contact sheet[2] for a long time and I know I can find it, but I suspect that in a whole lot of the pictures in that contact sheet, he will have been almost out of the frame at the last moment (laughs), as I was throwing these visual punches at him.

> What I was looking for is what I got. I was looking at something that had the intensity, that had the darkness, even the way he's smoking that cigarette with his wonderful hand satisfied me. I felt extremely fortunate to have gotten that and as I recall, I think it was one of the last pictures

in the roll and I think I moved in much closer on him than I had with the others. And then what he did was to present me with this wonderful mask, this wonderful sort of glaring mask.

The picture that was chosen for the book cover, naturally, became the image associated with Ladoo. One look at all the other images captured in that same session would show that this image was the least representative of how he really looked. But it was dramatic, intense and dark, not unlike the famous photo of Kafka (without the cigarette). I asked Peter Such which of the images he thought best represented the Harold he knew:

*Peter Such*: Well, you know the image he projected on the book is not really... I would say this is more like the Harold I knew. This one here:

and this one laughing, yeah, I would say that's closer.

*Christopher Laird*: But what was different about this image to the Harold you knew? The image projected on the book, what was different about it?

*PS*: Well, I mean, I was very conscious that Harold had these two sides, you know.

*CL*: Only two?

*PS*: (Laughs) That's simplifying life, because I knew him really... because the books are so harsh and vicious in a way, but I found him a very witty guy. And we had a lot of laughs together and we even made jokes sometimes quite macabre... You know, I think he had this other very, very nice side to him, a very charming side and when he felt comfortable with people, this side came out much more. I think he was really a very shy guy like a lot of writers are, and then with him, I think he sort of started to project this image once he knew the book was going to be published and, in a way, people kind of pushed him into this image, you know, this sort of somewhat menacing, mysterious image you know, the writer, kind of almost like the Hemingway style[3] (chuckles).

*CL*: Kafkaesque

*PS*: Kafkaesque, yes, that's a much better description actually, I was trying to search for that. And I had this feeling that there was this other depth to him really and I think that if he had lived he would have gone to that other depth, 'cause I think he had a great sensitivity. That inner sense was not revealed in his books. These books were a kind of rage and I think he was growing beyond that rage into a kind of wisdom when his life was...[4]

*Peter Such overcome by memories of his friend 2003*

Peter had to stop, put his hands to his eyes. The photographs, talking about Harold, the loss of a special friend and protégé overwhelmed him, caught him by surprise as these things do. Even to this day, forty years on, Ladoo still conjures raw emotion from those he got close to and even those who did not know him but just read his work.

When I showed the photos to Jim Polk, who edited Harold's second novel, *Yesterdays*, he was also stumped:

> *Jim Polk*: Well, I'm quite surprised. They don't look like the Harold I knew, and it's not just the suit and the tie and the white shirt, there is something very guarded about the expressions, as there might be from a guy who's having his book published and is taking author photos, and doesn't really quite know what image is expected or what to project. He looks quite serious, even when he's smiling, the warmth and the humour that I remember, the laughter isn't in the smile. I'm quite startled by these. I've seen them, they were on the book jacket, one of them certainly, the one with the cigarette, certainly he smoked a lot, as did I in those days. But this formal, serious, intense Harold is not anything like the man who came up the fire escape in sneakers, tee shirt. To be fair, it was very hot in my apartment, the summer was hot, there was no air-conditioning there and sometimes he'd take off the shirt. It was a very casual kind of Harold. I didn't know this one. Sorry.[5]

Harold, it is true, didn't like to have his photo taken. I am tempted to think that the reason is not the anthropological explanation that Peter Such ascribes to this reluctance but rather an instinct Harold had to maintain control of his image. There is just one photo his wife, Rachel, has of him and he is crunched into the edge of the frame, at a party, included in the photo as if by accident.

In his own life, Harold seems to have observed a separation between his family life, the life he shared with his Trinidadian friends, and how he wanted to present himself to his Canadian colleagues, none of whom, besides Peter Such, were afforded direct access to his family.

Professor Emeritus of English at the St. Augustine campus of University of the West Indies, Ken Ramchand and I interviewed Harold's sister Meena in 2003 and we asked her to talk about the Harold she knew, to explain the differences in the Harold of the photos, smiling, laughing but also stern and intense.

*Meena Ladoo:* Yes, he was a very joyous person, you know, my brother. Yes, and he can be that way too, very serious, very executive type person. Yes, he had those capabilities.

*Christopher Laird:* Talk a little about him as you remember him and what you felt. If you had someone say "Harold, what was Harold?" What epitomised Harold for you?

*ML:* A person full of life, that's how I would describe him, full of life. There was nothing dull about him. He was a very happy person, a very outgoing person, like a comedian type person too. He's a person he can bring you up from your saddest moment and he was also the type of person who could get very straight, very strict, very straightforward and put you right in your place; mind you he was very lovable.

*Ken Ramchand:* You never saw any cruelty in him?

*ML:* No, I never saw cruelty in him. For me, he was my brother, my friend, like we say, a combination, sister, uncle, aunt, mother, father, everybody in one. He would be there for you all the time, he would listen, he would tell you if you're wrong, his opinion and what he would think, but one thing he never did, for me and I look around at my other sisters, he will never condemn you. He will encourage you to think you're shifting, he'll try to get you to see it the other way, but he will not condemn you, he will always support you. He was like the knight in shining armour kind of person, he would be there to defend you, good or bad, you can count on him. [6]

So, Harold was 'ducking and weaving and defending', trying to keep control over the images he presented of himself in different circumstances, to different people. There is no doubt, looking at the reel that Graeme Gibson took, that Harold is almost chameleon-like in the way he appears so different from one photo to another.

The effort to keep track of the many histories he assumed for himself in the presence of the people and institutions that could affect his future became, I think, as much a creative burden as his writing. And the writing had to maintain a standard that would keep him a serious contender among his new literary comrades. The pressure to continue to earn the respect and attention of the writers he now counted among his acquaintances, if not friends, would have been constant. Writers like Dennis Lee and Margaret Atwood operate at such technically meticulous and scrupulous levels, deeply versed in the literary tradition that informed them, there was a great deal of 'catching up' that Harold felt he had to do to be counted among them. The early morning calls heralding a 'new novel finished' would be one way he must have felt would keep their attention.

How was he to follow *No Pain Like This Body*?

Endnotes

1.  Interview with Peter Such by Christopher Laird 2003.
2.  See Appendix Eight.
3.  Peter's allusion to Hemingway is telling. Hemingway was notorious for the way he manufactured his swashbuckling macho persona, one which he himself, later in life, began to believe.
4.  Interview with Peter Such by Christopher Laird 2003.
5.  Interview with James Polk by Christopher Laird, 2003.
6.  Interview with Meena Ladoo by Christopher Laird and Ken Ramchand, 2003.

CHAPTER TEN
YESTERDAYS

Shit talk back in town
Ah ha
Shit talk back in town
Ah ha
Shit talk back in town
And everybody shifting around
          — Trinidadian Limers' refrain

In May 1972 Harold wrote to Dennis Lee: "I APPOINT YOU DOCTOR OF THE NOVEL". The work with Dennis Lee on *No Pain Like This Body* had taught Harold what it takes to be not just a writer but a publishable writer, a publishable novelist. In a letter to Dennis Lee, August 1972, he wrote:

> I know for certain now that when I emerge from my apprenticeship I would be able to go into the ring as a champion. I think (do not think I am trying to praise you here) that any writer or poet who is tough and dedicated enough to stick with you would in the long run be a better artist. I know that PAIN would not have been the book it is today if you hadn't spent hours and hours with me in an effort to put the book in order. At times I wish I had your talent and particular kind of feel (not until I can somehow master some of your techniques would I be able to emerge from my apprenticeship);[1]

Having put *No Pain Like This Body* to bed in 1972 (and in keeping with the 'next novel' clause in the contract House of Anansi Press had with him) Harold had to follow up with a second novel. What should he lead with?
    As Peter Such said:

> In this country we are very vicious with people because if you do a really good first book you've got to do a really great second book and you have to do a magnificent third book otherwise you're dead.[2]

    Harold knew: "It is necessary for me to get two more novels out: three novels would give me the reputation that I need to establish myself."[3]
    As Jim Christy, of the *Globe and Mail* writes about *No Pain*:

If Ladoo can do it again he will have secured a place as an important young novelist. In the meantime, he has skilfully revealed new territory which if explored can only enrich fiction in Canada.[4]

According to his letters to Dennis Lee, he had finished at least two novels since August 1972, "Rage In Tola" (which he dubs: a "great novel", a "West Indian classic") and "The Intruders". And, if we give credence to his phone calls to Peter Such, Graeme Gibson and others in the early mornings after binge writing sessions announcing the completion of new novels, he should have had a number of options for his second novel. But he submitted what was initially titled *Mission* (after a suggestion from Dennis Lee that it be called *The Hindu Mission To Canada*) but was finally titled *Yesterdays*.

It is in *Yesterdays* that Harold has a lot of fun drawing on a sample of memorable characters from his knowledge of the McBean community. In its revised, published text, *Yesterdays* features three households straddling the Southern Main Road (as McBean does).[5] On one side is the homosexual shopkeeper, Sook, and his wife Rookmin and, next to them, the local 'village ram' the sexual opportunist, Ragbir, whose enormous testicles often dangle out of his clothes. On the other side of the road live retired cane farmer, Choonilal, his wife, Basdai and son Poonwa with their lodger, Tailor. The main premise of *Yesterdays*, the events of which take place some fifty years after *No Pain Like This Body*, is the effort by the main character, Choonilal, to hold on to his house which his wife wants him to mortgage to the corrupt local pundit in order to raise funds for their son, Poonwa, to go on a Hindu mission to Canada.

But House of Anansi Press rejected the "The Mission".

Harold chaffed at the rejection. He wrote to Dennis:

> When I wrote MISSION the book came out of a particular mood. There was hardly any time to sit down and view the book objectively or try to see where I had made errors in term of construction etc. As a poet you would be the first to understand the kind of artistic dilemma I am talking about. Many experienced veterans (my professors etc.) have read MISSION and seriously advised me not to rework or even revise the book. A few of them have even suggested moving to another publisher (RANDOMHOUSE for example).[6]

The rejection obviously sent him into a spin.

> ...and at one time when I became depressed, (I even viewed the idea as important and necessary for the wellbeing of my art. For more than a month now I had been at war with my own self and at one time or the other I had almost made up my mind to upset some of my philosophy and eat some of my principles. Out of boredom (and nostalgia) I had even planned to stop writing altogether. My life so far as you know has

been full of upsets and worries (it is a surprise to my own self that I have travelled so far). At times I worry very seriously whether my life is not perhaps more tragic than the artistic life of my own characters. Pessimism and nostalgia are so rooted in my whole life style and at times I question whether the sadness and longing are not the foundation of my own genius (if I have any). Life for me is a matter of moods.[7]

In a letter to Anansi's Managing Editor, Shirley Gibson a few days later, he protests even more vehemently:

I think that you know a work of art is really a feeling, regardless if analysis and criticism rip the work apart and doom the endeavour of the artist; still the work remains as a feeling, a vision; it is something total, aesthetic and unimpeachable; it is a mood, a vocation, a longing, and in the final analysis it is the digression of individualistic consciousness.

This (2nd) novel is a very important book in my saga. As I have told you, it took a particular mood to write the book in two minutes less than a hundred hours it was finished.[8] At times when I detach myself from the book I think that there are major things wrong with it. But each time that I attempt to rewrite the book my intuition steps in and I am unable to go beyond two pages. After over a hundred hours or so I have only written two pages and I have already destroyed the two pages. Daily I am growing more adamant to stick with the novel as it is. At the same time, I am quite willing to do some minor revisions here and there, I am even willing to make the novel a bit longer, but on the grounds of principle and the internal voice that gave it utterance, I am not prepared to change the structure of the novel.[9]

Harold would have to fight for what was now called *Yesterdays*. Dennis Lee had sent his feedback on the *Yesterdays* draft in May. Four months later Harold wrote to Dennis again:

I agree with almost everything you say, but only on a theoretical basis. Each time that I try to rework the novel something inside tells me not to make any drastic changes in the book. For example, I am prepared to rewrite (retype I mean) and change a few things around … but I am in no way prepared and even willing to change the structure of the novel. *Yesterdays* is not a plot novel like Faulkner's *The Reivers*; in *The Reivers* everything hangs together and moves along with grace and surprises until at the end we learn that everything (without too much sentimentality) sits squarely on the shoulders of a marriage. *Yesterdays* is not that kind of novel. It is an anecdotal book.[10] *No Pain Like This Body* is the kind of novel that is to be read and felt; it is dramatic and it is meant to excite the emotions (if it is legitimate to slap in Aristotle), but *Yesterdays* is not that kind of book. Nothing is meant to be experienced in it; it is a sort of ideological and anecdotal book; the style is neither dramatic nor epic; it is a very artificial style that cuts somewhere between Kawabata and Narayan.[11]

And as he continues to flail in defence of what he fears is an unpublishable novel, he takes refuge in his strength – storytelling – rather than novel form and structure, as he outlines his plans for extending *Yesterdays'* characters into sequels:

> Right now I am working on a draft of another novel The Hindu Mission to Canada. In that novel Poonwa will go into the village; there will be village council meetings; because in the other book we will learn that the village priest did not give Choonilal the money after all; Poonwa will have to get his money from the villagers; then we will have Poonwa going to the city to learn about women (he will go with Tailor) and then again we will meet with Phyllis (ex-wife of Balky, and Balky will be the son of Jadoo etc. which will take us right into Rage). And at the end of that book (If you are confused don't worry, I am all mixed up) which will be a plot novel in which I will slap in a very sentimental marriage between Poonwa and Phyllis and have them in conjunction with the village priest embezzle the funds of the villagers and run away to South City; and in a later novel I will have Poonwa dying in Toronto with a heart attack in Spadina Avenue, (Part of this story you already know – remember my friend who died with a heart attack a couple months ago; well that son of a bitch is going to give me enough material to deal with Poonwa in Canada... Perhaps a heart attack is too sentimental... perhaps I can have him go around Jew Market putting his hands into banana crates 'Chiquita' and have a deadly spider bite him and kill him and his mission in one lick... or perhaps have him go to the hospital and get treatment for the bite, sting? I don't know what –[12]

His delight is obvious in envisaging the fun of writing sequels for the dramatic stories he can tell. His dislike of Poonwa is delightfully expressed in envisioning his exotic and horrendous death. Nevertheless, I have found no evidence of "The Hindu Mission To Canada" among the fragments that survive. Presumably "working on a draft right now" probably refers to what he outlines in the letter and no more.

Just previously, he had written to Shirley Gibson and outlined another plan of sequels to *Yesterdays* slightly different to those outlined to Dennis Lee ten days later.

> You see, this novel (Yesterdays) is really the first novel in a trilogy concerning the mission to Canada. After this novel ends, Poonwa (the paranoid missionary, and fanatic) still has two weeks on the island before he leaves for Canada. In the other novel the approach will be different; there are so many surprises and disappointments yet to come. For example the Hindu priest will not give the money to Poonwa although he had had the audacity to make Choonilal (Poonwa's so called father) sign the mortgage papers. But these and other mishaps will only show up in the second novel of the mission trilogy. There are many things in Yesterdays that are merely touched upon (for example Poonwa is not Choonilal's son, he is really the son of the village priest; or Tailor who is planning to

defraud the Choonilals will have to leave the village in the other novel) only because of the vision that I have of my whole craft.[13]

I quote these passages at length, not for the plans Harold outlines in his defence but to give an idea of both his method and his state of mind ("If you are confused don't worry, I am all mixed up"). He also outlined the place *Yesterdays* and *No Pain Like This Body* had in his plans:

> *Yesterdays* is the first novel in the Vishnu of Tola series, and *No Pain Like This Body* is the first in the Panday series.[14]

The letters reveal his desperation to get his second novel published, not least because he faced the risk that his claim to have written a number of other ("great", "West Indian classic") novels in the interim could be unmasked as fantasy. He had to act. Things could unravel quickly. In a letter to Dennis Lee he gave a telling and probably characteristically charming account of a visit to House of Anansi which shows how conscious he was of the effect he could have on people and how he used it.

> One morning woke up thinking that the second novel is good just as it is. All day I worried about it until I finally remembered that you had told me that while you are away, it would be better to see the people at House of Anansi. When I remembered this I phoned up Shirley and told her that my "intuition" (ha!) tells me that the novel is a good one as it is. "Well if you feel it is good," she said, "you can bring it back and allow someone else to have a look at it: "All right," I said, confidence and authority trembling in my voice, " I'll be there." Quickly gulping some food down, I typed out a short letter and hurried down to Anansi, a feeling of achievement walking all over me. Once there I got down to business (my dark eyes flashing, my thin legs supporting me like a stork, one hand thrust into my pocket, the other holding the manuscript with the knowledge of a renaissance genius) I said, "This is a good book." Putting on the worried look (a look I have picked up recently from Choonilal) I added, "There are many authorities who have read it , and I am confident that it is publishable." "All right," she said, "we will take a look at it." Not a least bit worried, I walked over to Lions and powdered some beers. Confident that all my worries were over, I came home, played with my son, fell asleep on the carpet and dreamt that I was stabbing jello with a fork.[15]

Finally, House of Anansi Press (Shirley Gibson as Managing Editor) accepted the manuscript and designated James (Jim) Polk, Anansi's Editorial Director, to edit *Yesterdays* (Dennis Lee, the editor of *No Pain Like The Body*, had left House of Anansi Press by then). Jim Polk began working with Harold around June 1973. He recalled:

> My most vivid early memory of Harold is in my apartment, which was

a walk-up; it went up a fire escape on Burr Street, and he would be
waiting there at nine in the morning on the dot, a little early for me,
with a bag which had his sweet roll in it and a coffee and he was ready
to work, and I would make more coffee. Generally he would stay almost
'til three or four, in part because he had so many stories to tell.

I quite liked Harold, we got along very well indeed, in part because I
found him very funny, he had an amazing sense of humour and I had
read *No Pain* and expected a more tragic sort of figure, but no. He was
delighted to not edit anymore and tell me more stories about the island,
and his situation as a dishwasher, and people we knew, and it was kind
of very informal, almost an island experience I think, in that we just sat
there and shot the shit for far too long, and then we would turn to *Yesterdays*.
It was in pretty good shape, it had his voice, it had his sense of humour
certainly, the mission to Canada, the characters, all these things were
there. My job was to draw him out more, it was very short when it came,
it never got to be a big book and I wanted it slightly longer, just for
marketing reasons. But I did talk him into telling me more stories, some
of which got in there and we'd work on a sentence or two and he would
come back with a funnier version, or a better version, or a sharper version.
I was not a dictatorial editor at all. I led Harold, I pressed the button
and Harold had it to give, and I would sit there often and he would talk
to me and I'd type it out in patchwork to make the book hold together
a little better.[16]

*Yesterdays* was submitted to House of Anansi Press in a final draft just
before Harold left for Trinidad in August 1973. Apparently, Jim Polk was
under the impression he was to revisit the manuscript when he returned
from his fateful trip to Trinidad but as far as Harold was concerned he had
signed off on it in August. Polk again:

He decided in August that the book was finished. I secretly hoped to
increase the length to a more marketable size after he came back from
Trinidad. I know that he decided it was complete in August 1973, because
he immediately flew home afterwards. On the manuscript is this: "Note:
This is the final dedication for *Yesterdays*, 7-8-73".[17]

★

As noted in Chapter One, prior to the establishment of Hindu schools
in the mid nineteen-fifties, in rural areas and south Trinidad, the Canadian
Mission schools had offered the main opportunities for Indians to receive
an education – and when this was secondary education it was on condition
that they converted to Christianity. This provided the central motivation
for Ladoo's character, Poonwa, in *Yesterdays*, who is intent on going on
a Hindu mission to Canada to do to Canadians what the Canadian
missionary schools did to Hindus in Trinidad.

"But Poonwa say dat just how white people come here and teach we about Jesus Christ and ting, just so he go teach dem about Rama and Krishna."

"You tink white people want to read Indian books?" Choonilal asked.

"Well Poonwa say he goin to open a school and teach dem to read Hindi. I tink he could do it. How dem white people who come on dat Canadian Mission to Carib Island beat dem Indians and make dem learn English? How come dey make de Indians Christians? Well de same way Poonwa goin to beat dey ass and make dem learn Hindi. I tink he could do it."

"He go do it wen cock get teets," Choonilal said.

"You mean dat white people so bad, dat dey eh go allow him to open he school and ting?"

And Choonilal: "You don't know wot white people give, nuh. Dey want dis whole world for deyself, yeh. Poonwa only foolin around..."

Poonwa shouted from the next room, "Father why don't you shut up! Shut up! Just shut up!"[18]

*Yesterdays* could not be more different to *No Pain Like this Body*. It has none of the brooding violent atmosphere, none of its existential and metaphysical subtexts. Instead it is a rollicking farce, a tour de force of comedic writing, Trinidad style. While it no doubt disappointed the commentators expecting a sequel to *No Pain Like This Body*, to us, in Trinidad, it was a startling about-face in terms of genre and discipline that was nevertheless executed in style. It was a thrill to see a young writer bold enough to attempt a different genre in his second book and bring it off. It is as if Quentin Tarantino suddenly switched to making a Mel Brooks movie. It is very funny, especially if one has an ear for the dialect, yet it is not totally frivolous. In *Yesterdays*, centred as it is on the importance of his house to Choonilal who has toiled diligently all his life to be able to own his own house, (it could be called *A House for Mr. Choonilal*), Harold, who had V.S. Naipaul in his sights, takes a swipe at him and demonstrates that if he is as alienated from Trinidad as V.S. Naipaul, it is an alienation of a very different kind. If Naipaul attacks Trinidad from the metropole, Ladoo's critique is entirely from within. The portrait of Choonilal's son, Poonwa, who wants to take a Hindu mission to Canada could be aimed at Naipaul with his Oxfordian accent and language.

Choonilal berates Poonwa:

"Wen you de small you used to call me 'fadder', now you does call me 'father'. It look like English does flow from you ass. But all de book you read Poonwa, and all dat education you have in you ass is notten. In dis same island man wid dat education have to eat dey shit!"[19]

And again, Choonilal complains to his neighbour, Ragbir:

"Man Rag, wot I go tell you, man. Me son so educated dat wen he talk I does only feel to shit man. De boy talk some Latin just now man Rag. Man wen I hear de Latin, a shit take me one time."[20]

In Trinidad, (and many other places, I imagine) there is a mode of conversation referred to as 'shit talk'. In Trinidad, 'shit talk' is storytelling which riffs off the bizarre, the obscene, the sufferers of self-inflicted misfortune, the scatological, ideas of poetic justice and irony all to score maximum humour among 'limers' (groups – of mainly young men – exchanging anecdotes on the street corner, over drinks in a bar, or at home.)

Ladoo's *Yesterdays* is written in that vein. As such it is admittedly parochial and might well be misread or bewilder the foreign reader and critic. This is the novel's main fault as I see it. It is, in that sense, self-indulgent, but that speaks more to its marketability in foreign markets than to its artistry. It is 'write what you know' gone mad. *Yesterdays*, a Rabelaisian romp, is received by Trinidadians like a kaiso (calypso) – biting, funny, scandalous and inherently familiar. From the point of view of the critics who may have expected more in the vein of *No Pain*, *Yesterdays* may not have been the best choice as a second novel. The fact that Harold fought so hard to get it accepted for publication rather than the novels he had told people he had finished (such as "Rage" and "The Intruders") suggests that those novels were not in a publishable state, any more than the first draft of *Yesterdays* was, and may in fact have been no more than sketches for the proposed novels.

*Yesterdays* gives Ladoo (and the reader) light relief after the torment of *No Pain Like This Body* and furnishes him with the opportunity to exercise his formidable talent for his native dialect. Look at this passage, which I think is a gem of Trinidad Creole rhythm and syntax on the page:

"Dis world have too much trobble man Rag man. I tellin you boy Rag. Sometimes in de night wen I get up to pray to God man Rag, I does can't pray man. Look eh Rag, Tailor givin me too much trobble man."[21]

The use of 'man' and 'boy' in creating a beautifully timed rhythm may approach exaggeration but is perfectly pitched to communicate the speaker's anxiety and earnestness without making him appear ridiculous. Choonilal, at the centre of the novel, is the most sympathetic character. We laugh at the way he expresses his despair while at the same time empathising with his entrapment by Poonwa and Tailor; it gives us pleasure with the language while sympathising with the belaboured Choonilal. As Michaëla Danjé gushes in her review of the French edition of the book:

He (Choonilal) is besieged. He cannot shit quietly anymore. Besieged by the smell of the toilet outrageously blocked by Tailor, parasitic tenant. Besieged by his future missionary son, his wife and a rogue priest who plot to make him mortgage his home, the only way to get the money needed for the mission. He is tormented by his excessive faith, his credulity, and a sincere paternal love that is absolutely unreciprocated. The atmosphere is end to end lively, hilarious and worthy of vaudeville.[22]

Other publishers might have baulked at publishing a book whose dialogue is in such broad dialect, but Harold made none of the compromises that earlier writers from the Caribbean made and House of Anansi Press stood by him in this. True, he was standing on the shoulders of Selvon, who twenty-five years earlier had pioneered ways to convey the creole dialect while making it intelligible to the standard English reader. In *Yesterdays,* however, the narration is standard English, so the story is accessible, and the contrast between the narration and the dialogue adds to the scandalous effect.

Dennis Lee talks about the approach to language in editing *No Pain Like This Body:*

One place where I had nothing to offer really, except cheering from the sidelines, was speech patterns and the music of the language, of dialogue, but also the narrative voice since he got that located so close often to the actual speaking voice of vernacular. So there it was really just a matter of saying, "Look, push it, go further, you're doing fabulous things here." Sometimes, the interesting questions were spelling and things like that, but I mean that's all nuts and bolts stuff. I don't know, I think I was able at times to say – "but can we find some way of making a few things clearer to the reader who is not from this part of Trinidad?" There might even be some parts of the Caribbean where things that were in the first draft might have been a bit hard to follow. But it's also true you know that if some of these things are exotic or strange, foreign, inexplicable, that's not necessarily a bad thing some of the time, but if you're just totally operating in a sea of ambiguity or "what the heck is this all about", then that's maybe not a good thing. But for readers here the whole thing is an introduction into a world that most people here know nothing about, that's an invigorating thing more than intimidating.[23]

It is Ladoo's dialogue that drives his work. The energy of people undiluted by puritanical and colonial editing comes blazing through the Trinidadian landscape onto the page. You can hear and feel his characters as if you were right there. That is Ladoo's major stylistic achievement, it is a consequence of using the first language of Trinidadians, and Ladoo does it better than anyone.

His writing plays with the dichotomy with which Caribbean people live: a creole language for friends and intimates; standard English for formal communication, for engaging the establishment, the colonials and their inheritors. In Trinidad the 1970s was a time of confident and defiant experimentation in the use of Creole in a wide range of contexts. It was a time of great political turmoil especially among the youth in the Caribbean as the unemployed youth, the beneficiaries of the free education instituted a decade before, railed against a titular 'Independence' while the society remained under the control of neo-colonial proxies (*In dis same island man wid dat education have to eat dey shit!*).[24]

Ladoo could modulate his writing with a confident flair in both tongues, a flair that spoke one thing: truth; unwavering, in your face, stripped bare but rhythmically harmonised to beguile the reader. *Yesterdays* depends heavily on the humour, not only of the situations but of the language. As Eugene Benson and L.W. Conolly wrote:

> Ladoo himself professed Hemingway's creed of rendering experience in all of its immediacy and saw as his task the accurate presentation of rural Caribbean life. Although he definitely intends a critique of colonialism, his main concern is to immerse the reader in the particularities of his people's speech and customs in a manner that is less mediated than in the work of his Indian-Trinidadian contemporaries such as V.S. Naipaul (in his early novels) and Sam Selvon, both of whom are more overtly universalist and desire to bridge the gap between cultures either by assimilating minorities into a dominant Western cultural mainstream (Naipaul) or by creating a fluid cultural cosmopolitanism (Selvon).[25]

Perhaps because of its scatological colouring and sexual openness, despite (or because of) its astounding daring and its insistence on driving straight through the hypocrisy and sensitivity to image that Caribbean people, and especially 'fortress communities' like the rural East Indian community possessed, *Yesterdays* was dismissed by many as an inferior work. For instance, in a scathing review of *Yesterdays* in his paper, "Harold Ladoo's Alternate Worlds" (1982) Clement H. Wyke writes:

> In choosing to use the familiar territory of his native land as a mythological centre for later ethnocentric themes Ladoo is not original. His focus on the small East Indian village, for example, is more competently handled by fellow Trinidadians like Naipaul and Selvon and in a different setting by the noted Indian writer Narayan. The theme of pursuing the ethnic and cultural progress of the West Indian inhabitant through a cyclic pattern of history – by appealing to settlement history, to the problems of identity, and to the evolution of racial consciousness – has been more skillfully explored in poetry by Edward Brathwaite.
> The ironic clash between intruder and inhabitant, and the strange ironic mingling of the status of victim and victimizer, have received more complete and masterful treatment by Wilson Harris. It is against this dazzling firmament of literary stars that Ladoo's tame and unfinished creations stand. Clearly Ladoo's work is dwarfed in this universe; but it is dwarfed for reasons other than comparison with the works of more

mature artists. The reason also lies in the character and plight of the
author.

... This is not literary art but immature protest literature.[26]

Wyke seems bizarrely unaware of the difficulties of writing about
"Alternate Worlds", knowing only one first hand. His criticism is based on
value judgements that he assumes are axiomatic, as they are for those
writing from the point of view of the western literary canon.

   Though his own writing was mostly close to that western canon, the
Nobel laureate, Derek Walcott, provides an insight that can be applied to
Ladoo's writing:

> Those survivors, even in their mental and physical shackles, must have
> muttered to themselves that the nature which they occupied was not
> hostile to them for any reason, that before the sun became infernal and
> they moved through the cane harvesting like charred, black sticks, there
> was some benediction in the stupendous dawns and sunsets that had
> nothing to do with the boring evil of their servitude. Out of that condition,
> incredibly, came humour, mockery, and self-parody, an attitude
> incomprehensible to those who tortured them, a tone of voice in their
> music which is superior to tragedy – tragicomic.[27]

   The highly critical reception *Yesterdays* received in Canada for its apparent crudeness and lack of subtlety, for its negative attributes in relation to
the western literary canon, was not unanimous. There were other more
positive views. Mark Sarner wrote:

> *No Pain Like This Body* convinced even the wary that Ladoo was worth
> watching. *Yesterdays* establishes that he is worth much more than just a
> look...
>    Fortunately, it never becomes soapy. In fact Ladoo dazzles the reader
> with his control. The result is a beautifully paced book. We are entertained
> and enlightened by a community of charming and unusual souls, people
> intertwined in every sort of human relationship – financial, sexual and
> religious. Everywhere in evidence is Ladoo's tender understanding of
> his characters...
>    The dialogue is hilarious, the narrative just as much fun. Ladoo creates
> a comic vision with a flawless sense of humour, a delicate sense of irony
> that contains within it a love for his characters. It is hard to believe that
> Ladoo could achieve so much in so few pages; it is hard to believe that
> he is dead.[28]

And Roydon Salick in his "Bittersweet Comedy of Sonny Ladoo, A
reading of *Yesterdays*", writes:

> *Yesterdays* is a comic *tour de force* in the tradition of Chaucer's *The Miller's
> Tale,* Petronius's *Satyricon,* and in contemporary literature, Mordecai Richler's

*Cocksure* and Henry Miller's *Tropic of Capricorn*. It is therefore not for everyone; some will no doubt find it disgusting and obscene; others, a slight thing not deserving to be finished, let alone be read a second time. But the reader, familiar with certain aspects of the Hindu caste system and with the Indo-Caribbean peasant experience, will, I am sure, respond more fairly and intensely than the reader who assumes that Ladoo is indulging in prurience for its own sake. Accordingly, at the outset, I exclaim with Vergil's Sybil, "Procul este, profani" *(Aeneid* 4.258).

... *Yesterdays* is ribald, irreverent, and scatological; but it is neither deliberately disgusting nor gratuitously obscene. Its sustained verbal profanities are as appropriate as the genteelisms of Jane Austen's comic depictions of the landed gentry. Ladoo could not have employed any other linguistic register and achieve the same verve and success. *Yesterdays*, with its unrelenting pictures of human sexuality may be seen as a sort of linguistic version of the three-dimensional erotic sculptures on the temple walls at Khajaraho in India. The novel participates comfortably in an erotic and aesthetic tradition that has produced these famous sculptures, the *Kama Sutra,* the *Upanishads* and the unabashed poetry of Kali Das and Mira Bai.[29]

Both Harold's novels were translated and published in French. This, to me, is astounding, but proof of how Yesterdays, written in the broadest of Trinidadian creole, communicated across the language barrier. Here are some comments on *Yesterdays* from a French reviewer:

All my gratitude to the publishing house Les Allusifs for this precious gift: Harold Sonny Ladoo in French. Imagine that... The early 70's. An incredibly lively language nourished in oral and creole. Walking in the footsteps of the talented Sam Selvon while overflowing. More hot than, at random, a Chamoiseau almost 20 years before him. A text full of verve without respect, without taboo. The grotesque body, satire and laughter, invading. A Creoleness before the theories and more uninhibited still. Under the pen of the great Harold Sonny Ladoo, our committed Caribbean Sisters and Brothers from India are alive more than ever. Often invisible, ostracized, forced into an aura of pathological discretion, here they explode! And of what strength. A rage of life, bawdy, petty and fat, parasitized by Gods and great shenanigans. Trinidad.[30]

As Peter Such said:

But you know, ... they don't allow as they do in Europe and other countries artists to have a little trough of exploration while they build the quantum energy for the dynamic leap into the next phase, you know. And I felt *Yesterdays* was that. Still very good writing and very funny stuff and the whole satirical side and so on, the bawdy side and all that sort of stuff.[31]

I end this chapter with a quote from Victor J. Ramraj's paper, "Reinstating the Individual in Postcolonial Literary Studies", which gives us a sober concluding assessment:

Ladoo died before putting the finishing touches to this posthumously published novel. His premature death may have deprived West Indian-Canadian literature of a sequel that would have offered an absorbing, ironical evocation of cross-culturalism and as fascinating a postcolonial inversion of the imperial-colonial binary as Selvon's *Moses Ascending*, in which the Trinidadian Moses in London has an Englishman as his Friday. L.R. Early believes that, in this novel, Ladoo's "satiric intelligence has not sufficiently matured, or has been crippled by scorn." What we have is a relentless attack on those that debase religion and education, be they Hindus or Christians. There is a Juvenalian rawness to the work, which renders its vulgarity unmitigated and its satire blunt. It is the most savage, if unpolished, satirical piece (that can find its counterparts in works by such writers as Céline) in Indo-West Indian or West Indian writing at large. It is true, as some critics have pointed out, that Ladoo was untutored at the time he wrote these novels and needed editorial guidance, but there is evidence of his considerable native talent. *No Pain Like This Body* is a tour de force in Indo-Caribbean and Caribbean literature at large. And, however crude we may find *Yesterdays*, it is a strikingly original contribution to West Indian Indo-Caribbean sociopolitical writing – and, had Sonny Ladoo lived to write the planned sequel about his protagonist's realization of his vengeful aspiration to found a Hindu school in Canada equipped with whips and torture chambers, we would most likely have had one of the Caribbean's most Juvenalian pieces of postcolonial satire in Trinidadian demotic that censures a crucial aspect of the imperial-colonial divide, while subsuming the individual and personal...[32]

To extend the sobriety of response in a postscript, it is worth noting that, despite the rollicking farce, Ladoo cannot end *Yesterdays* as a 'Happily Ever After'. Choonilal signs over his house to the cowboy boots and diamond-ring-wearing Pundit who rides off into the sunset in his Cadillac with his lawyer. We are not sure, after all this, that Poonwa (who, it is implied, is really the Pundit's son) gets the money to go to Canada. The good, the pure, the innocent will always fall victim to the corrupt and the powerful.

When *Yesterdays* was published we were in awe of the audacity of this young author pivoting from the brutal *No Pain Like This Body* to the farcical *Yesterdays*. But Ladoo left another mystery: For a man who was seemingly known for his sense of humour and having displayed his comedic talent so joyously and self-indulgently in *Yesterdays*, how come there are no surviving fragments of his writing that continue in this humorous vein? Nevertheless, Harold was on a roll and in his sights was a towering body of work that would, he believed, establish his genius for all to see.

Endnotes

1.  Letter to Dennis Lee, August 1972.
2.  Interview with Peter Such by Christopher Laird, 2003.
3.  Letter to Dennis Lee, 1973.
4.  Jim Christy, *Globe and Mail*, 1972.
5.  The dangerous road that splits the action in *Yesterdays* (set in 1955) and the crossing of which risks life and limb is based on the McBean bypass section of the Southern main Road built in the late 1940s. It provides an underlying energy, humming and crackling like arc lamps on a set to the farce of characters scuttling back and forth to Choonlilal's house.
6.  Harold Ladoo letter to Dennis Lee, 31 August 1972.
7.  Harold Ladoo letter to Dennis Lee, 31 August 1972.
8.  Note that, despite this claim, a story featuring the characters from *Yesterdays* (subsequently rewritten) and titled: "an excerpt from his new novel – as yet entitled" was published by Patricia Gilhooly in her *Thirst* (1 April 1971).
9.  Harold Ladoo, letter to Shirley Gibson, 12 September 1972.
10.  Note again Harold's reference to an "anecdotal book" which is another way of describing what he refers to as an "episodic style".
11.  Harold Ladoo, letter to Dennis Lee, 22 September 1972.
12.  Harold Ladoo, letter to Dennis Lee, 22 September 1972. Harold's melodramatic plans to kill off Poonwa are a good indication of his attitude to Poonwa.
13.  Letter to Dennis Lee, May 1972.
14.  Letter to Dennis Lee, 25 September 1972.
15.  Ibid.
16.  Interview with Jim Polk by Christopher Laird, 2003.
17.  Harold Ladoo, A Timeline for *Yesterdays*, Jim Polk, email to Christopher Laird, 11 October 2018..
18.  *Yesterdays* (Toronto: Anansi, 1974), 67.
19.  *Yesterdays*, 76.
20.  *Yesterdays*, 34.
21.  *Yesterdays*, 22.
22.  Michaëla Danjé, "Harold Sonny Ladoo, filant dans nos nuits indo-caribéennes" (Harold Sonny Ladoo, Spinning in our Indo-Caribbean nights) "Review of *Yesterdays* and *No Pain Like This Body*", *Cases Rebelles,* April 2006.
23.  Interview with Dennis Lee by Christopher Laird, 2002.
24.  Probably the nearest comparable Caribbean novel in this respect is Jamaican, Anthony Winkler's *The Lunatic* (1987).
25.  Eugene Benson, L.W. Conolly, *Encyclopedia of Post-Colonial Literature*

*in English (*Routledge, 30 November 2004).

26. Clement H Wyke, "Harold Ladoo's Alternate Worlds", *Canadian Literature* No 95, Winter 1982.

27. "A Frowsty Fragrance", review by Derek Walcott of *Caribbeana* by Thomas W. Krise, *The New York Review of Books*, 15 June 2000.

28. Mark Sarner, *Books In Canada* Vol. 3 No. 5 Aug-Sept. 1974.

29. Roydon Salick, "Bittersweet Comedy of Sonny Ladoo, A Reading of *Yesterdays*", *ARIEL: A Review of International English Literature,* Vol. 22: 3, July 1991.

30.  Michaëla Danjé, "Harold Sonny Ladoo, filant dans nos nuits indo-caribéennes".

31. Interview with Peter Such by Christopher Laird, 2003.

32. Victor J. Ramraj, "Language and Perception: Reinstating the Individual in Postcolonial Literary Studies", *Cross/Cultures,* Jan 2, 2015.

## CHAPTER ELEVEN
## THE GRAND PLAN

But the books kept
pouring through your system like heart attacks,
nine in three years,
and the manuscripts rose in your bedroom, uneditable for
new ones came and
sabotaged your life…
— Dennis Lee, *The Death of Harold Ladoo*

In 1973, with one novel published and another soon to appear, Harold was ready to conquer the world. He had a jaw-dropping project in mind: an epic of some two hundred novels, dealing with the history of the Caribbean – his "Tola" saga. He had received a second Canada Council grant, this time for $4,000, and he intended to travel and do research. Jim Polk reports:

He got impatient with *Yesterdays* and was more interested in his 'Grand Plan', which was to write two hundred novels on the history of the Caribbean and the Western hemisphere, including the mythology, the history. His mentor was William Faulkner, the way he encapsulated the Civil War South and the modern South, and he had it all planned out. He showed me the plan, and to my shame I didn't keep a copy or make a copy, which was like a big tree and how characters would interweave and there was a historic line of dates; what novel would do what, they had titles, not all of them but there were some titles.

And I said, "Harold this is very ambitious [chuckles]. How can you possibly, how can anybody write two hundred novels?" And I tried to persuade him that maybe there were three novels or one. I would have liked a bigger novel from Harold, just as a publisher, to sell, and that was my hunch that this would be what would happen.[1]

He showed me one of the novels which he was working on; it was set in the eighteenth century and it was about a plantation owner and a slave in slave quarters and it was very interesting in the dynamic, the psychological dynamic between the two. There wasn't much of it and I missed the colour, the atmosphere of his writing in the present. I think he was a little uncomfortable with writing in the eighteenth century or about the eighteenth century and he agreed he needed more research time and more work on that.[2]

Trying to reconstruct Harold's 'Grand Plan' is where things enter a seemingly impenetrable maze. Harold, as Jim Polk says, always had his mind racing ahead to the next work, always had ideas for another project buzzing in his head, and couldn't stay focused on a specific piece without the carrot of imminent publication, and an editor. As one example, consider a note from Margaret Atwood to Dennis Lee, citing Harold's latest enthusiasm:

> The longest conversation I ever had with Harold was over the phone, a bad connection that kept fading out at the most sepulchral moments. He wanted to do a paper on Death in Canadian Literature... funerals, etc.[3]

So, despite his obsession with the Tola saga, the evidence of any actual, novel-length texts that pursue the Grand Plan is thin on the ground. I have not been able to find the manuscript of *any* unpublished novel, nor any short story longer than 32 pages. This is not to say they never existed; Harold might have completed one or more of the Tola novels, in first draft at least. They might even be still extant, in some undiscovered corner of his postmortem universe. But if so, the manuscripts are missing.

I believe this issue is central to any discussion of Harold Sonny Ladoo. As mentioned before, in addition to letters to Dennis Lee announcing the completion of a new book, Harold used to phone Peter Such and Graeme Gibson and others at ungodly hours of the morning, to report the birth of yet "another novel" after a binge writing session. He cultivated the mystique of these manuscripts with any of his Canadian acquaintances who would listen. Consequently, after Harold was killed, there was a wealth of lore about them, feeding the wishful belief in a trove of some six to eight full-length novel manuscripts (or maybe it was nine, as in Dennis's poem). But now, after half a century, there is still no evidence as to whether or not they existed in the first place. And if they did exist, where did they disappear to?

There were two separate occasions when writing by Harold was destroyed, or disappeared by other means. The first came in the fall of 1970, soon after he started at Erindale. After showing Peter Such the work in his "little brown suitcase", and then having his poetry manuscript rejected by Anansi, he told Peter, "I took the suitcase full of writing that I had and I tipped it down the garbage chute in my apartment building."

This is a stirring tale of brave new beginnings – and it might be true. The problem is that it's not the only account of what happened. In his memorial essay, Peter Such gave a competing version – in which Harold burnt his early work:

> Rachel tells me it took several hours to burn the manuscripts, two full suitcases of them. Everything he'd ever written up to that time.[4]

Which of these versions is true? The garbage-chute one? The fire? Both? Neither? This difficulty in determining the simplest facts is typical of the biographical quagmire that often exists around Harold's life. And it doesn't help that Rachel, despite what she told Peter Such, would subsequently profess to having no recollection of the burning incident. Here she is in 2002:

> *Ramabai Espinet*: He burnt his manuscripts? He burnt some stuff that he had written?
>
> *Rachel Ladoo*: I don't know, I didn't pay any attention to that one, I'm not sure if he did bring it up.
>
> *RE*: Do you know of him burning some of his writing out in the yard or something?
>
> *RL*: No, I don't know really.
>
> *RE*: Did he tear it up, you don't know of him destroying it?
>
> *RL*: No, I haven't any idea about that, no, or maybe he must have but I don't remember about it.[5]

So an iconic story in which Harold severs all connections with the past and strides unflinchingly into the future turns out to rest on shaky ground. But whatever the facts regarding the destruction of Harold's poetry in 1970, there would be far greater destruction after his death.

There were two posthumous episodes, followed by a coda. The first, which has not been reported until now, was at Rachel's hands. In a telephone conversation in December 2019, she told me that after Harold's death,

> I threw away a lot of his papers as rubbish. I couldn't tell what were manuscripts or not.

How much material disappeared in this housecleaning blitz? Ten pages? 100? 500? Rachel doesn't recall. And what did it include? Unpublished stories? Editorial exchanges with Dennis and Jim? Lecture notes and course essays from Erindale? Complete drafts of the much-trumpeted novels? Even his early poetry, if the destruction by garbage chute or fire was a fiction? There is no way of knowing what Rachel disposed of.

The second episode is more widely known, and forms a bizarre chapter in the Ladoo legend. After Harold died, Rachel says, an unidentified acquaintance made off with a box of his manuscripts "for safekeeping". Her rather evasive account goes like this:

> *Ramabai Espinet*: What happened to his manuscripts?
>
> *Rachel Ladoo:* To the manuscripts…

*RE*: How many and…?

*RL:* It was quite a few, like the one…

*RE*: A box? Do you know how many?

*RL*: About a pile, yeah, about a box.

RE: A pile?

*RL*: Because when he went to Trinidad [in 1973] he wrote his last book, "The Vultures" which he write exactly how he died, and how people taking the property, and how he was crying for help and how nobody help him and all those things. That's what I read, part of the book, I didn't read all of it, you know.

RE: He wrote it before he went?

*RL*: He wrote it in Trinidad. He stayed for a while and he wrote it and he left it there, and I brought it up back with me and I don't know, some people ask me to read it and I lend it to them and I never get it back. I don't know who I give it to and what happen to it.

RE: Who do you think you gave it to?

*RL*: That's what I don't remember, who was it now.

RE: Man or woman?

*RL*: I think is a man, but I don't know if it was an author or who was it because they were interested in his books and so forth, and they help me with those things, I lend it to them and I never get it back. So I never think about it, like, you know…

RE: You gave the person that one, or all?

*RL*: All the manuscripts to check it through because they were all mixed up, right. They say they'd help me put them in place and those things, because I didn't have time, I didn't, like, you know. So that's why I don't know who I gave it to.

RE: So, what do you have left?

*RL*: Nothing…[6]

Peter Such also speaks of a Trinidadian acquaintance of the Ladoos who took the manuscripts, promising to keep them safe from exploitation by Harold's conniving Canadian colleagues. He would see to it that they were treated properly, and would be published:

We were trying to see if we could get another book out of it but before we could get to it Rachel had got in with this guy, what's his name? Yes, [name mentioned]. I don't know if they were together very long. It was right after Harold died. And [he] took the whole suitcase. He said to her, "They will try to screw you out of this that or the other."[7]

Pondering this pile or box or suitcase of hijacked papers, we confront many of the same questions as with the material Rachel threw out. It was evidently fairly substantial – perhaps several hundred pages. But what did it include? Harold's "last book," apparently – "The Vultures", which he was working on in Trinidad just before he died. But beyond that, it's anybody's guess. There could have been anything from Erindale coursework to stories to complete novels in draft. Unless and until the shadowy friend comes forward, we will never know. And after half a century, that looks unlikely.

We come now to the coda – also unreported till now, and the only good news in this chronicle of destruction and chicanery. It comes near the end of the interview with Rachel above:

*RE*: So what do you have left?

*RL*: Nothing.

*RE*: Don't you have a binder?

*RL*: No, because some of the binders, some manuscripts like *Yesterdays* and those things, I think it's by my brother's place. Jeoffery lent it to my cousin and they say they have them in some stockroom somewhere. They wanted to read it and when they were living in that other place, Jeoffery and them, he lend them the manuscripts and they say they would've bring them back and they'd take them and they'd read it and probably it remain right there.[8]

So there was still a single "binder" (probably a file folder) in the hands of the Ladoo clan. Jeoffery, in a 2002 interview, reported:

Well, as far as I know there was a binder with his handwritten notes and some typed, so I left it at my uncle's house, so hopefully my uncle still has it so we could look through it, and if not, then I don't know what's left.[9]

Shortly after our interview in 2002, Jeoffery did salvage the binder from his uncle or cousin. And it is one of the two most important resources we have for exploring Harold's unpublished work – both the little that has survived, and (with guesswork) the much greater amount that has not.[10]

What *has* survived? All I've been able to track down are the contents of that folder, along with some typescripts in the House of Anansi papers at Library and Archives Canada in Ottawa, and one fragment in Dennis Lee's papers at the Fisher Library in Toronto.[11] Here's a breakdown:

1. The folder Jeoffery retrieved contains handwritten drafts of seven stories, ranging from one to 18 pages in length. These drafts provide an excellent tool to examine Harold's default process of building longer work from his short stories. These are explored in the next chapter.

2. The Anansi papers at Library and Archives Canada in Ottawa contain

typescripts of eleven completed stories, almost all dated early 1973. The shortest is a page, and the longest is 32 pages. Two were presented in Chapter Four of this book ("Lying Monroe" and "Jametin Laura"). They are almost all dated early 1973.

3. Among Dennis Lee's papers is a puzzling, untitled extract. It's nineteen pages long, numbered 116 to 132 (with two supplementary pages). There is a dividing line of asterisks at the beginning (page 116), and again at "THE END" (page 132). In content, it's not unlike his short story "Land of The Ancestors", where in a clash of time-frames, events like the British and Americans raping the land with bulldozers and DDT are contemporaneous with Columbus and his three ships, with slavery and the brutalisation of indigenous Caribs and Arawaks.

132.

Jackson, absolutely certain that it was himself he ~~was see~~ *saw* ~~seeing~~ in the face of the mutilated Scotsman, he dropped the blade. Then the ~~man-spirit~~ who had been watching patiently turned and glided into the rain forest again. With the corner of one eye, ~~he~~ *Gikonyo* saw the other whitemen coming towards the clearing, but he was already moving towards the forest, drawn by the tail-end of the lightning ~~and gre~~ of illumination and greater becoming.

\*\*\*\*\*\*\*\*\*                    \*\*\*\*\*\*\*\*\*

The End.

*The last page of the nineteen-page extract from an untitled novel, in Dennis Lee's papers.*

The extract is no longer than some of the other story manuscripts, but the page numbers and "THE END" give us pause. It is the strongest piece of evidence for a longer manuscript having existed. But there is little clue as to where the previous 115 pages may be.

A close reading of the extract however would suggest that this may well be surviving pages of a 'novel' titled "House Nigger" mentioned in a letter from Shirley Gibson to Dave Godfrey after Harold's death:

Re manuscripts: Harold submitted HOUSE NIGGER to us as his next work. He and Jim Polk did a lot or preliminary talking on it just before Harold left.[12]

The extract tells of a slave, Gikonyo who is forced by his masters to hunt and kill an Amerindian cacique. He hunts with two bloodhounds, Lucifer and Snake. Here is a quote from the extract:[13]

```
he was standing; right around there He had taken three
                             fourteen
right arms of Carib warriors twelve/years ago in order for
Spencer to make him a house niger. As he thought about what
he had to do just to get away from being a field niger
he cursed himself for having ever ventured out to get
the arms that the white people wanted to see so badly.
```

For ready reference, if not as a verified fact, I will refer to this extract as the "House Nigger" extract. Jim Polk doesn't remember seeing this novel or talking to Harold about it. No one I have spoken with has seen it and Harold never mentioned it in the correspondence that survives. Most significant is the qualification Shirley made in her letter:

He (Harold) felt that [it] was not good enough for publication and seemed prepared to use the best material for other works.[14]

And that is the sum total of Harold Ladoo's extant unpublished writing.

Overall, the shortage of evidence for completed Tola novels makes it harder to sustain the romantic image of long-lost masterpieces. If we're wedded to that idea, we could argue that the Tola novels are missing because Rachel destroyed them, or the nameless friend absconded with them. But it's equally possible that they're missing because they never existed in the first place – at least not as full first drafts, ready for reshaping and revision.

In any case, if we stick to the evidence and examine the stories and beginnings of novels that do exist, and if we keep in mind (as hinted in Shirley's letter), that Harold's default mode was to shape the world through the lens of short stories, we will discover something more limited, but more reality-based: solid evidence of a talent which was still developing, and which gave promise of major achievements.

What is also possible is to track the dates on the manuscripts. Those seem at first to suggest that between January and June 1973, Harold started four novels and finished nine short stories – three of them in less than four days. However, I must caution that the Library manuscripts are typescripts, and the dates they carry most likely refer to the day they were typed, not when they were written. It's probable that Harold Ladoo had written at least some of these stories before 1973, and was now typing them up and putting them in order.

What was in Harold's mind? The motive is clear: he was assembling a manuscript of short stories for submission to Anansi. Shirley Gibson would confirm this in a letter to Dave Godfrey on 10 September 1973, a few weeks after Harold's death: "He also gave me a collection of short stories." The eleven pieces at the Library are the manuscript he submitted (which was never published).

The handwritten stories in the folder Jeoffery Ladoo retrieved tell the same story – of a systematic review and stocktaking. These are first drafts, and many have a note scribbled in the margin: "to be worked on later." What's more, most of the notes have the same date: 3 March 1973.

*Last page of the manuscript of "1st Canadian Novel," in the folder recovered by Jeoffery Ladoo. (See the excerpts in Chapters Two and Three, the stories of Sohan and Sawak.)*

Harold was evidently doing a census and assessment of the short stories he had on hand (over and above the ones he'd typed up). Indeed, it's possible he was trying to put *all* his writing in some kind of order; there are handwritten title pages in the folder for novels for which there exist few, if any, pages of text.

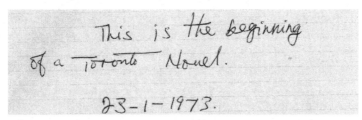

*Single page, unattached to any text, among the papers in Jeoffery's folder.*

Beyond the stories, Harold may have been trying to put his life in order that March – or at least, to hold it together. The pressure was coming from all sides. Money was a constant problem; despite the Canada Council grant, the Ladoos could no longer afford the rent at Roseneath Gardens, and they had moved into the basement of his sister's house in Scarborough. Harold was still a short-order cook, on the night shift at Fran's. Rachel was pregnant again. And he was going through the motions at Erindale, finishing the third year in a state of bilious alienation. He was also preparing to edit *Yesterdays* with Jim Polk, which would occupy him from May to August in 1973. And finally, as noted above, his mother's life in McBean had gone off the rails. She was being preyed upon by relatives (the "vultures" of Harold's final work), all trying to grab a piece of the inheritance from his father's estate. She was often seen roaming the streets of the village, drunk and begging. As the oldest son in the family, he had to do something about this nightmare situation.

Harold's colleagues at Anansi were both fascinated and concerned. Graeme Gibson said:

> It's too easy, I suspect, to feel that he had premonitions of an early death or whatever. I think it really was a kind of desperate seizing the energy when it was there, because it may not last.
>
> Georges Simenon said famously about his novels, if he didn't finish them in two and a half weeks he threw them away. Apparently he went in and had a full medical check-up, and then went and shut himself up and wrote a chapter a day. Ladoo was even faster than that; I think he wrote one of them in a sitting or pretty close to a sitting.
>
> He phoned me at about 2 o'clock in the morning once, crowing over the phone, "I'm halfway finished! I'm halfway finished! I'll be done!" And whenever it was, thirty-six hours later he phoned again and says, "I've done it! It's finished!" And there's always the danger of hyperbole, and maybe it was four days instead of two or three.
>
> I don't think it's because he felt he was going to die before he finished it, I just think that was the way he worked. But it's also in some way, obviously from our point of view, for those who knew him outside, he seemed to live that way too.
>
> ...I mean, it's like a natural phenomenon of some kind, like a kind of Jesuitical star, not thunder and lightning but there was this huge intensity and ambition.[15]

Or as Dennis Lee writes:

> But the books kept
> pouring through your system like heart attacks,
>                             nine in three years,
>     and the manuscripts rose in your bedroom, uneditable for
>                 new ones came and
>             sabotaged your life. And
>                     the life and the work wrenched farther apart;
>     you stabbed a man, berserk they had
>             doped your drink and you
> went on brooding on style, your ear emphatic with
>                             Faulkner, Milton, Achebe,
>                 Naipaul, Gibson, Harris, García Márquez:
>                     these men you meant to
>     write into the ground.[16]

Endnotes

1.  "He [Harold] unrolls a Scotch-taped patchwork of typing paper which is a map delineating the one hundred [sic] novels he intends to write, a Faulknerian mega-epic of Trinidad covering centuries." "A Very Fine Web – Half a Century of House of Anansi", Jim Polk, *Canadian Notes and Queries*, #100, October 2017.
2.  Interview with Jim Polk by Christopher Laird, 2003.
3.  Letter to Dennis Lee from Margaret Atwood (undated).
4.  Peter Such, "The Short Life and Sudden Death of Harold Sonny Ladoo", *Saturday Night* (Toronto) 89, 5 1974, and *BIM*, Volume 16 No 63, 1978.
5.  Interview with Rachel Ladoo by Ramabai Espinet and Christopher Laird, September 2002.
6.  Ibid.
7.  Interview with Peter Such by Christopher Laird 2003.
8.  Interview with Rachel Ladoo by Ramabai Espinet and Christopher Laird, September 2002.
9.  Interview with Jeoffery Ladoo by Christopher Laird and Ramabai Espinet, 2002.
10.  Jeoffery assures me that he could find no other papers or manuscripts at his uncle's where he found 'the binder'. Further we have the then managing editor of Anansi, Shirley Gibson, assuring the lawyer Max Gould in a letter after Harold's death: "There was no suggestion of work being in anyone else's hands."
11.  See Appendix Five for full lists of the work.
12.  Letter from Shirley Gibson to Dave Godfrey, 10 September 1973.
13.  Extract from 19 pages found among Dennis Lee's papers.
14.  Letter from Shirley Gibson to Dave Godfrey, 10 September 1973.
15.  Interview with Graeme Gibson by Christopher Laird, 2002.
16.  Dennis Lee, "The Death of Harold Ladoo", *Heart Residence. Collected Poems 1967-2017* (Toronto: Anansi, 2017), pp. 91-92.

# CHAPTER TWELVE
## STORIES INSIDE STORIES

and then the phonecall – one more
               livid book in draft: from the Caribbean to
Canada,
               the saga piecing together.

— Dennis Lee, *The Death of Harold Ladoo*.[1]

As noted in the previous chapter, no complete manuscripts for unpublished novels have been found to support Harold's claims. However, there are surviving manuscripts for shorter work because Harold never stopped writing. Even while working on his novels, he was writing short stories.[2] Examining these provides clear evidence of his novel writing method.

During his time at Erindale Harold had two short stories published as "excerpts from a new novel". These, in the first issues of *Impulse* and *Thirst*, were later repurposed for inclusion in *No Pain Like This Body* and *Yesterdays*.

> "All you chirens goin' to sleep in de rice-box," she said.
>
> She went inside the house and brought some rags. They were soaked. Rain water was constantly dripping from the rafters. Balraj went outside to get more leaves. Climbing on top of the box, Ma handed him the leaves; and he began to push them between the rafters and the grass. Nanny got a crate. He was standing on top of the rice-box when she came back. He told Ma to stand on the ground. Taking the crate from Nanny, he placed it upon the rice-box. He stood on the crate in order to reach the roof. The water started to drip less and less. He was working very fast. Then,
>
> "O God! O God!..." He shouted.
>
> Balraj jumped down from the rice-box. He fell on the ground, and started to scream; bawling as if he was going to die. We thought he saw a jumbie, because he was rolling on the ground. Nanny thought so too. Ma had the same idea. She and Nanny started to talk in Hindi; he was rolling in the water, keeping his hands high in the air. Lightning flashed again. He told Ma that his hands were on fire. Something fell from the roof. Nanny lighted the light again.
>
> We went closer to the box. There were three of them. Deadly. Full grown. Moving fast. Heading for the light. Black. The long legs were hurrying. They were there. Tails in the air. Moving faster and faster. Fire stingers -- little but deadly -- the scorpions. They kept running and running.
>
> "Mov' fass!" Ma screamed.

*A page from Harold's story in the first issue of* Impulse[3], *the scorpion/rice-box scene, is reproduced word for word in* No Pain Like This Body.

> Tailor sat with a worried face, counting the cars as they passed by. With an old embroidery scissors, he picked his teeth.
>
> Choonilal sat on an old potato crate, a few feet away from the barahar tree. He was brushing his teeth with a piece of guava stick. Occasionally, he glanced at Tailor with a worried face, probably thinking something bad; for there was a strangeness in his glance, as if his whole system of thinking was going out of balance. Chewing the stick with a type of irrational vengeance, he spat with pride upon an old sewing machine.
>
> Sometimes Tailor looked at him too, and spat on an old shirt that was hanging from a line in the yard. There was a Jandee pole in the yard. Every good Hindu in Tola had a pole like it, because it reminded them of their immortality. Choonilal in particular, was a very good man. He prayed with great effort to the gods. He did not want to be born again on this earth. Once he had already warned Tailor, but Tailor did not heed the warning. He kept glancing at the red flag that hung from the tip of the bamboo pole; as if, he was studying the impressive figure of the Hindu God Hanuman, whom he believed was going to help him out in his struggles in the next life. Hanuman was painted in white-painted in such a skilful way, that we got the impression that he was talking to Choonilal. Every Indian in Tola liked Hanuman, he was the God of Power, and they wanted power.
>
> 'Two years you livin' by me Tailor!'
>
> 'I is know dat!'
>
> 'You is man Tailor. You stones is hard just as my own. Even harder. Why you eh get a wife? Get one to cook for you. To wash for you. You modder ass chamar! You is hav' the same kin' of min' like Logan.'
>
> Choonilal looked at the outhouse. He looked at Tailor.
>
> Tailor looked at him.
>
> 'We is in war now Tailor!'
>
> 'I is know dat.'
>
> 'You stones gone today, Tailor.'
>
> 'Kiss my ass!'
>
> 'You does shit in my latrine, Tailor.'
>
> 'Yeh.'
>
> 'Well, clean it.'
>
> 'No.'
>
> 'Why?'
>
> 'De pit is yours.'
>
> 'But you does shit in it de most.'

*Again, the first page of Harold's story in* Thirst *opens exactly as his novel,* Yesterdays.[4]

On 24th November 1971, another "extract from a new novel" was published in the *Erindalian*, the college's student newspaper. It was prefaced by the following text (uncredited):

> Harold Ladoo, who is in second year at Erindale, has just completed his new novel, tentatively called *Rage*. In this small selection from the complicated mosaic of its four hundred pages, Vishnu of Tola, village mystic and storyteller, recounts for the young man, Balky, the legends of Balky's father, Jadoo.
>
> In all societies, including our own, the function of the storyteller is to infuse, synthesize, transmit, and thereby rationalize to society the themes of its culture. Through his stories Vishnu clarifies the self-destructive theme of *Rage* that is the Tola community's curse. His stories also show that this *Rage* has its roots in the slavery and brutality of colonial times. It is through men like Vishnu that a society can be redeemed.
>
> Flawed and human as they are, slippery and cowardly as they may be regarded by others, such men continue to seek enlightenment following the example of the great Buddha and also work to redeem their fellows

as did Christ. This West Indian fusion of the two great themes of history is the classic backdrop for most of Harold's work.[5]

The extract that the *Erindalian* published is in fact the first part of the short story titled "Rage: A Short Story", which is among House of Anansi's papers in the Library and Archives Canada in Ottawa. Harold also used it later as one of the stories told in the wake scene of *No Pain Like This Body*.

This was his mode of working. Short stories were connected to make *No Pain Like This Body* and *Yesterdays* is built around stories recalled by the characters.

As Peter Such says:

> Those short stories of his proved to be quick exploration passes over the material for his first novel, which he began almost immediately. This habit of getting into novels through his short stories was one he kept through his brief writing career.[6]

"Rage: A short story" in the Anansi papers is not one story but at least five shorter stories. Unconnected in terms of plot, they shared only a character, Jadoo, and examples of rage (a horse whipping, guns pointed at someone's head, ambush with cutlasses).[7] So, a credible conjecture would be that Harold salvaged these stories from a longer draft of "Rage" that he deemed unworkable[8] and, because they shared a character and a theme, he put them together for submission to Anansi as one the short stories he submitted for publication.

It is not unusual for writers to build their novels from short stories and Harold, as Dennis Lee has said, was probably was just beginning to realise that what he was doing

> was to generate batches of interrelated stories, and then weave a number of them together into something he could call a novel. That "weaving" involved time and craft, however, and he was short of both (though he was on fast-forward with the latter). So it's completely out of touch to imagine that any of his binge-generated manuscripts, whether or not they contained excellent writing, would have resolved the structural issues inherent in this way of working. They would have produced another batch of raw material, and that was fine. But he would still have had the challenge of selecting, shaping, adding, choreographing (where he might have learned to rely more on his film sense, if he'd survived).[9]

There is an even clearer example. Among the handwritten papers that Jeoffery salvaged there are three pieces: a short story entitled "The Agony" which is set in Toronto, about a relationship with a blonde girl who suddenly leaves him; "A Short Story" or "An excerpt from a Novel" which is about three characters in a Toronto strip club talking about liberating

South Africa from Apartheid; it ends with a handwritten note: 'Combine this with "The Agony"':

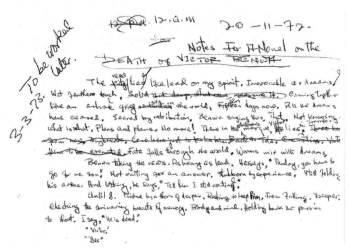

And then, in a story titled, "Notes for a Novel on the Death of Victor Benwa", the title changes after two pages to "The Agony – A New Novel". Here, in Harold's own handwriting, are instructions to start building a novel from three, rather different, stories. One couldn't wish for clearer signs of Harold's method.

*Note on the manuscript for "Notes on the Death of Victor Benwa" which becomes "The Agony, a New Novel"*

How Harold was going to weave these very different stories together is anyone's guess but his intent is clear.

But Harold was not only hoping to build longer forms (novel, novella, whatever) from short stories but he was also building a series of novels by linking characters. The story of the death of Victor Benwa which becomes "The Agony" seems to be setting up a sequel to *No Pain Like This Body*. Victor Benwa – who it is rumoured has died in Toronto where he went to study medicine and hasn't been heard from for four years – is the son of the stickfighter, Benwa, from *No Pain Like This Body*, who is mentioned in Chapter Seven as a model for manhood and briefly appears in one of the stories in "Rage":

> "Stick-fighter turned legend in Tola. Seventy-four years old; still strong. Carrying wounds in his memory. Stick-fighter turned landowner, building a house, a heaven on earth for Victor."[10]

The story of the death of Victor Benwa features Panday, one of the children in *No Pain Like This Body*, who is tasked to go and bring Victor's body back – and visit his sister Sunaree who lives there too. Ladoo is stringing characters together in pursuit of further episodes in building his series of novels. Significantly, in "The Agony" (the proposed novel), he is also venturing into creating a work that is set both in Tola and Toronto.

Harold's explanations about his planned sequels indicate ways in which he might have wanted to approach his 'Grand Plan' of 200 novels. Analysis of his letters and surviving manuscripts suggests that he was focusing on three prongs in his attack on this formidable target:

1: Novels encompassing the history of the Caribbean from pre-Colombian times to the modern day as evidenced by his fragments and short stories such as "Rage", "Chamar Tola 1940", "A New Novel", "Ashes and Blood", "Rage", "Land of the Ancestors" and "House Nigger", looking at colonialism, slavery and indentureship.[11]

2: The 'Panday series' of which *No Pain Like This Body* is the first and "The Vultures", "The Intruders", "The Death of Victor Benwa" and "The Agony" can be combined to fill out the next in the series.

3: 'The Vishnu of Tola series' or the sequels to *Yesterdays* of which Harold outlined various versions in letters to Dennis Lee and Shirley Gibson.[12]

The evidence that exists confirms that Harold had indeed a huge vision of a series of novels exploring Caribbean history. He even sketched them out and was gradually filling the sketch with short stories that would be developed and linked 'at a later date'. As Dennis Lee wrote:

> *No Pain Like This Body* came out, that spare and
> luminous nightmare and you
> went back to
> dishwashing, writing all night and flexing new

> voices, possessed;
> each time we met, your body was
> closer to skeletal fury,
> your eyes more
> deadly and on fire.
> And I watched bemused, and awed, as the circles grew
> tighter and tighter, those frenzied drafts more
> brilliant, and botched, and envious.[13]


## Endnotes

1.  Dennis Lee, "The Death of Harold Ladoo", 89.
2.  See Appendix Five for complete list of surviving publications and manuscripts.
3.  "From Yesterdays: a new novel", in *Impulse, First issue*, Editor Peter Such: The Heritage Press, 1971.
4.  "An Excerpt from a new novel", in *Thirst and Other Hungers*. Editor Patricia Gilhooly, (Toronto: Dorann Publishing Company, 1971).
5.  The preface quoted above could only have been drafted by Harold himself as the themes and the characters referred to in the preface do not appear in the story itself. This reinforces my suggestion that Harold wrote a review of his own novel (*No Pain Like This Body*) for *The Erindalian* – see Chapter 8.
6.  Peter Such, *The Short Life and Sudden Death of Harold Sonny Ladoo*.
7.  Three of these 'stories' involve a dispute over who is the beneficiary of the land left by the death of the 'whiteman, John Sharp'. Violence over a disputed inheritance was clearly a sensitive topic for Harold. Reports of relatives taking advantage of his mother over his late father's property kept coming from McBean.
8.  Harold had claimed in a letter to Dennis Lee in November 1971, that "Rage" was "A West Indian classic". A year later, he wrote to Dennis referring to "Rage" as a "dead book" that he would have to "bury".
9.  Email from Dennis Lee to the author, May 2022.
10. "Notes on the Death of Victor Benwa" which becomes "The Agony, a New Novel".
11. Letter to Dennis Lee, 22 September 1972 and May 1972.
12. Letter to Shirley Gibson 12 September 1972. See *Chapter 9 – Yesterdays*.
13. Dennis Lee, "The Death of Harold Ladoo", *Heart Residence. Collected Poems 1967-2017,* 92.

## CHAPTER THIRTEEN
## WHO WAS HAROLD SONNY LADOO?

### MANAGING THE MYTHS

"The most important single feature of Trinidadian culture is the extent to which masks are indispensable, because there are so many different cultures and ethnicities in his country that people have to play a multiplicity of roles, each of which has got its own mask depending on where they are. It's true of the whole Caribbean and Trinidad is the extreme case in my view."
– Lloyd Best[1]

Chapter 9, The Photograph, looked at how Harold was conscious of the need to control his public image and in the last two chapters I have tried to make sense of the stories that Harold told about his work. But it wasn't just his work that he embedded in myth. It wasn't just his writing that exercised his creative talent. He was also constructing his persona or rather his personas. While this may have begun as an instinctive, colourful way to present himself to his white friends, playing to their expectations of the exotic, as with most efforts to maintain fictions in real life, I think that this process became increasingly burdensome, psychologically demanding, and perhaps even fatal.

In McBean he knew everyone, and everyone knew him and his family since before he was born. Arriving in a big foreign city presented Harold with a circumstance that he may have fantasized about but had never experienced. For the first time in his life he could construct himself anew. With every new Canadian acquaintance, he must have relished the opportunity to present himself to people who knew nothing of his back story, his 'home truths'. He was presented with clean slates upon which he could exercise his talent for drama and storytelling in inscribing the Harold he thought would appeal.

Harold Sonny Ladoo was the consummate storyteller. He invented histories for himself and assumed personas, chameleon-like, to charm people. Chapter One noted that Harold was not, as he claimed, an adopted son, and the Canadian Missionary school (Exchange Canadian Missionary Indian School), he attended for a short time before the McBean Hindu school was established, was nothing like the school (with torture room and Canadian Teachers) he portrayed in *Yesterdays* and told Peter Such about.

It seems he was able to generate a past that synchronised with the experience and expectations of his listener. As Peter Such records,

> ... he did tell different stories to different people, but as far as I knew, he was raised in an orphanage and had a very abusive childhood. He certainly seemed to bear the scars of that both physically and emotionally, and I guess it was something that I understood because I had shared that too, you know. I was raised in an orphanage and went through a very violent period in my early childhood, was being bonged and so forth and so, you know, I think on the personal level, he had this healing to do and I think the writing for him was healing.[2]

Jim Polk speaks of another source of Harold's tall tales, a scar on his neck:

> *Christopher Laird*: Harold had this scar that he used to tell different versions of how he got it. Do you remember?
>
> *Jim Polk*: A knife fight. I saw the scar. There was also a tattoo of a cross, a crucifix with drawings with little rays, I recall. And the knife fight, he told me about it, I'm sorry I can't remember a single detail.
>
> *CL*: A knife fight in Trinidad?
>
> *JP*: I assume so.
>
> *CL*: 'Cause he told different people different stories (laughs).
>
> *JP*: Well storytellers often have different versions. They're artists.[3]

Peter Such expanded further:

> Yeah, well I call it the real self and the false self (chuckles). I think the real self was the one that I kind of knew, he was my friend. I think the false self was the one that... I call it the false self, it's the other self really, it's not a false self because it was in a sense constructed out of his pain and anguish, as all false selves are, you know. And I think the thing is that in some cases, it tended to overwhelm his real self, you know. He couldn't let his real self out and so he became in a sense, what we call here a "user" in some ways, because he got very cynical and used people. But on the other hand, then there was the real one, the real sort of loving self.
>     [... ]He told me all sorts of different stories about all sorts of things (laughs) and you know, the scar on his chest and so on. I mean he told me once that that was from an operation when he was a kid, from having rheumatic fever or something. And then he told me again that he got into a knife fight when he was on a banana boat coming back from Valparaiso (chuckles), which is much more dramatic. And so in a way, I think he was kind of constructing that, but he was very conscious, I think he was always conscious of this image, you know. So once that picture came out, he was always sort of smoking, but I think he would have grown

through that quite honestly. I think his real self was still there, really pumping it up.[4]

Harold's sister, Meena Ladoo/Jagroop tells how he really got that scar:

*Christopher Laird:* The scar on his neck, how did he get that?

*Meena Ladoo:* That was from my father. My father was a tempered man in a sense that you're his son or his child, you will listen to what he has to say. And we had this bull, and my father, whether he worked or not, he always made, you know, the oilcake, the oatmeal or whatever it is they take and make to give the animals; he told him prepare it and give it to the bull. He used to make it in two little loaves and feed the bull. So he told my brother to do it and my brother mouthed him off, and at the same time my father was standing there and he had a cutlass in his hand, and when he grabbed Harold and put his arms like that, (gestures) the cutlass was resting on his hand, and then next thing he saw blood, then he pulled the cutlass and it ended with a scar.[5]

*Meena Jagrup, Harold's youngest sister, demonstrates how Harold received the scar on his neck.*

And Graeme Gibson:

I think I have a sense, and I did not know him really intimately, I don't know people other than perhaps his family who did. I don't know what Peter Such's sense is or even Dennis's, what I felt I was dealing with was in the very best sense of the word: a mannerist construction on some level, someone who had decided that he was going to do and be something and that he had full conviction that he had the ability to do that, and that there was a burning sense within this construction, in the best possible sense of that, "construction" isn't the word I'm looking for, "persona" perhaps, that he would do everything possible and necessary to make it work and to get down on paper what he obviously felt he had to. And that he was hugely ambitious, I mean, he was after Naipaul, he was after everybody who wrote in a way or in an area that he felt he could and should measure himself against and he was after everybody (laughs).

*Christopher Laird*: Including you?

GG: (Laughs). Yeah. But that's great. It is and should be flattering.[6]

And Jim Polk again:

*Christopher Laird*: Were you aware at all that Harold had this ability to build different personas for different people he knew?

*Jim Polk*: I was surprised that he had a reputation for being rather grim and serious and intense, 'cause that was certainly not what I got, but maybe he knew I would like humour and stories and I did and that was it. As I say, my exposure to Harold was so limited, it was one or two months in the summer of '72 that I didn't see him interact socially. The Harold I knew came to my place and we had a good time and we got a book done, and the shock was just unbelievable when the news came. It was said to be an auto accident and I was just horrified. How can this be? That's all I can say. The persona part I'm sure, as a good mimic, a very good actor, a very good storyteller, he would do parts and dialects just like that. I suspect he was a shape changer, many are, but no, I can't give you help with that.

*CL*: If you had to describe Harold in a sentence as far as you knew him, what would you say?

*JP*: A very warm, very funny, very human, very humane person with a lot of gifts, a lot of talent, a bit hyper, a bit over eager, perhaps a bit over ambitious – if that's a flaw – certainly artistically his vision was enormous, was immense, but he had talent as well, to match it. I felt close to him, I felt we were friends and that's the Harold I remember.[7]

Based on the available evidence it would seem that the need to deliver what Harold promised and what his literary colleagues (and the Canada Council grants) expected, was a huge burden. Enough of a burden to push him into a bit of a corner out of which he assumed an attitude of what in Trinidad we would call *bravé danger* (disguising one's fear by adopting the pose of a warrior in the face of danger) or what is called these days (less dramatically) "doubling down".

This may be an assumption that appears uncharitable and unfair in the face of Harold's amazing accomplishments up to that time and the incredible pressure of his family life which worked against his dream of "writing V.S. Naipaul under the table."

Harold's charisma, his sensitivity and capacity for empathy enabled him to reach the inner core of those he encountered. This and his acute powers of observation meant that in his personal relationships Harold would *see* the other and the emotion that to this day still bubbles up when his friends remember him is testament to this sense of intimacy. This ability also is a key attribute of his writing and I believe it is central to Harold's development as a writer.

Quite apart from the different histories he may have conjured for himself he also had to juggle the Harold he presented to his Canadian friends and life at home with Rachel, Jeoffery and his stepdaughter, Debbie. His home circumstances were dire, Rachel was pregnant with their second son[8] (Jerry/ Durani was born on 4th May 1973) and, before he was born, Rachel brought her mother, Amin, to Toronto to help with the children. In November 1972 they moved to Harold's final place of residence at 787 Jane Street.

*787 Jane Street where the Ladoos lived before Harold went to Trinidad in 1973*

The family had little income, mainly from Rachel's job. Harold's own restaurant job was essentially part time. He had to attend to his studies at Erindale *and* he had to write. He also had to look after Jeoffery while Rachel was at work – until Amin arrived. Studying and writing in those circumstance must have been extremely difficult. But Harold was driven. He had left Trinidad with a 'suitcase' of his writing, with a dream of being a writer. If it meant locking himself away in the bedroom and typing or writing under the bed in all night binge sessions, then that is what he would do. But those conditions were certainly not conducive to a meditative analysis of his writing or to structuring novels out of short stories and fragments written in such binge sessions. The pressure under those conditions to satisfy his own expectations and those of his new comrades would have been horrendous.

If I ask, "Who was Harold Sonny Ladoo?" it is because he was impossible to pin down. Graeme Gibson who took the iconic photo of him for his book covers, described him as "ducking and weaving and defending" as he filled the roll of film. Graeme saw him during that session in a way no one else had the opportunity to see the camera-averse Harold. When I showed them the contact sheet of the roll of photos Graeme took, both Peter Such and Jim Polk were puzzled. Neither of them saw the chosen photo as representative of the Harold they knew.

Inventing stories about one's personal life is one thing, but Harold also acted out different personalities. One of the things that jumped out at me once I started to transcribe the interviews I did in 2002 and 2003 was the different ways my informants described Harold.

Have a look at three divergent perspectives on Harold: from his literary colleagues at Anansi, his Trinidadian friends and his family.

First, Jim Polk:

> I don't want to turn him into the Easter Bunny, but he was very, very fond of people and particularly of his children; he was very loving about his children and spoke of them with pride, showed me pictures of the son and how wonderful they were, how smart and this sort of thing. Not everybody liked everybody at Anansi, including everybody at Anansi, but he was quite forgiving and tolerant of us all and I remember him as being affectionate toward our follies and they were many back then in 1972. He seemed a kind man, perhaps an innocent man and maybe this was a persona for me, but I remember this and liked him for it.[9]

Compare this with how his Trinidadian friends and acquaintances saw him:

> It is difficult to become a friend of Harold. He had a difficult personality, you could not really relax with him he was always so intense, but intense to the extent that he would be talking very good sense, discussing really good issues, specially philosophical issues and always very very intense and therefore it was easy to get into an argument; he would explode and so on, so that is what he was like.[10]

Trinidadian/Canadian poet and novelist, Dionne Brand, in her introduction to a later edition of *No Pain Like This Body,* describes a dark version of Harold, as graphic and not dissimilar to Peter Such's first impression of him:

> …a brooding unhappy man. He smoked continually, his cheeks sucked into chasms cut out of a bony face, a permanent scowl etched there by the hard place he had come from in Trinidad, a place called McBean; mistrustful eyes made so no doubt by the same harsh landscape of subsistence agriculture he had hacked his way out of with a few others.

A dismissive turn to his equally bony compact body, he occupied the farthest corner of room in the cafeteria that we, a cosmopolitan group calling itself the African-Asian West Indian Association, had taken over, or liberated as we used to say. Ladoo sat there in the cloud of cigarette smoke working on *No Pain Like This Body*.[11]

And at home, here is Rachel:

*Rachel Ladoo:* Well, he start going to school and I think we move somewhere, …, to Roseneath Garden, Winona, and he start going to school. Then I get pregnant with Jerry and then I had Jerry and then my mother came.

*Ramabai Espinet:* So when did Debbie come?

*RL:* Debbie came before,

*RE:* And how did that work out?

*RL:* That work out not too good either.

*RE:* Why?

*RL:* Well, he didn't like Debbie that much really 'cause he didn't want her to come up and he used to get upset if I send money for her and those things. So then she came up and I still have to go to work again and leave her alone and she'll take care of Jeoffery.

*RE:* And she was how old?

*RL:* Nine years.

*RE:* And she was going to school.

*RL:* She was going to school, yeah (crying).

*RE:* It must have been very hard. You want to talk about it?

Rachel tearfully recalls the difficult times.

> *RL*: You want to talk about Debbie? (Sighs) When I used to go work,
> one day she came outside in the snow naked just with her underwear
> and said, "Mommy, don't go to work". I said, "Why?" She said, "I scared,
> I don't want to stay home." So I said, "I have to go to work, I cannot do
> anything about it," and then I said, "Go back home and stay" and then
> she went back home, but she never told me what she was scared of. So
> that's what happened there with Debbie.

> *RE*: Uhmm.

> *RL*: So Debbie now don't like Jeoffery too much, because Debbie used
> to get licks. Harold used to beat Debbie because of Jeoffery, because if
> he cry a little bit he want to know what he's crying for, like I say she
> was nine years old, and she have all the responsibility, because I'm working,
> and he used to take advantage, because Jeoffery used to cry sometimes.
> You have a little baby not even three years, he was about two years or
> something like that and he used to cry sometimes you know, he used
> to get upset with Debbie and take out everything on Debbie. Right now
> she don't like Jeoffery at all because of that, she thought he'll kill her
> because of him, and she grow up with that fear, he came out just like
> his father, he look like his father and everything, but she liked Jerry a
> lot, because my mother came and she take care of Jerry and he never
> take advantage too much again because [...][12]

Jeoffery remembers:

> I remember him writing a lot when I was younger. I remember him
> drinking alcohol a lot.
>     All I really remember is that he took me to buy stuff before he went
> to Trinidad and he dressed me in a girl's bathing suit and all the kids
> were making fun of me.[13]

Rachel's account of life with Harold is horrifying, but if we look at his
manuscripts we learn something very important about Harold the writer.
Harold was well aware of the contradictions between his work and his
domestic life. His commitment to truth in his writing was unequivocal.
Look at extracts from two drafts of the same story "The Teacher's Wife
Story":
First draft:

> Like a mule: summer and winter I worked as a waitress and a maid to
> support the man. For six years I never saw my pay check and even now,
> the seventh year, I can't see the money I work for. Horace collects my
> pay and if I talk he is ready to beat me.[14]

In the second draft the teacher is now called Sawak, the wife Indra –

characters from "New Novel" or "1st Canadian Novel". The teacher's wife tries to stop the teacher from abusing their daughter:

> I just simply say, "Sawak, left the gal. She not doin' you nothing." Sawak jumped like a horse and kick me in my face. Blood started coming down my nose. "O God Sawak!" I said. "You break me nose bridge." He said, "Get out of this house! I don't need you any more. You illiterate asshole!" My nose was bleeding real bad and I decided to call the police. Sawak took a pair of scissors and said he would stab me if I call the police. Luckily Vishnu of Tola came over same time... Vishnu turned to Sawak and insulted him, "You are a teacher at Humber College in Toronto and this is the way you are behaving? Have a conscience and respect your family. A man of your temperament should be kicked out of Humber College. You are out of the gutter, why not try to take the gutter out of you."[15]

It's as if he is writing about himself, accusing and berating himself in his literary space where the truth must be told. But then there was his public persona:

> Graeme Gibson: He talked a lot about his child, about when he was writing, I suppose the second novel, or it might have even been the first, of the child with its own beat up, old typewriter. He'd said he'd gotten a typewriter that didn't work 'cause he was looking after the child some of the time, or much of the time I think, when he was writing and that he put the infant in front of the typewriter while he was in front of his and wrote, and that I associate him with the child, I don't think I ever saw them together, but he certainly spoke a lot of this child and was very pleased with him. So, it's very complex on that level.[16]

Again, though Harold attended school, was from a well-to-do family and did little agricultural work, and spent no time in hospital, here is what he writes in a letter to Dennis Lee:

> Many years of my life have been wasted in hospital beds.
>     Even as a child I felt my life burning under the sky and my nights were filled of lamentations and doubt. Even as a child I have groped with the mysterious because even as a child I had the capacity to endure: my achievements (if they are achievements) can bear me out. I had no formal schooling, I had no money or encouragement, but I had the capacity to endure. I began to work when I was eight years old and I knew that one day I was going to leave the rice-fields and go out into a greater world. It was that thought that kept me alive. Many of my childhood friends are dead; too many of them are now behind prison walls, all because they were unfortunate from birth. But I had courage; I worked my way up; I learnt to read and write because I knew that when I got the opportunity to go out into the world I was going to devote myself to something that will matter to many people in this world. But today I am really in troubled waters.[17]

This statement from Harold is so delusional that it is not surprising that in his poem, *The Death of Harold Ladoo*, which moves through a wide range of responses to Harold, Dennis Lee expresses his hurt at Harold's attempts to manipulate his respect and affection:

And as for you, Ladoo! – you never missed a trick.
You soaked up love like a sponge, cajoling
hundreds of hours, and bread, and fine-tuned publication,
and then accepted them all with a nice indifference,
as though they were barely enough. You had us taped, you knew white
liberals inside out: how to
guilt us; which buttons to push; how hard; how long.
Three different times, in close-mouthed confidence you spoke of
three horrific childhoods; it was *there* you first
gave blood, now you could use it
to write. And I was
lethally impressed, and only later realised
two of the childhoods had to be somebody else's,
and all those dues you paid were so much literature.
You couldn't tell which one of you was real.
But I can, now: you were
a routine megalomaniac, taking the shortcut
through living men and women to try and make it big.[18]

Peter Such, in his personal memorial essay, "The Short Life and Sudden Death of Harold Ladoo" recounts a collision between Harold's private life and Canadian society and how he navigated it.

One morning the phone rang at an ungodly hour. Another novel? No, he was phoning from a police station. "Peter, Some kind of trouble. I'm in terrible trouble." I couldn't get him to explain. As I hung up I heard a news flash on the radio. A man had been stabbed, Harold Sonny Ladoo was being charged with wounding.[...]

Haltingly he told me the circumstances. He'd been dragged rather unwillingly to a party, dead tired, had had a bad time. He had run into arguments and had a couple of drinks. On the way home, as his brother-in-law said later, he seemed to grow strange and paranoiac. By the time they arrived home he was very agitated. He went downstairs to rest while the others chatted.

Ten minutes later he came up again with a breadknife, speaking incoherently and waving it around. He had cut himself, and his relatives – from what they could understand him saying – were afraid that he was going to kill himself. In the tussle to disarm him he stabbed his brother-in-law twice and cut himself again. When it was all over he fell unconscious. He woke up completely oblivious to what had happened, with the police all around him. He was convinced that someone had put drugs in his drink. (He avoided drugs like the plague.)

Dr. Elmer and I went to his trial as character witnesses. After hearing the general facts from Harold's brother-in-law; whom the prosecution put on the stand, the judge called both lawyers up to the front and chatted a while. The judge decided the case should proceed no further and remanded Harold until he had been examined by a court psychiatrist. A Clarke Institute psychiatrist examined him, pronounced him eminently sane, and kept him for ages talking about literature. Harold made that kind of impression on people.[19]

Harold had moved on from the paranoid immigrant looking over his shoulder for the authorities hunting illegals. He had learnt how to deal with Canadian society, he was confident in his ability to charm and impress. This is a man quite different to Sawak of "New Novel" or "1st Canadian Novel".[20]

As noted in Chapter Ten, Harold's consciousness of himself and his abilities to seduce is clear in his account to Dennis Lee of his trip to Anansi to convince them to publish *Yesterdays*:

(my dark eyes flashing, my thin legs supporting me like a stork, one hand thrust into my pocket, the other holding the manuscript with the knowledge of a renaissance genius) I said, "This is a good book." Putting on the worried look (a look I have picked up recently from Choonilal) I added, "There are many authorities who have read it , and I am confident that it is publishable." "All right," she said, "we will take a look at it."[21]

That image conjures up Anansi spider, the West African folk hero and trickster who travelled to the Caribbean. Many of us grew up with the moral tales of an Anansi, a Brer Rabbit or an Aesop but few have the ability and the charisma to spin a web of confidence the way Harold the storyteller could.

Harold's invention of alternate personal histories is by no means unique among artists, especially storytellers – Hemingway and the young Robert Zimmerman (alias Bob Dylan) are just two examples. It was not because Harold was pathologically delusional. He was taking mischievous advantage of liberal colonial stereotypes of the exotic and the other. Perhaps there were elements of suffering an "imposter syndrome" that drove him to manipulate others. Then again, it was, perhaps, simply because he could.

Harold knew he was under pressure to achieve the goals he set himself and produce those novels he called his Canadian friends about in the early hours of the morning. Maybe he was just enjoying being in literary circles, his dream, where he felt accepted as a writer by people who didn't know him as family, school friend or fellow villager – who knew nothing of his 'home truths'. At home, they knew the everyday Harold. That wasn't so nice. But Harold was still determined to escape his fate, the fate waiting for him back in Tola/Trinidad. That intensity, that urgency, that passion must have originated from a sense that a reckoning was coming closer and was inescapable ("I am really in troubled waters").

Endnotes

1. Economist and socio/political theorist, Lloyd Best interviewed by Patrick French (2004).
2. Interview with Peter Such by Christopher Laird, 2003.
3. Interview with James Polk by Christopher Laird, 2003.
4. Interview with Peter Such by Christopher Laird, 2003.
5. Interview with Meena Ladoo by Christopher Laird and Ken Ramchand, 2003.
6. Interview with Graeme Gibson by Christopher Laird, 2002.
7. Interview with James Polk by Christopher Laird, 2003.
8. Note: "I will really have to work fast, because it appears as if my wife is pregnant again, so if a baby is coming in the next seven or eight months or so, then I will have to work real fast." (Letter to Dennis Lee, 25 September 1972).
9. Interview with James Polk by Christopher Laird, 2003.
10. Interview with Lennox Sankersingh – fellow student at Erindale and friend from McBean, by Christopher Laird, 2019.
11. Dionne Brand introduction to the 2003 Anansi edition of *No Pain Like This Body.*
12. Interview of Rachel Ladoo with Ramabai Espinet, April 2003.
13. Interview of Jeoffery Ladoo by Christopher Laird, 2003.
14. "The Teacher's Wife Story" (first draft).
15. The Teacher's Wife Story" (second draft). *"He (Harold) even told me he married me for me to give him an education, that's it. That's what he needed me for.* Interview with Rachel Ladoo by Christopher Laird and Ramabai Espinet, September 2002.
16. Interview with Graeme Gibson by Christopher Laird, 2002.
17. Letter to Dennis Lee, 20 November 1971.
18. Dennis Lee, "The Death of Harold Ladoo", *Heart Residence. Collected Poems 1967-2017,* p. 90.
19. Peter Such, "The Short Life and Sudden Death of Harold Sonny Ladoo".
20. Peter Such, Ibid. Nevertheless, after this incident (November 1972) the Ladoos had to move out of Sylvia and Maniram's basement and move to 787 Jane Street – which was at least a little closer to Erindale. This would be the last move Harold would make before his final journey to Trinidad.
21. Letter to Dennis Lee, 25 September 1972.

## CHAPTER 14
## A KIND OF SENSITIVITY

"I think it was Ibsen who said that art must deal with reality, even if
reality hurts it must be portrayed."
— Harold Ladoo, Letter to Austin Clarke March 1973

Beyond any speculation about the reasons for his manipulation of others,
his presentation of multiple personas and sheer autobiographical invention,
there was one truth: the man could write. The reason that so many
people not only remember Harold after a half century but remember
him with a fierce mixture of fondness, awe (and sometimes a wounded
resentment), is because of his writing. I think Dennis Lee sums it up
best

> Harold had so much going for him in this way, because there was this
> vision of life in the place he came from and so much anecdotal material,
> just chock-a-block with vigour and passion and heartbreak and all that.
> You just have to read the two books to know.
> He had an artistic vision as well. It wasn't just a matter of being there
> to write sociological reports. He had a magic ear and I think that was
> true from the beginning. When the characters talk to each other but
> also in the narrative, the narrator of his books is talking; it sweeps you
> along. He had a gift for storytelling.
> He had this uncanny sense of the physical world and the way characters
> interacted with it. He had great ability to move inside and outside of
> characters, so things happened and then we get inside characters and
> get a sense for how they feel about it and what their thoughts are and
> back into it. He had enormous what seemed to be need of resources
> once he had hooked into what his calling as a writer was. The one thing
> that wasn't there yet was the craft to weave all these different chunks
> and bits and pieces and different strains and dimensions and streams of
> storytelling together, and it was partly because there was such a rich
> and sophisticated vein of storytelling that he had to get onto the page.
> That was a complex thing.[1]

Despite the awkward spot Harold may have felt he was in so far as
delivering the novels he said he had written, he was, as we have seen,
writing short stories and beginning novels at a fiercesome rate. Amid the
intensity and frenzy, he was undoubtedly maturing as a writer. Despite all
his *flimflam* about churning out one manuscript after another, something
was happening in Harold's writing that I believe he was conscious of and

working towards. Peter Such thought that Harold would have left the rage behind and developed stories that were *'not so violent and not so abusive, that had a kind of sensitivity'*.[2]

In the light of Peter's assertion, I refer to two events that occurred at the end of his first academic year in 1971. The first was the death of his father in August, followed by his traumatic trip home with his family to attend the funeral, and second, the loss of Peter Such as his Erindale mentor and touchstone when Peter's term as Writer in Residence came to an end. The death of his father obviously changed Harold's sense of his position in the world. No longer did he have to gauge his behaviour in relation to his father's expectations and demands on him. With his father's passing he no longer had a target for his rebelliousness and attitude. Instead, he could reassess his father's role and accomplishments with the understanding that now he was the successor, that he had to come to terms with the new family expectations of him as the person the Ladoo clan looked to for leadership.

Tola was recalling him, asserting its claim over him. But he was Harold Sonny Ladoo, who had studied hard, planted bhaji to raise money to emigrate to become a great international writer. He had stuff to write, and he would use all the time he could carve out to make headway in his "Grand Plan" – until events in Tola/Mcbean could no longer be ignored. In the process, I think his writing began to become more nuanced, less violently pyrotechnic, paying more attention to themes of family bonds, love and caring, in the face of social violence.

Two of the stories he wrote at this time (or dated this time), though contrasting in theme, display a different attitude to an oppressed Indian community, angry about its oppression, but more understanding of their difficulty in overcoming it and more ready to recognise the community's inherent decency. The first story, "Chamar Tola 1940", is set during the second world war and draws on the consequences of the 'Lend-Lease Agreement' made between the UK and the USA, when in exchange for 50 obsolete destroyers, the US was granted the right to establish bases is the British West Indies for 99 years. In Trinidad, the US established, two large airfields and a naval base. The largest airfield, Carlsen Air Base (now called Carlsen Field) was just a mile or two from McBean.

## CHAMAR TOLA 1940

The Americans had already passed in jeeps telling the people to leave Chamar Tola, because soon they would come with large tractors and level down their houses, and destroy their crops. And everyone believed it, because the tractors and other equipment were parked a little way from the village in a plot of open land. Everyone knew that the Americans were serious; Panday had already told them that there was a war going on with the Germans, and the Americans had come to Chamar Tola to build a base to fight the Germans; although no one in the settlement really knew anything about a war in which whitemen were killing whitemen, the peasants believed Panday. But when Panday had said that whitemen were coming from America to rape their women and destroy their houses, they had found that a little difficult to believe. But now they believe all that Panday had told them.

Yesterday for instance, Basdai and Chandra had gone to Saran Shop to buy flour. Since Basdai was twelve and Chandra was ten years old, Sampath and his wife Lotya became worried as night covered the village. Picking up a Poui stick, Sampath hurrying, going to Talia Junction to see what was detaining his two children.

As he walked along Chamar Trace, he saw a parked jeep, and the Americans were drinking and laughing When he saw that they were soldiers, he said, "Good night Sahib (whiteman)."

One of the soldiers gave him a pint of whiskey, and prodded him to the front of the jeep with his gun. Six feet from the parked vehicle, the light beams focusing on them, he saw two soldiers raping his children. Overcome with rage, he charged forward with his stick, but one of the soldiers struck him with a heavy object and sent him flying into the cane field where he lost consciousness.

When he recovered, he hurried home to tell his wife what had happened to their daughters. Villagers came with flambeaux to search for the girls, but all they saw was the blood on the ground. During the night they heard the tractors working, and Panday said that the Americans were digging a trench to bury the bodies, as they had done so many times before.

At daybreak Sampath had gone to Tolaville, begging the policemen to come to the settlement and put the whitemen in prison. When the policemen came the soldiers gave them cigarettes and whiskey. And when Sampath said that he would like to dig up the trench and carry his children home, the policemen, almost drunk now with the whiskey, told him to shut his mouth and go home.

At home the wind came through the small openings of the bamboo door, extinguishing the flame of the flambeau. A devilish darkness crept into the house.

"Get up and light de flambeau, nuh," Lotya said.

Sampath struck a match and relit the flambeau.

Lotya was sitting with her thin back resting against the old tapia wall. She took a drink and placed the rum bottle near the flambeau. Sampath sat facing her, his back resting against a potato crate; he shook his head from side to side, shook his feet and said, "Dem chirens can't remain in dat trench." Stretching his hands, he grabbed the rum bottle, took a drink, and remained quiet.

Lotya had already wept too much. So with her dry eyes and thin face, she said, "Basdai and Chandra done dead aready. But tink dat in de mornin dem soldiers comin to destroy de whole village."

Opening his eyes, Sampath yelled, "I have to take dem outta dat trench, because dey have to get a proper burial!"

His powerful voice echoed through the darkness as if the spirits of Tankee, those heroic men who had lived in Tola and watered the plantations with their blood and sweat were moaning in the night, lamenting the doom of their descendants.

"Shut you mout," she said. "Panday say de whitemen goin to come and shoot people in de village if dey hear any noise. Dey goin to shoot, because dey come here to fight de Jawmans."

"It have no blasted Jawmans in Tola!" Sampath shouted. "De Jawmans tousans of mile from dis island. Dey tousans of miles across de sea in white people country."

Sampath got up and went in the yard. The night was dark and the stars twinkled in the sky. The raucous shrieks of night birds hovered over the settlement. He scratched his bushy whiskers with his knotted and bony fingers as he walked to the cowpen. Shattered by the weight of the loss he had suffered, he took the fork and brought it into the house.

With her sad voice, Lotya asked, "Wot you goin to do, Sampath?"

"Just goin to dig dat trench and take dem chirens out. Dey have to get a burial in Tola bellin ground, Lotya," he said.

"But dem soldiers not goin to let you dig dat trench."

"If a man cant give he own chirens a decent grave, he dont have no right to be livin in de fust place."

As midnight passed, worn down by tiredness and sorrow, Lotya fell asleep on the earthen floor. Sampath drank the rest of the rum, put out the flambeau, and shouldering his fork, he hurried to re-open the trench.

At daybreak Panday took a mule cart and went to the white soldiers for Sampath: the soldiers had bayonetted his body twenty-five times, and the lieutenant said that he had been killed because he was found trespassing.

Since the tractors were already destroying the houses in the settlement, Panday took Sampath on the cart and brought him to Rajput Road.[3]

Harold was not concerned with providing a desirable image of his community to be presented to the world. He wrote it as he saw it, as his community made him live it. As he wrote to the Caribbean/Canadian novelist Austin Clarke in praise of his work:

> I think it was Ibsen who said that art must deal with reality, even if reality hurts it must be portrayed.[4]

The harsh truth of the story grabs the reader immediately. Surely, one asks oneself, incidents like this must have occurred. During World War II Trinidad was host to the largest US military bases in the hemisphere outside of the USA. Stories like these arise wherever there are military concentrations. How come, one asks again, we haven't seen such stories in our literature?

Friends in the Indo-Trinidadian community tell me of hearing stories like this quietly passed down inside families, but they have not appeared on a public forum. In the urban centres, kaisonians (calypsonians) sang of prostitution, child abandonment and the cuckolding of local men by the US military, but not of rape or violence. From the rural Indian community there was silence. Ladoo's encompassing rage at the hypocrisy around him, at the refusal to face our true selves (even, as we have seen, when it applies to his own actions) drove him towards his vision. It is possibly this characteristic that ensured that he would not be publicly recognised by his own community, and certainly it would not be far-fetched to suggest that it contributed to his untimely end.

But violence and rage were not all that Harold wrote about.

> *Peter Such*: Some of the short stories that he was beginning to write, I think he was getting more and more into short stories that had some kind of interpersonal level to them, that was not so violent and not so abusive, that had a kind of sensitivity there. I mean he was very young too when you think about it, he was twenty-six years old and were he my age now, (chuckles) that's another thirty odd years, people do change and heal and grow and I really feel he had this desire, I mean, I think he knew cognitively where his depression and his rage came from, you know.[5]

Harold was not all rage. "The Quiet Peasant", according to Peter Such one of his last completed stories (published by Peter in IMPULSE in 1973), is an iridescent example of Harold ability to express empathy, gentleness, caring, but all within a threatening, oppressive and demanding world.

## THE QUIET PEASANT

Gobinah wasn't the kind of man to eat in the dark. He used to say that night is the time for a man to sleep and probe the meaning of his dreams; it is a time too for him to think about his crops and meditate on the future of his children; life isn't worth living if a man prefers to wake after the sun has travelled far in the sky; a man is supposed to wake before the sun and feel the sweat streaming out of his body, and the mud caking his feet and hands while there is still the mysterious darkness, for without this exposure and personal closeness to the primeval earth, it would be totally impossible for any man to enjoy good health.

It was March and the tomatoes he had planted in the ratoon caneland were dying off for water. March is always a terrible month for planting things in Carib Island, and most farmers in Lima, fearing the dryness of the earth never bothered to plant a single seed during the dry season. Instead of trying to quarrel with the drought, the farmers in the area drank their rum, reaped their cane and looked after their animals. But Gobinah was different. Other men had their wives to help them in the fields, and their grown sons helped them with their cattle. Once Batulan had worked side by side with Gobinah. First it started as a little cough and Batulan drank bush medicine and consulted Bhola Saddhu, the village priest of Tola. Months later the D.M.O. in Tolaville said that Batulan had TB. Most men in Tola would have beaten their wife out of the village, but Gobinah didn't do this. He accepted her illness as his destiny and continued to work the soil. In order to pay medical bills he sold his crops and his cattle and never became depressed.

In the end he remained with the black double-jointed bull; he considered the animal his friend and he couldn't sell it. Some months ago a few wicked villagers had poisoned the animal. Most men in Tola would have gone on the warpath and kill somebody, but Gobinah believed in abstract justice, so be left the matter alone. Gobinah could have made some money, because butchers came to buy the dead animal to sell the meat in South City Market. Instead of selling the bull Gobinah dug a grave and buried it in the ratoon caneland.

In the night the butchers came with lanterns and guns, dug out the carcass and carried it away.

Because he had no money to pay someone to cart his cane to the derrick, he cutlassed down most of the ratoon cane, dug up the earth with a fork and a hoe and planted tomatoes. Sita, his eldest daughter, was already fifteen, and in May she would be married off to a crab-catcher in Jangli Tola. Although the crab-catcher belonged to the chamar caste (the lowest caste), he had demanded tilak (dowry). This dowry was important and Gobinah knew that only a madman would marry his daughter without it. His four other daughters were still too young to be of any real bother, and perhaps when they would come of age be wouldn't have to worry too much, because they were pupils at the Tolaville Mission School. Daily, girls with a little education were getting jobs in the cities and looking after themselves. Perhaps Sita would have had her fair share of education hadn't Batulan contracted consumption. With his whole mind centred on the work, and his powerful arms holding the fork, Gobinah continued digging the well. He had already crossed six feet, the earth became softer and colder, yet there were no signs of water. Long before daybreak he had started digging, but the top soil was hard like iron. Now however, it was easier for him to dig. The earth felt cold under his feet and his skin became taut as the direct rays of the sun hit his body.

Raju, the ten-year-old son of Gobinah, was weeding the yard with an old hoe. As he was putting some dirt around the small zaboca tree Batulan came out of the kitchen. Holding her chest she coughed. The boy heard the rackling inside her chest but he didn't look. Then Batulan spat out the phlegm and blood saying,

"Beta (son), time to carry some food for you bap (father) in the land."

"Ha (yes), Mai (mother)," he said, as he dropped the hoe on the ground.

When he approached the drain he saw the chunks of blood that had come out of his mother's chest resting like small red flowers on the parched earth. When he reached inside the kitchen, Sita handed him a basket. Inside the basket, the roti (unleavened bread) and fried allou (potato) were wrapped in banana leaves. Then she put some rainwater into the bolee (calabash) and handed it to him. Without saying anything to his sister, the boy walked out of the house.

He was going to meet his father in the caneland, and the land was a little over a mile away from the house. To get to his father he had to pass through the land of other farmers. Often the farmers cursed and swore at him, and many times they make their grown sons beat him with bamboo switches. To avoid the farmers he walked through the bamboo grass. Since he was barefooted and naked except for the short and torn khaki pants that were held up by the strand of corbeau liana tied around his waist, he felt the sun eating through his skin. Now he was near the two acres of land that his father rented from the whiteman. Thirsty, he drank some water from the bolee and looked up at the sky; it was blue, with hardly a strand of cloud anywhere.

When he walked into the land he saw the tomatoes' leaves all crumpled up; the leaves were pale, but here and there he saw little gold spots, and he recognised them as the tiny flowers. As soon as he reached the mound of freshly dug earth, he called out,

"Ay bap!"

"Ha beta," his father answered.

"I bring you food, bap."

"Send it down beta."

Slowly, carefully, the boy walked on top of the fresh dirt. The well was deeper than ten feet now, and still there wasn't any sign of water in it. Wearing a soiled and torn dhoti (loin-cloth), bare-back and barefooted, he saw his father inside the hole. Sweat was flowing from every pore in his body; with the earth caking his hands and feet, the man asked,

"How de tomatoes lookin, beta?"

As if expecting the whole plantation to change miraculously, the boy looked at the tomatoes again, before saying,

"De garden lookin bad, bap."

The man said nothing. First the boy threw the basket down inside the well; the man caught it, took out the food and flung the basket back for his son. Next the boy sent down the water. Resting the water at his feet, opening the roti and allou, the man asked,

"You go eat some food, beta?"

"No bap, I done eat."

With his toes hidden in the earth, with his back resting against the cold earth, the man ate his food. Raju stood at the top looking down at his father. He noticed that the man's feet trembled now and then, and his hands shook as he brought the food to his mouth. His face, neck and chest were red and his veins stood out as thick as corbeau lianas. Dropping the banana leaves inside the well, drinking the water from the bolee, throwing the container up for his son, Gobinah said, "So de garden lookin bad, beta?"

"Ha, bap."

Gobinah shook his head. "Soon as I get worta in dis well beta, everything goin to be oright. Wen I reap dis tomatoes I goin to pay de whiteman his rent. If I don't pay de rent, he goin to take away de land. Den I goin to give tilak for Sita to get married."

"Yeh, bap."

"Now beta, you modder kinda sickly. A few days every week, try and go to school and learn. Take education beta, so wen you come a man, you wouldn't have to kill youself for a bread like me." Wiping his brows with his soiled hands, he continued, "When you have education beta, you wouldn't have de cause to rent land from dese white people. And wen you come a man beta, try and make youself oright."

"Yeh, bap," Raju said sadly. Looking at his father, he said, "Well bap, maybe you could take a rest now. Tomorrow you could dig some more."

"No beta. I must get worta in dis hole, today Dem tomatoes deadin for worta. If dis crop dead off, beta, den de whiteman goin to take back de land, and de ten years dat I payin rent wouldn't stop him from takin it. Den dis crop have to make enuff money for you sista to get married. She is a big gal now, beta, and I cant keep she too long again in de house."

After the man talked some more, he took up the fork again and continued digging. Now the hole was too deep for him to swing the dirt up with the fork. He took up the dirt, made it into small balls, and flung them out of the hole.

"Lemme help you, bap."

"No beta, de so sun too hot. Go and siddown inside dem ratoon cane. Wen I get worta, I goin to call you."

"Oright bap."

Takes the basket and walks to the shade. Looks back at the balls of earth and dozes off

Exhausted by the heat of the sun, Raju took the basket and bolee and walked to the ratoon cane. Then he thrashed some dry leaves and sat on them. From his hiding place he saw the little balls of dirt darting out of the well: As he waited for his father to call, he dozed off.

Suddenly he woke with a start; during his sleep he had heard his father calling, just his eyes couldn't open at the time. Wiping his eyes with the back of his hands, he noticed that it was almost evening; he noticed too that no small balls of earth came flying out of the hole. Quickly taking up the bolee and the basket, he hurried to the well, calling his father. When he heard no answer, climbing the mound of dirt, he looked down inside the hole. Now the hole was much deeper, but there still wasn't, any water in it.

His father sat at the bottom of the hole; with his hands holding the fork, his head bent slightly to the right. Gobinah stared unblinkingly at the sky.

"Ay, bap!" the boy screamed.

"Ay, bap!" Was this a cry from Harold as much as from Raju? Was this a cry of abandonment, of grief for the innocence and carefreeness of youth who could still rely on a father (and mentor) to mediate the world for him?

Endnotes

1. Interview with Dennis Lee, 2002.
2. Interview with Peter Such by Christopher Laird, 2003.
3. "Chamar Tola 1940", short story.
4. Letter to Austin Clarke March 1973.
5. Interview with Peter Such by Christopher Laird, 2003.

## CHAPTER FIFTEEN
## THE INTRUDERS (SHORT STORY)

Everywhere in evidence is Ladoo's tender understanding of his characters.
…a delicate sense of irony that contains within it a love for his characters.
— Mark Sarner[1]

As we have seen in the last chapter, while he was drawn to write about
tragic violence with a sense of rage, Harold could also write with
tremendous empathy and respect. This is illustrated again in a remarkable
short story, "The Intruders". It is worth quoting at length because it
moves at such a considered pace, which is so different from the frenzied
earlier writing and, in its maturity, points to the direction Harold's
writing was taking.

★

There was a penetrating silence as if the night was resting. Suddenly
the silence was broken by sudden claps of thunder; it grew louder
and louder and almost without warning the explosion withdrew
into space. Sitting up on the bed Gonwa looked through the opened
window. The rain began hammering the galvanised roof, and he
heard the water falling into the concrete drain. Still peering through
the sodden darkness, he felt an unmistakable silence enveloping
everything. The rain and the wind with their fury and surging
power had always fascinated him. Lightning ripped through the
village in a bewildering swipe and continued its pilgrimage into
space.
     "Yazmin," he called his wife.
     There was no answer.
     Shifting a little on the bed, he called his seven year old
granddaughter, "Sita!"
     He got up from bed and put on his working pants. Without
switching on the lights, Gonwa opened the door and went and
stood in the gallery. Then he opened the hall door and walked to
the centre room's door.
     "Sita!" he called.

No one answered. Gonwa opened the door slowly. Standing near the four-poster bed, he called, "Yazmin."

They were asleep; Yazmin was snoring. Gonwa put on the light and looked. His granddaughter was asleep, next to his wife. Yazmin was a bad sleeper; one of her feet was resting on Sita's chest. He held her foot and pushed it away. On the ground there was a bottle of rum; the bottle was almost empty. A sudden rage came over Gonwa; he held Yazmin and shook her. She opened her eyes.

"I want to tell you someting," he said.

"Look here!" she said. "Look Gonwa, leff me life alone."

"I want to talk to you."

"I dont know why you dont dead, man. Dead and finish, den I know me trobble over."

"Why you dont stop drinkin dat rum?"

"Wen you dead den I go stop."

Sita turned on the bed. Not wishing to wake the child any more, Gonwa took off the lights and went back into the front room. He went and sat on the bed. Thoughts began to flow through his mind with a unique rapidness that astounded him. Scenes he had almost forgotten passed through his mind so clearly that he wondered whether he was not having a vision. Suddenly he heard a different kind of sound; the cattle were bellowing. Bareheaded, barefooted, shirtless, with only the tight khaki trouser pinching his waist, Gonwa walked out of the house. Quickly descending the fifteen steps, he walked into the yard.

Opening the door of his Land Rover he took out his working shirt. The shirt was dirty; there was a strong sweaty smell on it.

As he sat in the Land Rover the dogs began howling again. Same time the cattle started bellowing. No longer wishing to listen to these strange sounds he drove off.

There was about three thousand pounds of cabbage in the jeep. As he clutched the steering wheel he felt the strain on the engine. But it was a new jeep; he had bought it only six months ago. Instead of driving down to Atkinson Settlement he pulled into Lima Road and stopped in front of Beatrice's house. Switching off the vehicle he came out with two cabbages in his hands. Standing in the rain he looked at the house.

Beatrice was not asleep; it was her habit to be up late at night, because she was the village washerwoman. Lamps were burning inside the house; each time she moved Gonwa saw her shadow reflecting against the glass door and the windows.

"Maam!" he called.

"Who is dat?" she asked, her voice powerful and determined.

"Gonwa!"

The main door flung open; standing in the doorway she said, "Come, son. Don't wet in dat rain, Gonwa." While he was walking into the yard, she asked, "Like someting happen, son?"

After he had climbed the steps and reached the concrete porch, he scooped the rain drops off his forehead with his thumb and said, "Notten wrong maam. Just bring two cabbages for you."

"Wait lemme get a towel for you. You have no right wettin in dis rain bringin cabbage for me," and as she talked she walked inside the house. When she reappeared with the towel she was still talking, "...you too harden Gonwa. Wettin in dis rain like dat." She handed him the towel. Putting the cabbages on the porch he wiped his head dry. Then he put the cabbages inside the towel and handed them to her. "I goin now maam."

"You not goin no place till you have some strong coffee," she said. "Dem eight years I mind you wen you was a boy, is dat good mindin dat have you strong so. Oright. You over fifty now and you still movin like a bull. Come inside now."

Beatrice's hair was grey but she walked upright. Gonwa followed her. There were very few furnitures in the living room; except for four wooden chairs and a mahogany table, the house looked deserted. A small hurricane lamp hung from a rusted chain over the table. There was a religious painting hanging near the wooden partition that separated the living room from the bedroom. Gonwa sat on one of the chairs and allowed his memory to drift like a black shape into the night. From the hall he heard her heavy footsteps in the kitchen; now and then he glimpsed her as she moved with the oil lamp in her hand. At times he thought he heard the coffee beans percolating, but he was not certain, because the rain was still falling heavy. After a while she extinguished the lamp in the kitchen and emerged from the darkness with a cup of coffee in her hand. Steam came out of the cup, and though she was over seventy her hands didn't tremble. Placing the cup in front him, she said, "You drink dat coffee." Then she shuffled to the front door; Gonwa had left it open behind him. She pulled in the door, then walked slowly and sat on a chair opposite to him. Moths circled the hurricane lamp; weakened by the heat some of them fell on the table.

"I have to say de Lawd good to me," she said. "Goin on eighty and still goin strong. Yong yong people droppin down just like dat and deadin, but I still on me foot." She sat deep into the old fashioned chair. All the chairs had a semblance of agelessness; forty-eight years ago he had first seen them, and now they looked the same. "One ting I know," she continued, "me time nearin. But I wash meself in de blood of de Lawd." Her voice died out almost suddenly, just to begin again; not talking any more, but singing. Gonwa listened to her voice as it bombarded the house and the darkness in a sturdy harmony that came from the depth of her noble and primeval being. Suddenly she broke off, "I havin bad dreams dese few nights, Gonwa."

A moth fell inside Gonwa's coffee. He didn't see when it fell in, because he was watching Beatrice fixedly. When he saw it, the moth was floating trying to get out. With his index finger he fished out the dying creature, held it in his hands a little, then rested it on the table. By looking at the moth he knew that the insect had travelled a great distance towards death. The wings were stuck together, the legs moved slow at first, then they beat frantically, and in less than a minute it was dead. Gonwa took a sip of coffee and looked at Beatrice.

Beatrice fumbled into her pocket and pulled out an old clay pipe and some tobacco. Her long black fingers squeezed the tobacco into the pipe gracefully. Striking a match, lighting the pipe, she smoked contemplatively. At first the smoke came up in a bulk as she pulled hard on the pipe to make sure it was lighted properly. Now that it was lighted properly the smoke went up in thin puffs that obliterated her eyes and forehead momentarily. Without her shawl she looked impressive although her head was silvery white, the kinky hairs were still thick in spite of her age. Along the edges of her temples the hairs looked more ashes than white. Her eyebrows were puckered and grey; grey but still looking impressive and absolutely dignified; giving her black eyes a lustre of indomitability. Her cheeks were boneless, smooth, but there were wrinkles at the edges of her mouth. The flesh around her neck was loosed, stringy.

"Yeh," she said, "you must take care of youself Gonwa. Time for you to take a rest. Now you have money and you belly not heavy."

He sipped the coffee, then said, "You right, maam. No man never kill work yet. In de end a man does have to pass out and leff de work. Dis is de last big garden I make. After I reap dis crop I goin to rest. As you say maam, me belly not heavy." And unable to look at her he bent his head and stared at the floor. One of his large arms rested on the table, two fingers circling the handle-less cup the other hand rested on his right leg.

"Like someting worryin you?" she asked without alarm.

Gonwa released the cup and wiped his large handsome face with his left hand. Brushing back his thick black hair with his strong fingers he said, "Well maam, someting really worrying me bad. Most of me chirens away, maam, and I want to see dem. All dis property I have, I want to share it up. You know wot I mean. Just give a little to all de chirens."

Clutching the pipe between her strong teeth, she said, "But you dorta in law Jane stayin by she sista in Karan Settlement. She come from Canada on holiday."

For a moment Gonwa's large chest beat rapidly; his eyes looked terrible as if the news started a kind of abnormal thinking in his head. Looking at her, he said, "You know if me son come too, maam?"

Taking the pipe out of her mouth, she said, "No. Only he wife Jane come. She bring you little grandson wid she too." And she put the pipe back into her mouth, holding it between her teeth. Although the pipe went out, she clutched it with the strong teeth, not bothering to relight it.

"Four years now me son in Canada, maam, and in dat four years, he never write me one line. Now I have dis property to divide up, and none of me chirens around to get it." Gonwa shook his head; a kind of hopelessness and genuine sorrow spreading over his face.

Outside the rain and the wind rummaged the tall trees around the house. Beatrice rested the pipe on the table, cleared her throat noisily and said, "You must wear a hat, Gonwa. For fifty-six years old you lookin good. But take care of youself if you want to live as long as me."

"Yeh, maam."

A gust of wind shook the trees mercilessly. A window flew open; the flame in the hurricane lamp went up high, making the shade very smoky, then the flame came down, spluttered a few times and went out. A strange darkness descended upon the house and they felt the power and coldness of the wind on their faces. As the old woman began fumbling for the matches in her long plaid dress, Gonwa got up and bolted the window.

"Reach de lantern for me," she said.

Gonwa took down the lantern and put it on the table.

When she lighted it, she said, "Put it back now."

Gonwa hooked the wire handle to the little hook hanging from the rusty chain attached to the ceiling. "Well I tink I have to go now maam," he said. Walking to the concrete porch, he picked up the two cabbages he had brought for her and placed them on the table next to the empty teacup.

"How is Yazmin and Sita?" she asked.

Before he could speak, she said, "I hear you havin some trobble wid dat rum Yazmin drinkin in de house. But have some patience, son. Remember how she work so hard in she yong days. Now she want a little relaxation." She picked up the towel from the table and moved towards him. "Here, put dis towel over you head. Tomorrow evenin I comin to see you. Wen I come tomorrow, I goin to wash dem dirty clothes you have on you body."[2]

★

The story goes on to follow Gonwa to the Central Market in the capital in his green Land Rover full of cabbages where he negotiates their sale. The story paints a portrait of a respected farmer who can demand the price he wants and to whom other farmers look as a leader. The story also refers to Gonwa's son ("four years away in Canada without a word") and Gonwa's desire to divide his property before he dies.

It also mentions his intention to visit his daughter-in-law and grand-child who are in Trinidad from Canada for a visit. This latter reference seems to link to the short story, "The Vultures" (dated three days after "Intruders" and the longest fragment I have found – 32 pages.) which chronicles the return of Yasmin's daughter, Sarojini, with her daughters from Toronto to Tola.

Chapter Twelve noted how Harold planned the building of a novel to be called "The Agony" from three stories.[3] Combining the three stories from "The Agony" plus "The Intruders" and "The Vultures" provides a well of material from which Harold could have drawn an extensive family saga. "The Vultures" picks up after Gonwa from "The Intruders" dies and his widow, Yasmin, is being harassed and exploited by the villagers and her own daughter, Sarojini, visiting from Canada with her two and three year old daughters, Rose and Linda, who treats her mother like a servant. This calls to mind the predicament of Harold's own mother, Hamidhan, after the death of his father, Sonny. It is a set of stories and proposed novel that seems to parallel closely the fortunes of Harold's own family. In this he could not be closer to writing about "what you know".

But "The Intruders" is not restricted to its role in constructing a Ladoo family saga. There are many elements in this story which make it stand out above many of the other stories written/dated at this time. The portrait of Gonwa is unique in Harold's writing. It is carefully drawn in its detail, but cinematic, as elsewhere in his writing, narrating through action and dialogue and not pure description. One could construct a camera script from just reading it, a close-up here, a wide shot there. However, it is also written without satire, caricature or overt anger and with such humane reserve that one would find it difficult to attribute it to the author of *No Pain Like This Body* or "Rage". The two main characters are drawn with a gritty tenderness and an appreciation of an ageing strongman's vulnerability and weariness. The later part, when Gonwa is in the market, reveals a mature sensitivity to the isolation of a respected elder and of a father's distress when his children emigrate. Another thing that distinguishes this story is that its substance – the history of these characters, their faithfulness and mutual respect – is presented as a subtext not explicitly expressed in words or action.

It is tempting to believe that Gonwa is modelled after Harold's father. It is a respectful, almost loving portrait. It is so emotionally mature and so well executed that it supports Peter Such's belief that Harold was moving towards writing "not so violent and not so abusive, that had a kind of sensitivity".

What is also remarkable about this extract is that the Ladoo, who elsewhere in his writing is free with racist insults to Afro-Trinidadians as 'niggers' (or 'nigers' as he writes) or 'creoles', portrays Gonwa as finding comfort in an old retainer, "the village washerwoman", who happens to be an Afro-Trinidadian (and Christian). His description of Beatrice and her room is tenderly detailed even while, characteristically, attached to action. It comes explicitly through Gonwa's eyes as "he was watching Beatrice fixedly".

> "Beatrice's hair was grey but she walked upright."
> "Steam came out of the cup, and though she was over seventy her hands didn't tremble."
> […]
> Without her shawl she looked impressive although her head was silvery white, the kinky hairs were still thick in spite of her age. Along the edges of her temple the hairs looked more ashes than white. Her eyebrows were puckered and grey; grey but still looking impressive and absolutely dignified; giving her black eyes a lustre of indomitability. Her cheeks were boneless, smooth, but there were wrinkles at the edges of her mouth. The flesh around her neck was loosed, stringy.

Ladoo's portrayal of Beatrice is as respectful and as sympathetic as Gonwa's behaviour towards her and his trusting of her insights into his own vulnerability. Gonwa is a character whose inner life and existential fragility is exposed with such surefootedness that I think it gives a glimpse of Ladoo emerging from his 'apprenticeship'.

It is tempting to ascribe this 'literary graduation' to the death of his father. As mentioned in the last chapter, there can be little doubt that Harold was deeply affected by his father's death. As the son and heir he was faced with the daunting task of living up to his father's almost legendary accomplishments and community prestige. He now had to face the world on his own terms as an adult, as a father and above all as a writer. Besides, everyone was looking to him to see to his mother's care and deal with Sonny's estate.

There are two glimpses of how Harold responded to this challenge, made more difficult because he was going through some rough times in Toronto. Further to the calamities he reported in his letter to Dennis Lee about his trip to his father's funeral, on his return to Canada he was so short of money that the family had to move from 21 Roseneath Gardens, where they had lived since the fall of 1970, back to Sylvia and Maniram, this time to the basement of this couple's new home at 1309 Victoria Park Avenue. Unable to afford his own car, Peter Such rented transport for him and helped him move. Peter told a revealing anecdote about the move:

> I had a chauffeur's license then because I used to drive trucks so I rented a truck and drove the truck.
> He had quite recently before that been to his father's funeral. It's a bit macabre but this is the anecdote:
> In those days apartments didn't come equipped with stoves and fridges. He had a stove and a fridge so we had to move them out of his little house and in order to get it out we had to tip it and finally the only way we could get it out was put it on his back and the three of us carrying it. We were carrying it on our shoulders through the door and down the stairs and Harold said, "I've just come back from carrying something like this in Trinidad." He was referring to his father's coffin. For some reason his friend thought this screamingly funny, and it was all we could do not to drop the fridge. And he was laughing too. So, we had this giggle fit and had to stop and put the fridge down otherwise we would have definitely dropped it, you know. But I mean, it just blew me away that he would come up with this.[4]

When Peter told me this I was intrigued, not so much by the story but that Peter found it remarkable. I can only put this down to the difference between a Canadian and a Caribbean or, more specifically, a Trinidadian, sense of humour. To me, Harold's black humour is typical of the way that Caribbean people, long used to having some slaver, overseer, colonial policeman or neo-colonial exploiter's boot on their necks, not to mention natural catastrophes such as annual hurricanes, occasional volcanoes and earthquakes, mourn with humour, following the age-old adage, "If you don't laugh, you cry."

Nevertheless, the incident shows one thing clearly: in the midst of moving his fridge, his father's death and funeral were not far from his thoughts. It is the beginning of his awareness of his father's ghost which would lead him to write the moving, nuanced portrait of Gonwa in "The Intruders". After the passage quoted earlier in this chapter, Harold describes Gonwa's visit to the "Hindu cremation ground" on the Caroni/Carib river where Sonny Ladoo was cremated:

Exhaustion began to overpower him. Instead of running the risk of falling asleep behind the steering wheel, he stopped near Carib River; pulling off the road, he drove on the muddy trace along the riverbank, finally parking near the Hindu cremation grounds. It was the first night he had come to visit the resting place of human ashes and dreams. Pulling up the hand brakes, he released the steering wheel. He knew all about the ceremonies for the dead, he had witnessed many cremations in his lifetime. Strangely, he felt warm, comfortable; everything took on a proportion of peace and solitude; even the rain drops looked like dancing spirits. No longer wishing to be an intruder in an area of ashes and bones, he reversed the jeep and came out on the new road again.[6]

It is tempting to read this evocative description as reflecting a visit Harold himself made (or later imagined) to his father's cremation site.

The quality of this story, unedited as it is, points to the tragedy for himself and for Caribbean literature of the shortness of Harold's life. The existence of such work offers strong evidence of a maturity and ability to write about real people and relationships way beyond the violence and paranoia of his earlier writing. He seems to be pivoting towards a more nuanced appreciation of the community and family he left behind in McBean.

This story (and the "Quiet Peasant" dated three weeks later – at least in typescript form) show a writer who is beginning to understand his talent beyond writing melodrama, who is beginning to explore a balance between violence and human respect and care. This story is a true glimpse at what we have lost with Harold's death.

## Endnotes

1. Mark Sarner, *Books In Canada* Vol.3 No. 5 Aug-Sept. 1974.
2. "The Intruders", A short story. Why it is called "The Intruders" is a bit of a mystery. Who are the intruders? Maybe this was to link up for the novel he bragged to Dennis about and for which there exists only a handwritten title page.
3. See Chapter 12, *Rage in Tola and other Novels*.
4. Christopher Laird interview with Peter Such 2003.
5. "The Intruders" (short story) 13 March 1973.
6. E.g., in "The Quiet Peasant", Harold writes sensitively and gently about a long-suffering but loving family trying to make it by doing the right thing but the world around them crushes them: the mother's TB, the rich landlord's sons bully the boy taking food for his father, thieves steal the father's bull and Death steals his life.

CHAPTER SIXTEEN
## THE KNIGHT IN SHINING ARMOUR AND THE VULTURES

... uprooted
we have survived
the piercing morning
we have survived
death in the backdams and the hovels of hope
we have survived
we are the surviving
we who know the snake's fangs
the tide's and the season's treachery
the boot the fist the spit of the British Empire

"We have survived", Arnold Itwaru (1987)[1]

Harold was a man in a hurry to achieve his ambitions as a writer but he seemed also to sense that the fate he had escaped from in McBean/Tola was catching up with him and his time was somehow limited. The powerful forces of his real history lay in wait in McBean and it was only a matter of time before he would have to deal with them.[2]

He no longer had to travel out to university at Erindale, to do assignments for his professors; he had two novels behind him. The future was his to make, but, according to Peter Such:

> ... it was summer and he needed work. Harold Sonny Ladoo, B.A., probably a genius, by now about 110 pounds of sinew, couldn't get a job anywhere. He went back to washing dishes. Then the first half of his Canada Council grant came through – $2,000 worth of freedom.[3]

This was the situation in which he decided to face his fate. He could return to Trinidad with copies of his acclaimed novel in his suitcase, the Canada Trust grant in his bank account and a sense that, with a second novel about to be published, he no longer had to write himself into myth. Now was the time for action. He was by no means naïve about his return. He was well aware of how little his success in Canada would mean in McBean and how easily it was for that community to discount him as a returnee with airs and pretentions.
Graeme Gibson remembers:

GG: And again, it's very hard over so many years; he talked about having to go home and his fear of it and his frustration that something was being done to his mother and that it was up to him to...

CL: Right the wrong.

GG: To right the wrong and you know the terrible ending of this story of him being killed; particularly for fiction writers it's likely to reconstruct the past in a way, but I have a very clear, a very clear sense that he conveyed to me and I'm sure to others, the fact that he probably wouldn't be coming back, that he wasn't going to be able to do anything about this but he couldn't not try. I never knew exactly what that was. We heard rumours afterwards about who was supposed to have done it, etc. etc. But there was something really fated in the scene as I remember it, that this had taken him over and that he had resisted as long as he could, accepting the implications. [4]

## Rachel remembers:

... It was only before he go to Trinidad he have changed, he tried to be a nice person, tried to treat me very good before he went Trinidad. A few weeks before he was going, he changed to be a different person altogether. He talk nice and we get along very good after. And when he was going I ask him when he's coming back, he say he don't know, he don't know if he'll be able to come back or not, he don't think he'll come back, he not sure yet what's going to happen.

*Ramabai Espinet*: Why?

RL: I don't know what make him say that, and he bought all dark clothes, purple clothes, black clothes, which he never used to wear before, I say why you buy those clothes for, he said he feel to wear them, those colour clothes. He never like to wear dark clothes, he was a boy who like to wear pink shirt and that kind of thing.[5]

## Peter Such took Harold to the airport in August:

When he went to the airport, ... he started to tell me about all his troubles in Trinidad, and they mostly were that somebody had taken over the whole estate, had taken the Land Rover when they shouldn't, etc. and that his mother was being cast aside and she was being drugged and fed booze, she was sleeping in ditches and so on. And this woman Phyllis who – I don't know her relationship – ... kept sending him these letters and he said, "I've got to go back to Trinidad and sort this stuff out".
He never told me about inheriting any money or anything else, and that's because I thought well, because (chuckles) he's not the real son. But he did tell me his mother, his adopted mother you might want to say it, was in this distress and that's why he was going back. He was going to sort it out, and he said to me, "I may never come back", and I said, "Well, you're doing so well in Canada, why would you stay in Trinidad?" He said, "No, what I mean is I think I may never come back because

I'm going to be killed when I go there", and I said, "Harold, why are you going there?"

And he had just gotten notice that the Canada Council Grant had come through, his second book was about to be published, things were going really well, you know. This was his aim, his ideal; he'd graduated from university; he had a life here if he wanted it, and I begged him not to go. I said, "If you have that kind of premonition, you know, you're a writer, you're very psychic like I am and you can stop this. Don't go." And I went up to the airport with him and as he was putting his ticket in I said, "Harold, come back home with me now. Don't go." Three days, four days later, I got the call. He was dead.[5]

After his father died and his mother was wandering the village demented, the taking of his father's new Land Rover became a symbol of the way his father's legacy was being appropriated at the expense of his mother. As his sister, Meena, who lived in the family house, says:

*Meena Ladoo*: When my father died, there was money, there was crops in the field, there was a lot of worth involved and the land always had money's worth, and people just tried to get all they can, what they can, and it was not an easy thing to try to stand up to these things. Oh no.

*Christopher Laird*: Tell me, there is a question of a Land Rover that keeps coming up in his writing and also when he talked to people, there was a Land Rover as part of your father's estate?

*ML*: Yes, my uncle had that. I think that is what really made him go that way that eventful night.[6]

Apart from a mention in "The Intruders", the Land Rover also features in another of his unpublished short stories, "The Vultures". The main character, Sarojini, has just returned to Trinidad from Canada and is met at the airport by her mother, Yasmin, who, as a widow, is being ruthlessly exploited by everyone:

Sarojini walked slow, stamping her feet hard upon the concrete sidewalk. When she reached by the Land Rover, she said, "So this is the jeep Dad died and left? My Christ, it's almost new." Shaking her head now, she asked, "Haven't you all brought a car to drive me to the village?"

"Me chile," Yazmin said, "you coud go home wid we in de jeep. You fadder buy dis jeep new brand in February and now is only November. Notten wrong to travel in it. If you fadder was livin, he woudda be glad like hell to see you travellin in he jeep. Look Sarojini..."

"Shut up!" Sarojini yelled. "My bloody name is Sandy, and don't you or anyone go calling me by any Indian name!"

"I sorry, me chile," Yazmin said. "You forgive you modder, because you modder never go to school." Yazmin pulled out a small kerchief from her bosom. Untying the knot, pulling out a twenty dollar bill, she handed it to Sarojini saying, "Go and get a car me chile."

"What did she say, Mohammed?" Sarojini asked, and before he could answer, she added, "Her bloody accent is so terrible that it gives me the creeps."

"Your mother said to take the twenty dollars and get a taxi."

"I need more than twenty dollars, Mohammed."

Turning to Yazmin, Mohammed said, "Lady, you dorta say dat twenty dollars not enuff. She want more."

"Oright," Yazmin said, as she handed Sarojini two more twenty-dollar bills.

As Sarojini walked away to get the taxi, Mohammed, scratching his enormous belly, said, "Lady, I want a few dollars from you, lady. You see I not workin dese days, and I want you to lend me a few dollars."

"Boy Mohammed, you know dat me husban done dead. Now I don't have money comin from no place," she said, loosing the knot on the kerchief. "How much you want?"

"Lend me one hundred dollars, lady. I go give you back one of dese days."[7]

– *The Vultures* (18 March 1973)

Harold's sister, Meena, picks up the story of Harold's last days when he came to spend his final nights with her in McBean:

We had those scales that you have the weight on it, five pound, ten pound, but it's just a little weight and he was holding one, like a five pound weight, turning it in his hand and hefting it, and I was like, "What are you doing that for?" and he said, "I'm just looking at the weight on it" and out of the blue he asked me a question like, "You think if I hit a man with this I can kill him?"

For me it was an odd question, so I say, "I suppose so, but what would make you think that you will have the need?"

It seems like, for me, something wasn't right and in that same night he said, "Can I sleep with you in the bedroom?" and I'm like, "What! No!", you know, but he had this fear. There was something he wasn't telling me. I said, "No, you can sleep in the front room, and there's three rooms, the door is open, believe me, I can see the bed from here, whatever makes you comfortable, and with that in mind he took his weight and he went to bed.

I was very concerned. For me, I was kind of concerned with the oddness in the question, the uneasiness in him, like he expected something to happen to him or something like that. Something wasn't right. But I told him, I say, "To give you an assurance, trust me, nobody is going to come here to do you something and I'm here. You're my brother. They'll have to do us something both." You know, I mean, no way.

The fear, he definitely had fear, there was a lot of fear there and he's not the type of person to show weakness; my brother is not the type of person – this one I know – to show weakness. For him to talk like that or make a statement like that, yes, something was very wrong.

He got up early in the morning and he leave and I asked him, I say, "When you coming back? Should I cook or something for you, what?" because I don't know what his timeframe is, what he's doing. And he

said to me, he says, "I have to go see some friends in the old road. I'll
come back. I have some things to take care of."

He came back about 5.30 in the afternoon and I said, "You were gone
for the whole day. You really have a lot of catching up to do." He say
"Yes, but I have to leave to go to find out some stuff," and I say, "What?
You've been gone all day." He say, "I've been hearing some stuff and I
want to go check it out," and I says, "Personally, I don't want you to go
check out nothing. It's late, it's coming to night now, coming to nightfall.
Leave that for tomorrow." He say, "No. This I have to do."

There was nothing I could say to change his mind, he was set on
whatever course he was going to take. So I asked him, I say, "Where are
you going?" He say, "I'm going up the road, I'm going to see [name]",
because I think some things were involved concerning properties and
stuff like that. I was very worried then and I practically begged him not
to go and he said, "No, no. This I have to take care of."

You know, the odd thing about it is, I looked at him walking away;
it's like a feeling that I would never see him again, and it's only twice
in my lifetime I've had that feeling. When my sister was in the hospital,
I went to see her and she died. When I was walking away I looked at
her and there it was. When he was leaving, I looked at him, and there it
was.[8]

Harold had no illusions about the danger that he faced. The boy who had
walked these streets like a Steve Reeves with a comic book folded in his back
pocket and dreams of heroism, righting wrongs and taking revenge, walked
away on that fateful evening in his specially bought mourning-colour
clothes, probably conscious of the fact he didn't have the scale weight in his
pocket. As we can see from the extract from "Rage", below, the hefting of
the scale weight, that Meena describes, would be perfectly appropriate in
terms of arming himself for his confrontation.

I am a container of violent energies, apocalyptically I dream in blood.[9]

Harold, forever one to chronicle his own myth, in his unpublished short
story, "Rage", seemed to envision his demise, but one must resist the
temptation to join the chorus of those who "drink the Kool-Aid" of
Harold's myth-making. "Rage" was written two years before his death,
even before No Pain Like This Body, and in fact one can also find the story
in abbreviated form in the wake scene in No Pain Like This Body.

## RAGE

One night Jadoo is walking along Jangli Tola Trace. The night is cold. Jadoo listens. He thinks he heard something. He listens again. Yes. He is hearing something. A man is begging; begging and begging and calling for help. The voice is coming from near the mangrove. Now the person is calling loud as if life is already coming out of him. Jadoo runs towards the mangrove. He thinks perhaps a drunk man wants to fight with another drunk man. Now he is close up. Four men are beating one man. Jadoo is young. He cannot just stand there and see a man get himself killed just like that; he cannot see advantage; he feels his head spinning. Feeling a rage building up inside him, he says, "All you leff de man! Maybe he have wife and chirens, so don't beat him no more."

But the men continue to beat the man.

Jadoo cannot control himself any longer. "All you leff de man! If all you don't leff him, it goin to have trobble here tonight!"

When Jadoo talks like this two of the men run away, but two of them remain standing on the trace. And the two men call the two who are running, but they keep on running. Now the wounded man gets up from the ground and runs away also.

The two men are close up to Jadoo; almost too close. He has a chance to run, but he decides to stand up and fight. Jadoo is strong; he is sure he can beat the two men.

One of the men stretches his hand. Jadoo feels something warm like sweat running down his back. It is sticky and very uncomfortable. Now he feels something warmer than sweat; something warm as warm water running down his spinal column and settling on his pants waist. Jadoo knows he is not sweating, because the night is too cold for a man to sweat. He put hands by his waist and feels the sweat; it is warm and sticky. He lifts his fingers to his eyes. The moonlight is bright. He is bleeding.

The tall man with the blade is standing in front of him; the other man is standing at his back with a stick. Jadoo is penned like an animal. Now he knows that the two of them are seriously planning to kill him. He begs, "Gimme a chance, bredders. I is a poor man from Tola. I is a Indian like all youself bredders..."

The man with the cutlass has a heavy smell of alcohol. Jadoo sees the blade; the man is using the blade crazily. He feels the blade eating up his flesh. Each time that the blade comes down, the other man with the stick, pounds him from behind. He can feel the stick and he can feel the blade, but he is not worrying about the stick; he knows that the blade is more dangerous. And the cutlass is devouring the flesh around his navel. Now the man with the blade makes a swing at his belly; Jadoo draws back and swipe! the blade separates his leatherbelt. "Oh God gimme a chance nuh, man," he begs again. "I is a Indian like all you bredders!"

"Finish him fast!" the man with the stick encourages his companion.

The tall man is moving faster with the blade. He is more careful now. He makes another swing at Jadoo's belly. Jadoo jumps back just in time, but the blade digs into his toe, and the man with the stick strikes him hard in his back. Jadoo wants to fall, but he has to balance himself, if

he falls now, he is going to die, and he wants to live. So he stands up;
Now the cutlass looms before his eyes. There is more pain as the blade
shaves the skin off his forehead, he lifts his arm to protect his head.
Nine times the blade comes down on his left arm. The strength in his
arm is going fast; his whole body is growing weaker and weaker; he
knows that he cannot take this much longer if he really wants to live.
His feet are giving way, but he wants to live, so he has to stand up. Now
the blood is flowing from his forehead; falling and going into his eyes.
He can hardly see. He makes a desperate effort. Jadoo times the stick,
as it falls on his back, he grabs it with his right hand and pulls it away.
He strikes the man with the blade watap! and the man falls to the ground.
Jadoo drops the stick and begins to run; he is running but he knows
that he can hardly make it to the village. He is half mile away from the
closest house. Jadoo runs inside the mangrove. The tree roots in the
swamp are thick with sharp oyster shells. He is moving as fast as he
can, and the pointed shells are ripping the skin off his feet. His hanging
toe gets entangled in a root; it rips off and remains somewhere in the
bluish mud. Hundreds of mosquitoes are biting his face. With blood
still in his eyes, he clutches his chopped arm with his right hand, trying
hard to keep it from falling off. He knows that the two men are following
him; he hears them cursing and swearing.

   The tide is rising, and he can hear his blood falling drip! drip! in the
salt water. He moves on until he comes to the mouth of Jangli Tola
River. Wiping his eyes, he looks back. The two men are searching the
mangrove with a torchlight. They are near the river now. They are talking;
just talk how he cannot escape. Jadoo is hoping that they are going to
turn back.

   Jadoo buries himself into a cluster of roots. But he is still not safe.
He looks; the men are still searching, and they are close to him. They
are not leaving the torchlight on any spot for long; they are merely scanning
the mangrove. Now they swing the light in his direction; he buries himself
deeper into the mud, and remains still.

   It is very uncomfortable in the mud. The pain is unbearable; he wants
to scream, but he cannot find his voice. He feels faint as the mud stifles
the mouth of his wounds. Devilish crabs are chewing his chopped flesh
in the water. The salt in the muddy water is burning him, travelling up
his bones and mixing with his marrow. The men are coming closer and
closer; they are about five feet away from him. Jadoo closes his eyes;
he is just waiting to die.

   But the blade does not fall upon him.

   The men turn back.[7]


   Phyllis's husband, Shaffir Sarafat told me that he and Harold went to a
party at the home of one of Harold's uncles. Jeoffery picks up the story:

   My uncle told me that the party was really nice. All the Ladoo family
   was there to see him and were very proud of his success. My uncle had
   to work in the morning and said that he told my dad, "Lets go," and my
   dad said, "Hush your ass we having a good time dancing and singing."
   So my uncle assessed that my father was safe and he left the party and

told me he couldn't sleep but felt my dad was safe, he told me my dad had a revised copy of "Vultures" and was showing everybody.[10]

Harold's battered body was found next morning beside the Southern Main Road less than a mile from his family home. His head was so damaged he could be identified only by the scar and tattoo on his body and his jewellery.

There are weighty issues involved here. Not being a legal expert nor a criminal investigator, I cannot indulge in my own speculation. The official (police) story is his death was the result of a 'Hit and Run' vehicular accident. However, speak to anyone in McBean and you will be sure to be told various versions of a story of murder by a relative over the issue of his late father's property. They can name names of culprits, now deceased. His wife and eldest son can point to those they accuse but in 1973 they bowed to the official verdict to protect the infant children who were also perceived to be in danger and to secure payment of the insurance policy in order to survive.[11] Jeoffery told me:

> [...] there's a lot of rumours about his death. One rumour is he got hit by a car, another rumour is he got beaten up in the cane field and shot on the road to make it look like a car accident, and another rumour was I heard that he got a cutlass on his head, so I don't know. A lot of people that I meet they would always give me different stories and different theories, but I really don't want to say who I think did it, because I really don't know and I don't want to step on anybody's toes.[12]

That is where our story ends.
What a life!

Harold Sonny Ladoo screamed across the sky like an angry comet, searing his way into the hearts of everyone he met and those who just read his writing. He, who could wrestle rage into poetry on the page, could not withstand the forces of history and greed at play in the community he thought he might escape.

I have tried, here, to place his extraordinary story on record but, more importantly, to give a glimpse of the Trinidad he saw, in all its darkness, brutality, love and dignity, and I was determined to place it within our literature and that of Canada, the place that gave him the opportunity to realise his ambition.

I also wanted to paint his life with the words of those whom he touched and who still live with the indelible memory of the "little coolie boy from McBean" who, driven by his dream of being a writer, lived inside one of his own violent and tragic stories. I leave the last word to Dennis Lee:

Harold, how shall I exorcize you?
      This is not for blame.
            I know that
    *it* lived *you*, there was no
choice; some men do carry this century
        malignant in their cells from birth
    like the tick of genetic stigmata,
  and it is no longer
        whether it brings them down, but only
    when. You were a fresh explosion
of that lethal paradigm: the
        Tragic Artist, *yippee* and
    forgive me friend.
But you heard your own death singing, that much I know.
    And went to meet it mesmerized – to get
        the man that got your mother, yes, but also plain
          wooing it, telling Peter you'd
  never be back alive. The jet's trajectory
    a long sweet arc of dying, all the way down.
And whatever the lurid scuffle that
    ended the thing – your body
        jack-knifed, pitch dark, in the dirt –
  it was after the fact; you had
    lived that moment for years, you were
      already one of the chosen.
    Your final legacy
two minor early novels, one being nearly first-rate.[13]


"Only by dying brutally can man become equal to mystery."
— Harold Sonny Ladoo, *A Short Story,* 22 January 1973.

Endnotes

1. Arnold Itwaru, "We Have Survived", *India in the Caribbean*, ed. David Dabydeen and Brinsley Samaroo (London: Hansib Publishing, 1987), 292-293

2. Harold was apprehensive about his return and his account of a dream in his short story "The Agony" written in June 1972 seems to provide a metaphorical interpretation of his escape from McBean in 1968: "I had escaped when I found a poisonous spider weaving a coffin-like web above my head in the tropics. Eye to eye I had faced the spider and, frightened, I had journeyed beyond the seas."

3. Peter Such, "The Short Life and Sudden Death of Harold Sonny Ladoo." *Saturday Night* (Toronto), 89, 5, 1974; and *BIM* (Barbados), Volume 16 No 63, 1978.

4. Interview with Rachel Ladoo by Christopher Laird and Ramabai Espinet, 2002.

5. Interview with Peter Such by Christopher Laird, 2003.

6. Interview with Meena Ladoo (Jagru) by Christopher Laird and Ken Ramchand, 2003.

7. Interview with Meena Ladoo by Christopher Laird & Ken Ramchand, 2003.

8. Harold Ladoo, "A Short Story" or "An Excerpt From a novel".

9. "Rage", a short story 1971 (excerpt).

10. Notes from Jeoffery Ladoo, October 2019.

11. Estimated to be about $20,000CA according to Peter Such who was working on it. Letter from Peter Such to Rachel Ladoo, 24 August 1973.

12. Interview with Jeoffery Ladoo, 21 September 2002.

13. Dennis Lee, "The Death of Harold Ladoo". *Heart Residence. Collected Poems 1967-2017*, pp. 102-103.

EPILOGUE
RAGE AND CARE

...all our yesterdays have lighted fools
The way to dusty death. Out, out, brief candle!
Life's but a walking shadow, a poor player,
That struts and frets his hour upon the stage,
And then is heard no more. It is a tale
Told by an idiot, full of sound and fury,
Signifying nothing.
— William Shakespeare, *Macbeth*[1]

We who did not know him personally knew him through his writing and through Graeme Gibson's photo of him on the back of his novels.

Yes, he was intense (glowering through the cigarette smoke). The intensity was dramatic in a sort of a 1950s Hollywood way but that was only a way of hiding his real understanding of seriousness. Serious because, as a history buff, if not from personal experience of his community, he knew western society from the position of a descendent of indentured servants of empire. He was a fun-loving, hard-drinking, quick-with-a-quip Trinidadian when socialising with friends but he knew the horrific roots of his community back in McBean.

It seems that Harold did not actively participate in the political discourse that would have dominated the "Caribbean Table" at Erindale College (see page 71), much of which was in response to the turmoil of the 1970 revolution in Trinidad, but he was there and would have heard it roiling around him. As Dionne Brand writes ironically, in her introduction to the 2003 edition of *No Pain Like This Body*:

> We others, with our mix of pan-colonial desires, political awakenings and unbridled ambitions, left him to his writing, sometimes giving it the respect of a sacred act, sometimes grumbling and arguing with him about what seemed Ladoo's disengagement with what we considered real and urgent political issues. We were going to liberate the world and how could he be writing a mere book?[2]

*The Caribbean Table, with Ian Jeffers and Dionne Brand in discussion and Harold (reading the newspaper and almost out of frame).*

Ian Jeffers' comment on the picture of Harold seemingly 'disengaged' was: "The photo you have is classic Plato. You will notice that there are no cups in front of him. I guarantee you that he is listening intently to the conversation, and I also guarantee you that he would share his thoughts, a cup of coffee and a cigarette or two while having animated conversation with me at a later time. He would have listened and analysed every opinion, and shared his."[3]

Despite the impression Harold gave of being disengaged, he was politically aware. In fact his whole aim as a writer was to explore the human consequences of genocide, slavery, indenture, imperialism and colonialism.

From his writing and from his conversations with Peter Such it is clear that he was aware of the absurdities, the violence, the intrigue, the poverty, and greed he saw around him in his village, but was also clear that these were the legacies of indentured migration and the servitude of bond labour. Nevertheless, he was also proud of the dignity, humanity, astuteness, and ability to survive exhibited by his family and neighbours in McBean.

According to his eldest son, Jeoffery (who was only three when Harold was killed), Harold was a part of a committee to free Nelson Mandela. While I have been unable to verify this, it does seem possible on the evidence of one of the fragments of writing that remains: a draft of "A Short Story", (January 1973). It features his favourite Toronto female lead, the prostitute, Laura (of "Jametin" fame), and a South African Indian called Santosh Anand. It is a meandering conversation in a strip club between Laura, her pimp/lover, Suraj (in the first person), and Santosh. Rather like a freestyle doodle – some of it incomprehensible – the conversation circles around a half-baked plan to travel to South Africa to join the revolution to "beat the Europeans".

"I can die for justice." This is Laura talking. "Why does the white man have to be so oppressive? Everywhere he goes there is injustice. Santosh, you and I could fight…"[4]

Harold, the avid student of history, was incensed by oppression, especially as it pertained to those who had suffered slavery and indentureship. He was obsessed with his 'Grand Plan' of a series of 200 novels that would span the brutal history of the Caribbean. He was conscious of the way his fellow villagers in McBean were imprisoned in the echoes of indentureship and he cared. He immortalised them as unforgettable (and sometimes unforgiving) characters striving with humour, violence, and cunning in the face of the tempting nihilism of history.

But there is caring as well as rage in his treatment of his characters, so that, for example, even that most violent and amoral figure, Pa, in *No Pain Like This Body*, can be seen as a victim of a dehumanising system.

Even in the ridiculously brief time between meeting Peter Such and his violent death, Harold grew as a writer. He began to privilege his caring at the expense of his rage, or at least his rage became more controlled, so that in stories like "The Quiet Peasant" or the story of Gonwa in "The Intruders" he could explore compassion, loyalty, family and responsibility, skilfully contextualised by reminders of the oppressive social background, *sans humanité*. Hence Raju, the ten-year-old son in "The Quiet Peasant", while carrying out his filial duty, taking food for his father, Gobinah, is harassed by the landowner's sons who pelt him with stones. And if the powerful don't get you, nature (the drought and the heat) will.

Harold Ladoo knew the fate of those who tried to do the right thing in the face of greed and the "crab in a barrel" desperation to secure a future in a society that offered none. He was under no illusion about that, and, when he chose to return home to sort out his inheritance, he warned his friends that he might not return alive. At the same time, he cultivated the image of the writer/artist as hero and mythmaker.

"The artist is strong. He can fight and fight until he becomes a myth."[5]

And:

"It is natural for the strong to build mythologies."[6]

But despite the weight-lifting in his teenage years with his friend, Chanlal, he was no Steve Reeves. As he recorded in *No Pain Like This Body*, Rama's encounter with the evil king Ravan/Pa could prove fatal, despite the victory promised in the *Ramayana*. He was evidently aware of the threat but could not ignore the call of McBean/Tola any longer. As he left his sister that final day and walked away from his family home down the streets of McBean he must have felt very alone, maybe leaning too hard on his fantasies of heroism and making the mistake that other artists have made before him, of believing their own mythology. Did memories of the McBean of his childhood swagger invade his thoughts as he walked? Did images of his doomed characters rise before him fighting for their place in the world: Choonilal, Raju, Gobinah, Jadoo, Ma, Sunaree, Poonwa, Monroe, Sampath, Laura…?

> "Like a magician I form reality into dreams but cannot do it the other way."[7]

He had duties as the eldest son to rescue his mother (though save for his Canada Council grant he was desperately broke) and despite the risks of intervening and the probable fate of so doing (like his character, Jadoo, in "Rage") he may have believed he had no choice. He must have been very aware that dressing in the funereal colours of purple and black and being a "knight in shining armour" did not make him invulnerable. In fact, it seems he was certain that, like his characters, he could not stand against the powerful and a system that exploited the weak.

> "At times I worry very seriously whether my life is not perhaps more tragic than the artistic life of my own characters".[8]

Even as the Caribbean literary establishment treated Harold as a footnote, there are signs that a new generation of Caribbean writers, especially the increasing number of women writers, are determined to move Caribbean Literature out of the shadow of the 1950s and 1960s. The promise of a new way of telling our stories we saw at *Kairi* in 1974 is being fulfilled. The book, *No Pain Like This Body* and the writer, Harold Sonny Ladoo, whose literary "matryoshka dolls" of stories embedded in stories are inhabited by people who speak history as folklore, who live it with violent defiance, resilience, and humour, are, half a century later, quietly becoming cherished icons in the forging of a new Caribbean canon. With yet another edition of *No Pain* being issued, this time by Penguin Random House[9], this biography, and a forthcoming film about him by Richard Fung, Harold Ladoo has perhaps finally achieved his desire to move into the world of myth.[10]

In my Introduction I asked why so many of us remain captured by Harold and his writing, even after half a century. I believe that despite Harold's 'ducking and weaving' and his masquerading with different personas and fake biography, we recognise not only his enduring determination to succeed as a writer under punishing circumstances but, more importantly, we recognise his caring and his commitment to truth as a writer, to his community, country, and region. We are transfixed by the way he uses his nascent talent and skill in their service. But above all, we are both horrified and awed by his determination to carry his caring to its fateful conclusion in the real world and to face it through a final intervention on behalf of his family.

Harold Sonny Ladoo – Equal to Mystery.

Endnotes

1. *Macbeth*, Act V, scene 5.
2. Dionne Brand, Introduction to Anansi's 2003 Edition of *No Pain Like This Body*, p. viii.
3. Email from Ian Jeffers to author, November 2022.
4. Letter to Dennis Lee, 25 September 1972.
5. Ibid.
6. "A Short Story, an Excerpt from a novel", (January 1973).
7. "A Short Story, an Excerpt from a novel", (January 1973).
8. Harold Ladoo in a letter to Dennis Lee, 31 August 1972.
9. Ironically, Harold had threatened Dennis Lee with moving his second novel from Anansi to Random House: Harold Ladoo letter to Dennis Lee, 31 August 1972.
10. "The artist is strong. He can fight and fight until he becomes a myth". Harold Ladoo, "A Short Story", an Excerpt from a novel, (January 1973).

## ACKNOWLEDGMENTS

I am not a writer. I am a filmmaker. In writing this book I had to learn a lot about writing and about biographies. Writing a biography to be published as a text demands much more research, detail and precision than writing a biography for a film. It also requires one to be literate enough to keep the reader engaged.

The first drafts of this book were transliterated directly from the scripts for the six-part documentary serial of the same title that I wrote and filmed in the first three years of this century. Converting it into a book took a lot of guidance from editors. In the five years it took me to write it I came to understand what a writer is and know that, while I may not be a professional writer, I had to develop enough of the necessary skills to make at least this one book publishable.

In this I was aided and spurred on by the strength of the story, but it was the generous mentorship of the poet and editor, Dennis Lee, who despite initial protest that he didn't have the time, stuck by me as *de facto* editor by email for the five years it took before we considered it in good enough shape to be submitted to a publisher. He worked closely with me particularly on the first twelve chapters. Dennis's incredible empathy and incisive engagement kept me on my toes, ingrained in me over the years a new discipline and made this process a privileged masterclass and one of the most memorable periods of my life. I cannot overstate what it meant for me or the book (not to mention his permitting me to quote extensively from his poem *The Death of Harold Ladoo*).

With the acceptance of the manuscript by Jeremy Poynting of Peepal Tree, Dennis stepped aside as editor. Then Jeremy took over. Jeremy brought his publishing experience with the added value of having some expertise in Indo-Caribbean literature. He was thus able to help me minimise any literary *faux pas* while, at the same time, indulging my sympathy for Harold's challenge to the canon. How could I have been so fortunate to have had such experience, learning and skill to assist me in this enterprise?

Poet and novelist, Ramabai Espinet has also stuck with me as sounding board, advisor and comrade (Ramabai *is* a writer). Over the years I pestered her often with questions and drafts. She was always supportive (e.g. driving me all over Toronto to film Harold's residences and Erindale College or interviewing Rachel and Jeoffery) and encouragement through all the setbacks initially with the documentary film project and then when it morphed into a literary one. Having her selfless friendship and insight to rely on helped to keep me going.

There is one person who is at the centre of this book apart from Harold, that is Peter Such. It is Peter's memorial essay *The Short Life and Sudden Death of Harold Ladoo* (1974) that cemented my obsession with Harold and his story. Peter's pivotal role in Harold's life as a writer, through their chance meeting in a bus station in 1970, points not only to one of Caribbean literature's most significant literary encounters but also, probably more importantly, to Peter's emotional generosity and loyalty, factors that provided Harold with enduring mentorship and solid reliable friendship in the Canadian world. This story would probably never have been told without Peter Such.

Without novelist Graeme Gibson's photographs of Harold for the cover of *No Pain Like This Body* we would also be bereft of a proper image of Harold who seemed to shy away from the camera. Graeme generously gave me the negatives from the roll of film he shot in that session with Harold and, ever the gracious gentleman, submitted himself to an on-camera interview with me about Harold.

Novelist, Jim Polk, who edited *Yesterdays* with Harold also graciously resigned himself to an interview. There is no doubt that Harold enchanted him as he did many others, Jim remembers his sessions with Harold with enthusiastic nostalgia, Harold's storytelling, humour and ambition had impressed and excited him. Harold had even invited Jim to Trinidad. I contacted Jim many times when the project was transformed to text and despite the almost half-century distance in time, he did his best to respond constructively to my pestering questions seeking to pin down dates, events, and other details.

The Ladoo family, Harold's widow, Rachel Khan, and eldest son, Jeoffery, whom we interviewed in 2002, his sister-in-law, Phyllis Siewdass and her husband, Shaffir Sarafat, Harold's only surviving sibling, Meena, her step daughter, Maria Jagroop, his cousins Lily Parmasad, Ramdaye Jogie, and husband Basdeo Ramlochan were all gracious and helpful, welcoming me on numerable visits to McBean, helping to fill in the Ladoo family tree and tell stories of the family in the community. Rachel and Jeoffery have persevered with me in the 20 years since the first interview, enabling this book to eventually see the light of day by giving me permission to quote extensively from Harold's unpublished texts, texts that Jeoffery was able to recover from his uncle which, along with those in House of Anansi's archives at the Library and Archives of Canada, are the only copies of Harold's writing we have been able to find.

They must all have wondered if I was crazy, but they humoured me.

Other McBean villagers also went out of their way to assist this mad stranger. Neil Dookie introduced me to villagers who knew the Ladoos and through him and his contacts I was able to meet Hugh and Chandra Ramdeen who were inexhaustible reservoirs of community history, also childhood friends, Sarjoo 'Chanlal' Ramsumair and Remy Khan.

Through a notice kindly inserted in Indo-Caribbean World by editor Romeo Kaseram I was put in touch with Puran Ramlogan who was a member of the McBean 'study group' with Harold. Thank you also to Pundit Parasram who taught Harold at McBean Hindu School and whom I had to call on often to clarify memories and facts relating to McBean.

House of Anansi has over the half century since Harold's death been extremely supportive in all my efforts, from Ann Wall in the late 70s who sent me copies of some of Harold's short stories, to Bill Hanna in the 80s who helped me take an option on *No Pain Like This Body* for a feature film and Matt Williams this century who entertained my Quixotic efforts to make the film documentary and later this book.

Professor Ken Ramchand was a source of literary wisdom and personal interest in Harold who first took me to McBean to interview Meena and the Parasrams in 2003 and continued to encourage me in my efforts to bring Harold's story out of the historical void that threatened to subsume it.

Adding depth and nuance to the book were the libraries that held the papers of Dennis Lee (Fisher Library, thanks, Catherine Hobb), Peter Such (McMaster library, thanks Gillian Dunks) and the Library and Archive Canada in Ottawa where House of Anansi's papers as well as those of Shirley Gibson are held. Much appreciation is due to Sophie Teller at the Library and Archive Canada who, always the professional librarian/archivist, went beyond what may have been expected of her to seek answers to questions I had not even thought of. This book owes her deep gratitude.

I also acknowledge the assistance of artist Jamelie Hassan (and Shira Taylor who drove me to London to interview her in 2002) who allowed me to interview her and who gave a me a copy of the notes she made when she visited McBean in 2002 as part of an artist in residence attachment to the Caribbean Contemporary Arts that she dedicated to Harold. Also Sally Stollmeyer who was a generous and supportive host for me on my two trips to Toronto in 2002 and 2003 to shoot footage for the documentary and most of the interviews that are referenced in this book. Thanks also to Paul Barrett for his picture of The Ladoo residence at 21 Roseneath Gardens.

Generous assistance was also provided by people who had either taught Harold at Erindale or who were acquainted with him and his work while there: Ian Jeffers (Harold's friend at Erindale who named him "Plato")Brian Corman (Harold's professor 18th century English literature), Richard Greene, Randall Mcleod, Douglas Hill and Mark Levene as well as Lorretta Neebar, Registrar at the University of Toronto at Mississauga who helped me gain access to Harold's university transcript.

I have here to also express my deep appreciation to those who have helped me in my quest over the past half century and through the many attempts to bring Harold's story and work to light. Dionne McTair who in 1986 joined me in drafting out my first draft of the screenplay for *No Pain Like This Body*; film producers, Roger McTair and Clair Preto who entertained the notion of producing a feature film of *No Pain Like This Body* with me in Canada in the 90s. To Tony Hall and Errol Sitahal who co-wrote with me the *No Pain Like This Body* screenplay commissioned by UK's Channel Four an initiative of Equal Media and the indefatigable Parminder Vir who in 1999 spearheaded the (ultimately unsuccessful) attempt to bring *No Pain Like This Body* to the screen.

## BIBLIOGRAPHY


## I. BOOKS BY HAROLD LADOO


### 1. *NO PAIN LIKE THIS BODY*

1a. *No Pain Like This Body* (Toronto: Anansi, 1972).
1b. ———————— (London *et al*: Heinemann, 1987).
1c. ———————— (Toronto: Anansi, 2003), Introduction by Dionne Brand.
1d. *Nulle douleur comme ce corps,* Tr. Marie Flouriot and Stanley Péan. (Montreal: Les Allusifs, 2006).
1e. ———————— (Toronto: Anansi, 2013), Introduction by David Chariandy.
1f. ———————— (London: Penguin Random House, 2022), Introduction by Monique Roffee.


### 2. *YESTERDAYS*

1a. *Yesterdays* (Toronto: Anansi, 1974).
1b. _____, Tr. Stanley Péan (Montreal: Les Allusifs, 2007).


## II. SHORT FICTION

1a. "The Quiet Peasant". *Impulse: Vol. 2, Numbers 3&4*. Editor: Peter Such. The Authors. 1973
1b. _____. *Canada In Us Now*. Editor:Harold Head (Toronto: New Press, 1976).
1c. _____. *Trinidad Noir: The Classics*. Editors: Earl Lovelace and Robert Antoni (New York: Akashic Books, 2017).
2. "An Excerpt from a new novel". Thirst and Other Hungers. Editor Patricia Gilhooly (Toronto: Dorann Publishing Company, 1971).
3. "From Yesterdays: a new novel". *Impulse* First issue, Editor Peter Such (Toronto: The Heritage Press, 1971).
4. "Rage, Extract from Novel & Short Story by Harold Sonny Ladoo". *Erindalian* (magazine of Erindale College), 24 November 1971.

## III. A CHRONOLOGICAL SEQUENCE OF REVIEWS, ESSAYS, AND CRITICAL COMMENTARY

1. "No Pain Like This Body: A review". Uncredited (possibly Harold Ladoo), *The Erindalian*, 6 December 1972.
2. Frank Birbalsingh, "No Pain Like This Body – a review", *Open Letter Vol.2 #5*, Summer 1973.
3. Bruce F. Bailey, "No Pain Like This Body – a review", *Canadian Forum 52.48,* March 1973.
4. Neola Vieira, "No pain Like This Body – a review", *Canadian Reader Vol.15 #4,* May 1974.
5. Victor Questel, "When Gods Have Fallen: A Review of *No Pain Like This Body*", Kairi, 1.74.
6. "Yesterdays – a review", *Canadian Reader* Vol.15 #6, June 1974.
7. Mark Sarner, "Bright Flash from the Dark – Review of Yesterdays", *Books In Canada,* Vol. 3 No.5, also *Saturday Night 89:37,* Aug-Sept 1974.
8. Peter Such, "Harold Sonny Ladoo – *Yesterdays*", *Tamarack Review #68*, October 1974.
9. Peter Such, "The Short Life and Sudden Death of Harold Sonny Ladoo", *Saturday Night* (Toronto), 89, 5, 1974; and *BIM* (Barbados), Vol. 16 No. 63, 1978.
10. Christopher Laird, "The Novel of Tomorrow, Today – A review of the novel *Yesterdays*", *Kairi 1.75,* 1975.
11. Ronald Hatch, "Yesterdays – a review", *Canadian Fiction Magazine* No. 18, Summer 1975.
12. Brinsley Samaroo, "The Presbyterian Canadian Mission as an Agent of Integration in Trinidad During the Nineteenth and Early Twentieth Centuries", *Caribbean Studies,* Vol. 14, No. 4, 1975.
13. Dennis Lee, "The Death of Harold Ladoo", *Kanchenjunga Press,* 1976.
14. Boendranath Tewarie, "The Work of Harold Sonny Ladoo – The Drama of the Low Caste Hindu Peasantry, the Last Terrible Victims of the Colonial Experience in the New World", Paper delivered to Conference on East Indians in the Caribbean University of the West Indies, 1979.
15. Samuel Selvon, "Review of "Canada in Us Now", *Canadian Ethnic Studies,* Vol. 11, Issue 1, January 1979.
16. Clement H Wyke, "Harold Ladoo's Alternate Worlds", *Canadian Literature* No. 95, Winter 1982.
17. Christopher Laird, "Compassion in a Sans Humanité World: Harold Sonny Ladoo's unique perspectives", *Divali Magazine*, Trinidad, 1987.
18. Suwanda Sugunasiri, "Reality and Symbolism in the South Asian Canadian Short Story", *World Literature Written in English* 26 (1986),

*98–107.* Web,1986. Also: *Step Down Shakespeare, The Stone Angel is here. Essays on Literature: Canadian and Sri Lankan* (Nalanda Publishing, 2007).

18. Sue N. Greene, "Review of *Facing the Sea: A New Anthology from The Caribbean Region*", *New West Indian Guide/ Nieuwe West-Indische Gids* 61 (1987), no: 3/4, Leiden, 1987.

21. Josef Skvorecky Papers held at Fisher Library, Toronto and University of California Digital Library – Hoover Institution Archive, 1919-1994.

22. Stephen Cain, "Tracing the Web: House of Anansi's Spiderline Editions", *Studies in Canadian Literature*, Vol 25 No.1, 2000.

23. Christopher Laird, "An Uncompromising Eye", *Trinidad & Tobago Review*, December 2002.

24. Geoff Hancock, "Harold Sonny Ladoo", *The Oxford Companion to Canadian Literature* and *Encyclopedia of Literature in Canada*, ed. William H. New (Toronto: University of Toronto Press, 2002).

25. Dionne Brand, "Introduction to *No Pain Like This Body*" (Toronto: House of Anansi, 2003 and 2013).

26. John LeBlanc, "Ladoo, Harold Sonny (1945-73) Trinidadian/Canadian Novelist", *Encylopedia of Post-Colonial Literature in English*, Editor, Eugene Benson, and L.W. Conolly, 2004.

27. Marina Salandy Brown, "No Pain Like This Body – My Chutney Mind". Review of *No Pain Like This Body,* 20 January 2008.

28. J. Vijay Maharaj, "A Caribbean Katha Revisioning the Indo-Caribbean Crisis of Being and Belonging Through the Literary Imagination", PhD Dissertation, University of the West Indies, 2011.

29. Shona N. Jackson, "The Baptism of Soil: Rooplall Monar and the Aesthetics of the Kala Pani, *Journal of Caribbean Literatures – University of Central Arkansas,* 2011.

30. "The Experience Of Indian Indenture In Trinidad: Arrival and Settlement", Cruse & Rhiney (Eds.), *Caribbean Atlas*, 2013.

31. Ramchandra Joshi and Urvashi Kaushal, "Indo-Caribbean Canadian Diaspora: Surviving Through Double Migration and Dis(Re)Placement", *Journal of Indo-Caribbean Research,* Vol. 8, No. 1, 2013.

32. "Harold Sonny Ladoo's *No Pain Like This Body* : The Ramayana and Indo-Caribbean Experience". Shalini Khan, *Wasafiri Volume 28, 2013 Issue 2: Brighter Suns: Sixty years of Literature from Trinidad, Canada,* 26 March 2013.

33. Introduction to *No Pain Like This Body*. David Chariandy (Toronto: House of Anansi, 2013).

34. Anita Baksh, "Reconsidering the Folk in Peter Kempadoo's *Guyana Boy* and Harold Ladoo's *No Pain Like This Body. Unhomely Stirrings: Representations of Indentureship in Indo-Caribbean Literature from*

1960 to the Present". Dissertation submitted to the Faculty of the Graduate School of the University of Maryland, 2014.

35. *"No Pain Like This Body* by Harold Sonny Ladoo, book of a lifetime". *Newspaper article: Independent.co.uk* (newspaper), 10 July 2014.

36. S.P. Moslund, "Place, Language, and Body in the Caribbean Experience and the example of Harold Sonny Ladoo's *No Pain Like this Body*", *Literature's Sensuous Geographies,* 2015.

37. Victor J. Ramraj, "Language and Perception, Vernacular Worlds, Cosmopolitan Imagination", *Brill,* edited by Stephanos Stephanides, Stavros Karayanni, 2015.

38. Alison Klein, "Tangled Up: Gendered Nationhood in Indo-Caribbean Indenture Narratives", *Anthurium: A Caribbean Studies Journal*, Vol.12 Issue 2, December 2015.

39. Abigail Ward, "Indian-Caribbean Trauma: Indian Indenture and its Legacies in Harold Sonny Ladoo's *No Pain Like This Body*", *Postcolonial Traumas* (London: Palgrave Macmillan, 2015).

40. "Norah's Pick: *No Pain Like This Body*". Online Article *Broken Pencil.com,* 23 March 2016.

41. M.L., "Harold Sonny Ladoo, filant dans nos nuits indo-caribéennes (Harold Sonny Ladoo, Spinning in our Indo-Caribbean nights)", *Cases Rebelles,* April 2016

42. Daniel G. Ross, "Remaking Downtown Toronto: Politics, Development, And Public Space On Yonge Street, 1950-1980", A Dissertation Submitted to the Faculty Of Graduate Studies in Partial Fulfillment of the Requirements for the Degree of Doctor of Philosophy , Graduate Programme in History, York University, Toronto, Ontario, March 2017.

43. Kumar Mahabir, "V.S. Naipaul: Childhood and Memory", *Multiple Identities: Essays on Caribbean Literature* (Indo-Caribbean Publications, 2018).

44. Rabindranath Maharaj, "Dark Imaginings – Harold Sonny Ladoo's *No Pain Like this Body*", *Canadian Notes & Queries.* 50th Anniversary issue (#103, Fall 2018).

44. Monique Roffey, "Introduction to *No Pain Like This Body*" (London: Penguin Random House Vintage Classics reprint of *No Pain Like This Body,* 2022).

45. "Review of NO PAIN LIKE THIS BODY". Blog by Parasuram Sirju.

46. Adama Coly, "The Tragic Vision in George Lamming's *Natives of my Person*". Paper of Department of English, Ecole Normale Supérieure, Dakar, Senegal.

# APPENDICES

APPENDIX ONE Dennis Lee's response to Ladoo's submission

31/5/71

Harold,

I hope you'll allow me to set down my reactions to ALL OUR YESTERDAYS on paper, even though we'll be meeting in person. I find it easier to think onto paper, and if you find anything to agree or disagree with strongly in what I say, it may be useful to have a record.

First off, you are a natural writer! Sections of the novel come on like a house on fire. You obviously have a beautifully firm sense of the reality of what you're writing about. I kept getting a sense of excitement, from time to time, at realising that this was someone writing who probably had a really fine body of work ahead of him--I think you are going to write some excellent, moving books.

But--to swing around almost (but not quite) 180 degrees --I don't think you have a publishable novel on your hands yet in YESTERDAYS. I think there's one there (I want to qualify the form I sense in it, in a moment). But I don't believe it's fully emerged yet.

The problems I felt--and I take it that you are enough of a writer already to recognise that serious criticism is the sincerest kind of respect you can get from other writers—had mostly to do with pacing, and with tone.

At the stylistic level, I found the clipped and simplistic style wrecking very well over short periods, especially where the material was itself quite painful and the laconic understatement threw that into high relief. But as a medium for the whole book, I eventually found it chopped up

everything into discrete little units which came
at me with a flat relentlessness, and which
levelled out all the highs and lows of the book
into something that began to approach tedium. I
can't believe that this was your intention--even
though I recognize that the style is appropriate
to Panday's childhood consciousness--and I
noticed with delight your gift for irony, as in
the high-flown terms of the indirect narration of
conversations at times, as in the latrine
episode. So I think you miscalculated--there is
just more variety of tone needed, so that the
rhythms and pacing of the book can get unjammed.

I found the same thing, at a different level, in
your pacing of the incidents. Item after item
flashes by, and Panday can only record what is in
front of his eyes apparently at each given
moment. I can see this working if he is to be
seen as either totally numbed by the brutishness
of much of what he lives amidst, or as a near-
idiot, perhaps in the style of Benjy in SOUND AND
THE FURY. But as it is, I have more the sense
that you wrote a fixed amount each day for a
number of months, and covered the ground you'd
sketched out at the same pace, no matter whether
it was description of a scene, comic or painful
interaction of people, casual perceptions of
natural objects, climactic events in people's
lives, etc. It seems to be ground out of the same
cloth (to bugger a metaphor) somehow.

If you'll allow me to say so, this is not at all
unusual in a first novel--in fact what is unusual
is the amount you've conveyed about these
people's lives within the confines of a
convention that did become rather restricting.

I remember your saying that you are now into 2
new novels, and I'm not sure what I can suggest
with this one that will be helpful. But if you
feel like it, I'd think that you might achieve
your aims--both of conveying the day-to-day
texture of these people's lives, and of giving A
sense of dynastic continuity (which I think
misfires completely as it is--the outlines of
genealogies in the text just stay inert)--you

might conceivably achieve that better by doing it ss a series of apparently loosely-related stories, zeroing in on strategic times in the lives of people over a couple of decades, and eventually conveying a sense of the past, the presents, and the changes that time brings to people's lives, Your feel for this is marvellous, but you just haven't recreated it yet.

This would also enable you to omit a lot of the connecting material that tends to stay inert, and -- finally, what I've been trying to work up to -- would let you treat each episode/story as a thing in itself. You'd then be free to blow it up more (I don't mean make it artificial), to let it find its own proportions & modulations & specific tones. I can sense some absolutely breathtaking episodes here—the rain, the latrine, the village poets, the contest to stay alive, etc. -- which could well be 2 or 3 times as long, and explored with much more verve and panache and subtlety. Sometimes they'd be just as clipped and cryptic as they are now. In others, I suspect, you'd find that you wanted to just spread your wings and take straight off. The scene with the 2 village poets seems to me one that could gestate a marvellous episode. And you'd both be able to extend your own resources in each individual tale, and convey--I think much more effectively-- the panorama that you're after.

Harold, I can't step up & offer to publish YESTERDAYS as it stands. (Apart from my editorial reactions, there are financial barriers which we'll maybe get onto briefly, but they aren't the crucial thing.) You therefore have every right to submit it elsewhere as is, to see if you can get it published. I'd very much hope, though, that you'll pat yourself on the back for having accomplished far more in your first book than the great majority of writers do, and then either go back at it or grow past it in the new books (I must say, I hope you can eventually bring it off, whether right now or later--there's a splendid book here). And if you are inclined this way, I'd like you to let Anansi see further drafts or new mss. as they emerge. This has to be without

commitment on either side, and I'm not trying to
bind you without giving you any solid promise in
return. But if you do want to keep working
knowing that Anansi (in the person of me, for the
moment) respects what you're doing a lot, and
will talk candidly about anything else you show
us & hope to be able to publish you when the
time's right ... if that informal kind of
situation interests you, I'd like that alot.
That's something to mull on, in any case-- it
doesn't require any sort of solemn undertaking--
more a matter of mutuality.
Thanks for letting me see the book.

APPENDIX TWO: Dennis Lee's editing letter 1

2 March 72
YESTERDAYS: notes on pp. 1-40

Harold, this is just fine! As you'll notice, I have
virtually no suggestions of any size to make; it's
almost all a matter of polishing here and there.
Don't, by the way, let the fact that everything
marked down is a negative comment, depress you;
that's the point of editing, but of course my major
feeling is enjoyment and respect for what you've
written. I just haven't set that down on paper.

Here are the main points; there are a series of
line-by-line comments as well, for which you should
see the pages.

1. The title, dedication and epigraph are all
manifestations of the pre-Raphaelite Harold Laddoo,
and jar grotesquely with the primitive starkness
and gutsiness of the actual book. The dedication is
easy to prune (see my suggestion on that page). The
epigraph, I suggest, should be either replaced or
just dropped (the sentiment is fine, but the
expression leads into a different book altogether).
The title: Rage is the kind of stark title I think
you need for this book too, though I don't suggest
you use it here of course. Yesterdays sounds like
the title of a sentimental pop song. If you can't
find anything better you might think of In Tola
Trace; but I suspect you can improve on that a good
deal.

2. There is a certain amount of confusion on a
simple physical level, which you would do well to
clear up. What is the relative position of the
house, the mango tree, the rice-field, the sugarcane field? If you could establish that (tactfully!)
the physical layout fairly early on, it would help
at this mundane level.

3. As we've discussed, you get mired down in the
details of execution of an action fairly often. A
lot of my little cuts are directed to this. There
are a few notes and pleas on pp. 32-3 in this
connection.

4. I cut out alot of 'he said's'; think you could be more sparing with them?

5. There are some typographical matters for typing. Could you take note of these things?

- Indent every new paragraph, whether or not it is a line of dialogue.
- If a paragraph ends with a quotation, you normally include the speech as part of that paragraph.
- Space between paragraphs the same amount as between any other two lines, unless you want to indicate a larger space; then use double the usual space.
- Use double quote marks to enclose quotations.
- In the following case, "I'm coming." he said... the period after 'coming' is wrong; it should be a comma.
- leave one space after a semi-colon or a comma. Like so; get it?

6. I would suggest not italicizing the dialect words (i.e. delete the underlining), and printing the sound-words (splash) in lower-case but italicised (i.e. in the manuscript, underline them).

7. We might think of a brief glossary, though only for the more out-of-the-way terms. Such as jackspaniard, fireside (?), Tola Trace, orhni, change (a cow), poor-one.

8. Let's talk about the style for changes in the text.

APPENDIX THREE: Dennis Lee's editing letter 2

14 March
Chapter 6: 98-138
I find myself making a more major suggestion about
this wake chapter--which is clearly one of the
centre-pieces of the book--than I had anticipated.
I think it's well written in itself. But it could
fill a much finer function in the whole novel than
it does now, and I wonder if you'd consider revis-
ing it with some of these things in mind. (You may
agree, or you may want to discuss it.) ... I have
gone through and made minor editorial suggest-ions
throughout, but in fact most of them may be superseded by this more radical proposal.

The thing about the wake here is that a reader gets
almost no sense of its process. You occasionally
describe the activity of everyone at it, but most
of the time you concentrate on a group of 2 or 3
people, or else open out into one of the tales. The
result is that all the background--the people
carousing and laughing and farting and bad-
mouthing--is so indistinct as scarcely to be there,
and the wake doesn't really distinguish itself very
much from what came before in the book and what
comes after. I suspect that you really meant it to
lift into a kind od desperate conviviality. But
that hasn't happened.

I also suspect that, consciously or not, you had a
few things from La Guerre, Yes Sir! in mind. I
think this is completely fine, provided that you
make the thing your own--remember Eliot saying that
bad poets borrow, good poets steal. I think you
haven't stolen enough, in fact; you can make
Carrier's strengths more wholly your own in your
wake scene. The basic thing he does that you
haven't is to keep up a series of mountingly-
frenzied (though short) descriptions of people's
external activities, including all the repetition
and confusion of them. You do do it in the
paragraph on the top of 123, and again on top of
124. I would say that if' you do want this sense of
mounting activity this kind or description should
be orchestrated all the way through, and should
also re fairly stylised--there are probably 4 or 5

basic things that people keep doing, including
pouring rum into Ma, stepping around the corpse,
hawking, going to the latrine, slapping each
other's backs, etc. These things need to enter and
re-enter enough that one gains the sense of them
never letting up--the real thing now is that you
have a feeling that a series of individual things
happen at the wake, in an end-to-end fashion; but
you have no sense that a whole series of things are
going on simultaneously. So even during the stories
I'd drop some of this in. And of course you want to
build it and choreograph it, not just shove it in
by the yard from time to time.

The next thing is that I would suggest letting the
reader experience the lighthearted part of the
evening more from the vantage-point of Pa and his
cronies. That is, I'd make at least one of the
tales much more comic and bawdy, so the reader
himself breaks out laughing (I'd wonder about using
that latrine story you had before, made absolutely
ridiculous). There are a couple of reasons for
this. One is that the book as a whole is so
harrowing and unrelenting that you may lose the
reader, cause him just to go numb, if you don't
permit him to ease up for a spell. (The result of
changing the pace, in fact, is to let the reader
experience the horror of these lives more fully--
otherwise he may just tune out.) A second reason is
that at the moment, the nastiness and betrayal of
Pa and the others is done completely from the
outside--we have no difficulty in judging them to
be heartless and wicked, and the whole thing is
just a little facile. But if we (the readers) were
ourselves drawn into the merriment, the recognition
later of how lousy a thing it actually is would be
much more chilling. To make this work, I'd suggest:
  a) getting Ma drunk more as a prank at first,
  with people parading by (at Pa's apparently kind
  urging) on and on, and it only gradually
  emerging that this keeps her shut up, lets Pa
  tell lies about himself and then lets the others
  treat her like dirt.
  b) have Pa express some things that are either
unforcedly funny, or even--I would take this
seriously--kind of tender, almost remorseful. I
don't mean a great deals but just enough to

disorient the reader, break down the monolithic
good guy/bad guy dichotomy that now functions. No
one is really unrelievedly horrible, even if their
good impulses are nothing but impulses and usually
get sold out in practice. It would be interesting
if one of the kids was tempted to believe Pa, decided he/she couldn't, maybe one of them does, and
then later sees it all go up in smoke (this would
be different from Pa on the riverbank pretending
that he isn't going to punish Balraj--at the moment
he would really believe in his own good intentions,
or he might be embarrassed enough to express something tender that he would be clearly not conning--
in a sense he'd be trying to leave it unsaid.
   c) only gradually having the mood of the evening
   turn sour and vicious to the extent that it
   does. More honest condolence, more genueine good
   spirits, at the beginning--then modulate it
   gradually, so the reader can't say precisely
   when it's passed over into the other.
   d) against this continuing background of party-
ing, have (as I suggested) at least one of the
stories a great earthy sprawling bawdy piece of
high-kinks -- and then the vignettes you give with
Panday, Sunaree, Nanna, etc. will also stand out in
bolder relief (at present they are not lit up
against any background, really--they occupy almost
the whole focus of attention themselves.

Another thing you'll have to be conscious of: the
business of Panday refusing to understand (or not
being able to) that Rama really is dead, is very
touching and in a way amusing. But I think you need
to control it a bit more--by the end of the book it
has come in too many times in the same form. I'd
drop one or two cases of it, and you might also
consider having Panday develop a more and more
self-contained fantasy about it--he does now, as I
recall, but somehow you want the reader to be able
to step into the fantasy with him, and not feel
each time he starts it up again that he is being
exhibited by the author for the sake of pathos.
Perhaps one would do this by, an at least one
occasion, having the people around him fall silent
and not try to contradict him--both out of sympathy
for him, and in a way half-wishing they could keep
Rama alive themselves as he is.

Let me know what you think about all this. It does
involve rewriting the chapter, though of course you
could use a good deal of what's here. Is it a
possibility? I think both this chapter and the book
as a whole will be greatly strengthened if you can
do this.

# APPENDIX FOUR
Letter to Austin C. Clarke

787 Jane Street,
#207, Toronto,9.
26-3-73.

Hello Austin,

I have read your interview in <u>Eleven Canadian Novelists</u>
and I am very impressed by the things you had to say. As one of
the torch bearers of West Indian writing you have already established
yourself as a writer of great stature.

So far I have read all of your published work and I am impressed by your talent and technical writing skill. You have a very
unique way of putting your observation on paper and your use of
dialogueis superb. I think that you are writing about the condition
of West Indians very beautifully. You understand the dilemmas of
coloured people in this hemisphere and with your ability to give
articulation to simple people (like Bernice and Henry and Estelle
etc...) you are constantly opening up new grounds. In all of your
books you deal very effectively with the anguish and ironies of
our time; in every story, in every novel, you get to the gut of
the dimensions of loneliness, joy, frustration etc... and you weave
a very complex but fascinating picture of people as they live.
I think it was Ibsen who said that art must deal with reality,
even if reality hurts it must be portrayed. Your books are real
and fascinating and they matter at the deepest human level. It is
not very often that a writer can keep putting out works that matter
at the deepest human level, yet judging from your output you seem
to manage quite well. I personally wish you well with your next
book.

Harold.

APPENDIX FIVE

Manuscripts and typescripts in Anansi's papers rescued by Jeoffrey Ladoo:

**Anansi's papers** in the Library and Archive Canada in Ottawa contain only typescripts of a few short stories. The dates most likely relate to the date of typing (for submission to House of Anansi Press for possible publication of his short fiction) rather than writing:

1. "The Intruders" (short story), 15 March 1971, 20 pages
2. "Rage" (short story), 1971, 18 pages
3. "Land of Ancestors" (short story), 7 June, 11 pages
4. "The Vultures" (short story), 18 March, 32 pages
5. "Jametin Laura" (short story), 1 May, 5 pages
6. "The Trial" (short story), 15 March, 4 pages
7. "Spadina Boarding House" (short story), 2 May, 7 pages
8. "The Quiet Peasant" (short story), 3 March, 4 pages
9. "Chamar Tola 1940" (short story), 5 March, 3 pages
10. "Lying Monroe" (short story), 2 April 1973, 4 Pages
11. "The Quarrel" (short story) July 1971, 7 Pages

The Folder that Jeoffery salvaged contains manuscripts and typescripts of short stories and the beginnings of novels.
1. "The Teacher's Wife" (short story), undated deleted draft (1 page) second draft 1½ pages.
2. "The Agony", a short story, 5 page manuscript, 24 June 1972
3. "A New Novel" (tentative title: "The Agony") combined with "The Death of Victor Benwa". Note: "To be worked on later (3 March), total 12 pages.
4. "New Novel" also titled "1st Canadian Novel to be worked on later", 18 Pages the story of Sohan/Sawak.
5. "A Short Story, An Excerpt from a novel" (short story) 22 January 1973, 10 pages. Note: "To be worked at a later date! – combine with "The Agony" Jan 28". (*Not satisfied with the perspective. Needs time to plan and sort out the facts, to understand everything better*")
6. "Second Canadian Novel", three page manuscript, "*To be worked on later*", 3 March 1973
7. "Ashes and Blood" (beginning of another novel) 25 January, 10 pages. Note: "To be worked on later" (3 March)

Among Dennis Lee's papers at the Fisher Library in Toronto is an an 18 page typescript numbered from page 116 to page 132. Page 116 starts with a line signifying a break (★★★★★) and ends with another line ★★★★ and "The End".

APPENDIX SIX: Review in KAIRI 1.74

NO PAIN LIKE THIS BODY
Harold Sonny Ladoo
House of Anancy Press 141 pp.
A review by Victor Questel

### WHEN GODS HAVE FALLEN

Last year Ladoo died under very violent and mysterious circumstances in Trinidad. Born in Couva, Trinidad, in 1945, he had been living from 1968 in Toronto with his wife and son. He returned to settle some pressing family business, and consequently met his death. His first published novel, NO PAIN LIKE THIS BODY, spearheads a series of novels spanning life in the Caribbean and Canada. His sudden death has obviously put an end to what promised to be a new and important contribution to the West Indian novel.

Unfortunately, NO PAIN LIKE THIS BODY (referred to from now on as NO PAIN) is not available in the bookshops here, and I thus beg that book dealers order copies as soon as possible from the House of Anancy Press Ltd, Toronto. NO PAIN is set in Tola Trace on the imaginary Carib lsland in August of 1905. Carib island is really Trinidad and Tola Trace could easily be Caroni.

The story is the recording of a battle between an East Indian family and nature, and a battle between Pa and that family. The details are recorded by a child, with a child's simplicity, but without the inhibitions peculiar to a child. The novel strikes one with the same force as Orlando Patterson's CHILDREN OF SISYPHUS. What the reader has to decide is whether the novel is wilfully obscene or if the violence of the language is an integral part of the experience explored by Ladoo.

Here is the novel in brief. It is the height of the wet season in 1905 and rain is beating down on Tola Trace. Pa is drunk and beats up Ma. The children run through the rain in fear. The grandparents Nanny and Nanna do their best, but Rama contracts pneumonia, is later stung by a scorpion and dies in the district hospital. As a result of young Rama's death, Ma finally breaks down and goes mad. The novel ends with Nanny armed with her drum going off with the children into the forest in order to find Ma.

Ladoo's first novel NO PAIN, adds a new dimension to the West Indian novel. It is the kind of dimension that complements Michael Anthony's exploration of the world of the child and the adolescent as seen in THE YEAR IN SAN FERNANDO and GREEN DAYS BY THE RIVER. NO PAIN is also very instructive for any reader coming from a sitting with a novel like Shiva Naipaul's THE CHIP CHIP GATHERERS. NO PAIN explores a fragment of the world of the Trinidadian East Indian which has not been previously done. Selvon has skirted around the area but never really got into it. I am referring to life for the first and second generation Trinidadian East Indian practising subsistence farming here while their gods fall around them and the middle-aged and the young move around without meaningful points of reference and standards. Ladoo shows us that such a world is really a world of anarchy in which one has three choices: patient suffering or madness or an early death.

The grandparents Nanny and Nanna have an unshaken faith in the sky god, and in the integrity of the drum. In fact despite the hostility of the rain and wind Nanny and Nanna do not ever find the situation insurmountable. Ladoo seems to imply that they have faith in their gods from India. Ma, the daughter of Nanny, wants to believe in those gods or even the God of the Western world, but does not see any reason why she should. Pa, her husband, does not want to believe, in fact he does not believe in anything. Thus, without any frame of reference he finds himself a violent anarchist bent on brutalizing his family. The children are bewildered and their sudden realization is that they are both children and imitation adults trying to work the land, while their father is constantly drunk and waiting to beat both their mother and themselves. The children are four in number: Balraj, who is twelve and is the eldest, Sunaree, Rama and Panday. They all work in the rice paddy, though they are constantly on the run from Pa, the most violent father in West Indian fiction. The novel opens:

> Pa came home. He didn't talk to Ma. He came home just like a snake. Quiet. (p. 13)

Pa is a snake. He is the one who beats up each member of his family. He is the one indirectly responsible for Rama's death and Ma's madness. In fact, Pa can be seen as the reverse side to the indifferent invisible God in the sky. Pa is a snake, the agent of evil, a devil figure; a directionless individual on a violent rampage of violence. Thus, if God is presented as the indifferent agent of destruction, then Pa is presented as his opposite number on earth.

As things get progressively worse Panday asks

> "Wot God doin now?"
> "He watchin from de sky."
> "God still watchin"
> "Well God playing de ass now!" (p. 56)

This feeling that the persons in authority do not care, but are simply "playing de ass" runs throughout the novel. Each member of the family looks upon the other with suspicion and with the feeling that he or she is both exaggerating his or her pain or irritability. Thus, when Ma is drunk during the wake for Rama, her child Panday says,

> "Ma you drink rum and playing in you ass!"
> Ma was getting on; bawling and swearing and getting on. Pa came inside the kitchen. "Keep dat bitch quiet!"
> "But she chile dead," Soomintra the wife of Sankar said.
> "Yeh. De chile dead, but she eh have to get on like a ass." (p. 98)

Most of the action in the novel is played out in rain, Ladoo's characters are seen as trapped in the wires of rain, and therefore fixed in time, in the wet season, which is presented as the more aggressive of the two seasons. It is significant that Ladoo traps his characters in the rain and then closely examines their lives, since it allows him to make his point by exaggeration for once trapped he places them under a microscope. One can see that this writer has imposed all his memories of grim wet seasons onto that one wet season of his fictitious Carib Island. The result is a reign of terror that reigns supreme.

So far, in West Indian literature our writers have used the sun as the symbol of suffering and hot indifference. The cold of the rain in Ladoo's novel is even more biting. Hence, we can get the following:

> The sky rolled as an endless spider and the rain fell like a shower of poison over Tola. The darkness was thicker than black mud, and the wind howled as evil spirits. (p. 57)

The counterpoint of irony is what knits the novel together. The central irony being that nature for the trapped in Tola Trace is hostile, yet nature is all they know, and their ability to tame nature determines their degree of survival. The result is that we get descriptions of the hostility of nature, even the evil in nature, while alongside these are passages which show the characters becoming part of nature. In an attempt to show both the hostility of nature and the evil it can contain, Ladoo floods his novel with such creeping and crawling things as snakes, rats, worms, ants, spiders and scorpions. The following passage on the other hand shows Ma, a woman who fights against the odds of an apparently hostile yet indifferent natural world, as well as a violent husband, becoming part of nature.

> A greenish juice leaked out from her palms and fell on the ground. The juice smelt as something to eat. Ma looked at her right palm; the leaves were ground enough: *it looked as if moss was growing in her palms.* (p. 27. My emphasis)

Many passages also show Ladoo comparing how his characters behave to that of animals or insects.

The other irony is that the children talk, work and behave as adults, then suddenly realize that they are only children. It shocks us as much as it shocks them. The following passage traces Panday's refusal to plant rice.

> "Look wot you doin Panday!" Sunaree said.
> "I not doin notten. Dis rice could kiss me ass! I is a chile."
> "If Pa  hear you he go  beat you Panday!"
> "But I is a little chile!"
> Pa stood on the riceland bank by the doodoose mango tree. He heard Panday. He jumped as a bull on the riceland bank. "Panday shut you kiss me ass mout boy! Shut it boy! Me Jesus Christ! If you make me come in dat wadder I go kick you till you liver bust!" (p. 65)

The central irony is really Ladoo's presentation of comedy as being part of tragedy, or at least related to it, while not arriving at say the tragi-comedy of V. S. Naipaul. The best example of this is the wake scene. Incidentally, Ladoo has been quoted by Darryl Dean, a Trinidadian journalist based in Toronto, as claiming that,

> "In one chapter about a wake which included the folk lore of the people, many sections were deliberately chopped out because the publisher felt it would be better to leave it out."

Before singling out any of the action at the wake scene I should first record the reaction of Ma and Pa to the death of their son Rama, since their reactions are related to Ladoo's implied question – "who is to blame?"

> "Me son dead widdout seein he modder face. Two days he live in dat hospital just waiting to see he modder. He wait till he dead. Which part in dat sky you is God? Me chile not even leff a trace in de world. He just born and dead. Dat is all. And he own fadder kill him too besides!"
> "I tell you God kill him!" Pa shouted. "Yet you sayin I kill him. Well me eh doin one kiss me ass  ting for dis wake and funeral!" (p. 71)

At the wake stories are told and jokes exchanged, and Pa sees that Ma gets drunk so that only his version of the death can be told. Furthermore, Ladoo uses the wake scene to show how the gods have fallen. No one including the priest has any faith in the ritual performed. In addition to this, the priest's authenticity is questioned by the group and by extension what he

represents. The priest claims that he is a Brahmin but the one-legged
villager says:

> "He is a modderass chamar and he playing Brahmin. Bisnath
> Soddhu is not a priest. He fadder used to mind pigs in Jangli Tola.
> He modderass chamar come to Tola playing holy."
> And Pulbassia laughed and said, "Yeh one foot. Give him in he ass!"
> Bisnath Saddhu the village priest said, "Shut you one foottail! I
> not from Jangli Tola. Me fadder and me come from de Punjab."
> "Punjab me ass Punjab!" Pulbassia shouted. "You son of a bitch
> Baba all you used to mind hog in Jangli Tola."
> "Who say dat?"
> "Me Pulbassia."
> The priest sat up, wiped his eyes with the back of his hands,
> yawned and said, "I de born a Brahmin." (pp. 98-99)

Given the intensity of the traumatic experience that the children and Ma
experience because of stupid brutality of Pa, the children soon begin to
create their own reality and Ma goes mad. For example, Balraj insists that
Rama is not dead and buried but is "still in the dead house in Tolaville".

> "All you cant fool me," Balraj said, "By dat haspital have big big
> rats. I see dem rats wid me own eyes. I tell all you dat Rama still in
> dat dead house in Tolaville. Rat eatin him. Nanna never bring Rama
> home. I never see Nanna bring dat boy on no horse cart. So Rama
> still in dat dead house. Rat still eatin him" (p. 112)

For Panday, "Rama was living in the water. He drowned in the riceland
because he had a long cut in his belly. Rama was buried in the water. The
water snakes were searching for him…" (p. 112)
Ma throughout the novel takes her licks from Pa and God, staying with
Pa for the sake of the children. After Rama's death she goes mad. Only her
mother Nanny with the aid of the drum is able to find her, when she
wanders off in the forest. In fact Nanny and Nanna have a confidence in the
sky god that nothing can shake. They follow the old values brought over
from India, and are thus always in control of both themselves and their
environment regardless of the hostility of things. Thus, we can have,

> … This time she [Nanny] beated for the tadpoles, the scorpions
> and the night birds; she beated not only for the living things of Tola;
> she beated a tune for all that lives and moves upon the face of the
> earth. She beated and she knew that the great sky god was watching
> with his big big eyes. (p. 42)

It is because the Gods have fallen or maybe ignored that the environment is haunted by spirits and jumbies, or rather, the characters are haunted by the fear of spirits and jumbies.

One of the starkest of passages in the novel is the description of Rama covered in a ricebox. Rama is sick with fever and is placed in a covered ricebox very much as if dead and placed in his coffin. He is later stung by a scorpion and dies in the district hospital. It is as if his burial is rehearsed. The placing of Rama in the covered ricebox gives some more support to the tentative theory of re-burial mooted by some commentators on West-Indian literature,

The only works written in the English-speaking West Indies which come closest to this novel in so far as we are talking about man versus nature is Roger Mais's THE HILLS WERE JOYFUL TOGETHER and Derek Walcott's THE SEA AT DAUPHIN. To Afa, "the sea it have compassion in the end"; to those in NO PAIN, the rain does not care, nor does the wind or the land.

> The rain didn't care about Tola. Rain was pounding the earth. Ma and Balraj saw the drops; they looked like fat white worms invading the earth from above. God was trying to tie the earth and the sky with the rain drops. The whole of Tola was dark and dismal. (p. 27)

Furthermore, the wind is seen as blowing "with such force and temper; blowing with the intention of crippling even the trees, blowing just to cause trouble and hate."(p. 43)

One area of weakness in NO PAIN is that Ladoo overdoes his attempts to capture sound. The novel is top-heavy with sounds such as 'tuts', 'splunk', 'slap' and 'toots'. I understand his need to capture sound in that rain-drenched setting, but it ends in near-parody. Moreover it too often interrupts the flow of the descriptions. For example,

> A large cockroach with long wings flew *flut* over the light. It settled *taps* on the earthen wall. It was wet; it came from the rain to shelter near the light. Nanny took the brown hand-drum and crushed it *crachak!* (p. 42)

If Ladoo had omitted the 'flut' and the 'taps', that 'crachak' would have been more dramatic. As it is, it is just another noise.

Since Ladoo is now dead, it is difficult for anyone to make claims for him since he cannot now fulfil them. All that can be said is that Ladoo has pointed another dimension that is open to the young West Indian writer. If the novel reads as if it is unfinished, it is because it is the first in a projected series which Ladoo's untimely death has brought to a very premature end.

The novel really does not attempt to answer some of the questions raised; maybe the later novels would have cleared up some of the areas of vagueness. One of the questions not answered is what kind of belief must one have to survive in a hostile environment in which standards are non-existent, but in which one must create new standards so that the next generation can survive?

The strength of NO PAIN is its directness. It is a novel stripped to the bone of pain. Ladoo by looking back steadily at Tola Trace has made it the earth's centre, and that is a success that few first novels can boast.

APPENDIX SEVEN: REVIEW IN KAIRI 1/75

THE NOVEL OF TOMORROW, TODAY
A review of YESTERDAYS
a novel by Harold Sonny Ladoo
Anansi Press 1974
by Christopher Laird

*Yesterdays* is the last published work of Harold Sonny Ladoo who was killed under mysterious circumstances in Trinidad in 1973. This novel was published posthumously and represents the second of a series intended to span life in Trinidad and Canada. We thus only have two novels by Ladoo to work with but in these two short works I believe we have the most significant contribution to Trinidadian literature since the fifties.

In his first novel *No Pain Like This Body* (reviewed in **KAIRI** 1-74 by Victor Questel) Ladoo blazed a furious path across "the Caribbean literary scene in "what is probably the most violent work of Caribbean fiction". A work that, despite its brevity, is of such energy and complexity that continued analysis reveals more and more of its intricate symbolic structure and condensed and organic vision of an existential nightmare. Though I do not intend to elaborate on Victor's observations in KAIRI 1:74, I will in the course of this essay refer to *No Pain* as it is impossible to appraise *Yesterdays* without reference to the only other published work of the author.

Probably the first thing that can be said of Yesterdays (probably the most scatological work of Caribbean fiction) is that its mood and its narrative technique are startlingly different to that of *No Pain*. The complex system of simile e.g.
Pa is like a snake
Streaks of lightning are like long green snakes
or
Tadpoles are black like rainclouds (clouds like black rice)
   or black like tar
   or black like drunk people (Pa)
Sunaree's hair is like grass
   or black like the sky
   or blacker than a dream of snakes and evil spirits (Pa)
This series of similes represents only a small portion of the whole scheme but provides an example of the complexity of the structure. In Ladoo's work everything in the environment is equal importance with the people; the whole world is an organic capsule of seething, struggling life. One device Ladoo uses to encapsulate his location, is to set up a series of

balanced points of reference, a series of reflections or mirror images.
So in the similes quoted above, the sky is black and so is Sunaree's
hair which is like grass so the sky is black and is like the grass and also
like the tadpoles which are like tar (the road). So already there is a
great crotch of blackness with the horizon its apex and in the sky there
is lightning, on the earth there is Pa, and later on Pa is likened to Satan
(in Hell) and God (in Heaven). The whole novel is set in rain described
as "God trying to tie the Earth and Sky with rain drops."

This system of balance (the rotting body of Rama in the rice box coffin
(rice like worms) balanced with the rotting insides of the belching, farting,
stink breathed Pundit; the Sun like a fat worm crawling over Tola; ties the
whole of *No Pain* like a tight ball of string.

Even though *Yesterdays* is almost totally void of such explicit similes, a
close look at the work reveals the mirror image again, but this time not so
much a cosmic one but one that is used to dramatise and elucidate the
internal structure of the novel by being localised to the very specific
landscape of *Yesterdays*. This landscape consists of a section of Tola consist-
ing of three buildings, really four homes, separated by the main road which
is a searing strip of modern death splitting the community, a relentless
symbol of the world outside Tola passing by. On one side is Ragbir and
Sook who runs a shop with his wife Rookmin. Ragbir is the village ram and
pimp, Sook the village homosexual who has an arrangement with his wife
Rookmin who stays with him because he is a good businessman. On the
other side of the road is the building housing the main characters of the
novel, Choonilal, his wife Basdai, son Poonwa and his lodger Tailor who
lives downstairs. Choonilal is the hardworking, hen-pecked, neurotic hero
of the novel who is under attack from everyone else in his house to
mortgage the house to get money for his son Poonwa to go to Canada to
launch a Hindu mission to do to Canadians what the Canadian missionaries did to Trinidad's Hindus. Basdai wants Poon to go because otherwise
he will just stay and drink rum and 'bull' in Tola. Tailor wants him to go
because he sees himself taking Poon's place in the household and getting
maybe to move upstairs. Poon wants to go because he is essentially
psychotic and has a thing about a buxom aryan Canadian teacher who used
to beat the hell out of him (literally) at school. (I use 'aryan' here in the sense
of blond/blue eyed – this ghost contrasts with the Aryan gods who haunt
Choonilal). Choon is afraid to mortgage the property because the pandit
from whom the money will be borrowed is 'a smart man' and may end up
stealing the house entirely. The whole action of *Yesterdays* is built around
this conflict. But, as can be guessed, this central action is but one significant
event upon which Ladoo hangs a number of issues and it is with some of
the main ones I will attempt to deal.

To return to the main mirror image – on one side of the road is a scamp

Ragbir and a genuine shopkeeper Sook with his wife, on the other is the scamp Tailor and the genuine cane farmer Choon and his family. There are two lavatories on each side of the road. On one side the latrines of Sook and Ragbir and on the other side the filthy latrine of Choon which is used by all the household except Poonwa who uses the other lavatory, a modern w.c. upstairs. It is at the risk of spiritual defilement that a traditional Hindu may use the w.c. while it is at the risk of physical defilement in the form of homosexual 'affair' (or 'bull') with Sook that use is made of Sook's latrine.

Secondly there is the sterile and increasingly impotent Choonilal who is always kneeding his balls and scratching his 'bald' head on one side and the oversexed Ragbir who is constantly fingering his balls and wiping his face or wrapping his head in a blue towel on the other side. The sexual looseness of Tailor on one side – who has caused the diversionary neurosis of Choon by bringing whores home to mess up the latrine – is balanced by the sexually deviant Sook on the other side. There are many other details which increase the mirror image on that scale, but Ladoo also brings it down on a smaller scale too. The first four sentences of the book illustrate a small scale balance:

> Tailor sat under the chataigne tree; with a worried face he counted the cars as they passed by. With an old embroidery scissors, he picked his teeth.
>
> Choonilal sat on an old potato crate a few feet away from Tailor, and brushed his teeth with a guava stick. Occasionally he glanced at Tailor with a worried face.

Here, on one side of the road are Choon and Tailor, each carrying out similar tasks in different ways. The chataigne/potato balance and the tooth cleaning balance with the man of the world, technological Tailor using an embroidery scissors while cane farmer, rooted Choon, uses a guava stick. Both have a worried face. It is as if they were facing each other in a mirror. Which one is real? Are they both the same?

The mirror image is only one aspect of Ladoo's writing and the evidence for the existence of such symmetry is strong enough to suggest that what appears at first to be merely a short bawdy tale is deep down more than that. Everything that is said is significant on many levels. The work's very brevity demands that every word work overtime. Ladoo has taken his comment beyond the simple(!) analogous structure of *No Pain* and extended his range by making use of more subtle devices while at the same time retaining the energy and organic vision of the world centred on Tola that appears in the earlier work. If *No Pain* called to mind the works of Caldwell or Kafka in their treatment of violence and the arraignment of forces against the individual, *Yesterdays* touches on a possibly much more worn path of satire and irony travelled by Fielding, Swift, and closer home, Naipaul.

An essential element of much satire is the author's ironic comment, seen only in puzzling flashes in *No Pain*:

The music of the flute was sweeter than sugar; than life even.

(This while Rama is dying, they are beset with violence and sorrow) and again when Nanny "beated a tune for all that lives and moves upon the face of the earth" and immediately afterwards uses the drum to crush a cockroach *crachak!* it returns as an integral part of the style of *Yesterdays* showing itself clearly by the fourth paragraph:

> And at times Choonilal wept as he offered water to the Aryan gods in his brass lota; he did this because he felt that the gods were going to recognise the weeping Choonilal after death...

and is thereafter ever present especially in the author's description of present and past action. Probably the point at which Ladoo really casts all satiric restraint to the wind is in his handling of the scenes at the Choonilals' after Basdai announces Poonwa's "death". It is worth quoting at length:

> When Tailor ran upstairs he found Basdai screaming hysterically and pounding her head violently against her son's door. For a while Tailor wondered what to do. Now that Poonwa was dead, it meant that he would be able to live comfortably with the Choonilals. Tailor thought a little and decided not to weep. But as the prospect of homelessness came to him, he decided to weep, because by weeping he would be able to influence Basdai. Behaving as though Poonwa was his child Tailor burst into tears. He was weeping and weeping, weeping more than Basdai even. Realising that it was all going unobserved, he quickly embraced Basdai in a motherly fashion and pounded his head against the door. This new development had the desired effect. Basdai gripped Tailor and said, "O God Tailor! You cryin too Tail."
>
> Wishing to sustain Basdai's vision of the weeping tailor, he pounded his head with a savage determination. Each time that he drummed his head against the door he screamed. Sometimes he bent his head in such a way as to see his landlady's breasts as he wept. Now and then he abandoned the pounding of the door to strike his head against softer material. Once or twice he struck his forehead against Basdai's breasts.

The scene builds up and up as the other characters come in and join the wailing; Sook and Rookmin come in and proceed to butt the wall then finding that too hard they butt the chairs and the wooden partition:

> Ragbir was the last to reach. He stood for a moment and viewed the situation. He farted and slipped into the mood of the evening. Eager to kill two birds with one stone, he went down on the floor to weep. Gradually he crawled until he came by Rookmin. Then he slipped his head under her dress, and with his eyes to heaven he, wept and wept.

Fielding uses a similar technique in *Joseph Andrews* when Pastor Adams is told his favourite son is dead only to find out afterwards it was a mistake. The Pastor's actions during that time highlight his well-meaning hypocrisy as his human concern overcomes his pompous religious rhetoric. Basdai's tactic is intended to cut through Choonilal's professed stand in the same way, by appealing to his compassion he may relent and let Poonwa go to Canada.

But Ladoo's satiric stance is as unique as his cosmic blues were in *No Pain*; it is essentially Trinidadian and tied closely to his personal attitude to Trinidad. What he uses satire for here is not to deflate or highlight hypocrisy – Ladoo's work assumes this as given, as all Trinidadians do – but to rejoice in the opportunism of his characters when the demands of convention provide the opportunity for the fulfilment of desires; whether long range as on Tailor's part or short range as in the case of Ragbir.

Again, though Ladoo's 'excremental vision' displayed in *Yesterdays* calls Swift immediately to mind, Ladoo is not using the reference to anal functions, products or deviations to shock sensibilities or to make a statement about what he thinks of 'Man', he is merely using an aspect of everyday life in Trinidad as he used violence in *No Pain*. He uses it pointedly to comment on the world and the people he portrays. It isn't so much that he exaggerates that aspect but he filters out other aspects much as a printer may do to obtain three-colour separations of a full colour scene, each in one of the primary colours. Bawdy satire becomes a parameter in *Yesterdays*, it is the colour used to paint the scene and becomes close to being his medium.

It is impossible to analyse *Yesterdays* without looking for the significance of shit. If *No Pain* was set in a cosmic swamp beleaguered by the elements and everything hostile in the Universe, then *Yesterdays* is set in a latrine and it seems at times that the characters had already suffered the worse fate possible – "to be born back a blasted worm in a latrine". The scene where Tailor and Ragbir eventually clean the offending latrine that forms the centre piece of the novel seems to place humans in their evolutionary perspective in an incredible but typical conversation between the cleaners:

Worms were running all over the place; they were trying to climb up on Tailor's rubber boots. Ragbir moved away a little. "Man Rag, like dese worms want man in dey ass."

"Well bull dem, nuh," Ragbir declared.

The stench from the pit was almost unbearable. "People shit is de worst kinda shit to smell," Tailor said. "Cow shit does smell nice. Horse shit does smell good too. Goat shit and sheep shit is nice shit to smell. But dog shit does stink like people own, you know boy Rag."

"Korek."

"You know wen I de small boy Rag, we de have a goat. Wen I de small man sometime I used to eat goat shit man Rag."

"Wot make you stop?"

This is a passage that echoes Swift but the spirit is so different, we are dealing with recognisable people here not symbols of misanthropy.

The latrine incident whereby Tailor's drunken whore friends broke down a wall one night and left the facility in a mess is used by Choonilal, who refuses to clean it on principle, as a release for his anxiety and preoccupation over the Poonwa problem. This is recognised by the other characters, even his friends, and later acts as an ego comforter for Choon when he has to back down on the main issue to know that Tailor backed down on the latrine issue. Until then the stinking pit stands as a bone of contention in the middle of the scene and Choonilal has to risk his life crossing the main road (where "twenty people had been killed on one spot within 15 years") when a shit takes him to use Ragbir's pit. Basdai's threat that she go give him pressure till he shit he pants, and everybody's advice to "give him pressure in he ass" almost pay off as Choon nearly asphyxiates in his own shit near the climax of the novel,

Poonwa depends on the latrine or lavatory for security. It is the place where he hid in school – "The toilet was a safe place" – he ate there and later when working as a lawyer's clerk he had lunch there. Poonwa becomes accustomed to the smell though it is the smell of the latrine that has Choon in trouble from the gods and his dreams throughout the book. So Poonwa eats in the lavatory, a very significant image as when Poonwa speaks he speaks shit. In fact he is the only character in the novel who speaks English; this has a devastating effect on Choonilal – whom he calls "father".

"Man Rag, wot I go tell you, man. Me son so educated dat wen he talk, I does only feel to shit man. Dey boy talk some Latin just now man Rag. Man wen I hear de Latin, a shit take me one time."

Ladoo spells out the symbolism as Choon shouts to Poonwa later:

"Wen you de small you used to call me 'fadder', now you does call me 'father'. It look like English does flow from you ass. But all de book you read Poonwa, an all dat education you have in you ass is notten. In dis same island man wid dat education have to eat dey shit!"

It is also significant that Choonilal was more interested in sodomy than learning English when he was attempting to learn it. Choonilal's rebellion (bulling on the altar instead of English lessons) instinctive though it may be is more subversive than Poonwa's.

Shitting is important to the characters, but bulling is the lowest activity on the moral scale, yet is indulged in by all the males (this is what Basdai is afraid for in Poonwa' s case – though going to Canada does not help, he is seduced before he goes and advised to continue by Basdai's own ally, the Pandit). There are three ways to lose one's shame: to abandon the gods; to urinate close to the house; and to practice sodomy. Tailor has done all these, Poonwa none of them – though using the indoor toilet may theoretically be considered near the house –, yet Basdai can say, "Sook should be shame, why he don't kill heself?" though throughout the book the only one who plays with suicide is Poonwa. This irony is typical of Ladoo's work as it appears in *No Pain*, also in the ambiguous relationship between the all-seeing but unhelpful God (who 'playing in he ass') and the devil; between the God and the very effective aryan tradition of Nanny and Nana. In *Yesterdays*, the counterpointing of official religion and human values reoccurs. The aryan gods are again just watching, recording your deeds on your heart, but Choon's personal preoccupation with the gods, specifically Hanuman, is very different from the way Poonwa or the Pandit uses the gods. According to Poonwa his mission will "teach the white world compassion" when he has shown himself void of that attribute. It is Choonilal and to some extent Sook (from whom Poonwa is to be 'saved') who of all the characters exhibit compassion. It is this compassion that Basdai and the others work on to obtain their ends, such as in the pretended death of Poonwa quoted above.

In fact, the contrast between the official spokesman for the gods (the Pandit) and ordinary human values is highlighted continuously and prob-ably becomes most pointed as the climax approaches and the signing of the mortgage is to take place. For example. the Pandit's advice to Poonwa:

"...Take dis as you feelosofee in life: If a woman lie down for you, ride she! If a man bend over for you, bull him!
Never spear de rod!"

is most unbecoming a man in his position and embarrasses the Choonilals.

The passage from the Holy Book that Pandit reads shows life not unlike life in Tola but with one difference: friendship. Where Hanuman "couldn't allow a friend's wife to be seduced", Choonilal, whose own wife was seduced by countless men including Pandit Puru (who is most likely Poonwa's real father) never had such a friend to call on except maybe Sook, to a very slight extent. Compassion again is what is missing.

When Poonwa (who can't even read Hindi, despite his missionary zeal) says: "With the paper of ownership in a drawer and the Bible under his head, …the witeman sips whisky as he dreams of peace," he is unwittingly talking probably more of the Pandit than anyone else, now that the Pandit has the mortgage on Choon's house.

On and on the ironies converge and illustrate Ladoo's statement. (Check out Poonwa's comparison of his ideas to those of Hitler and Mussolini.) *Yesterdays* seems, despite the laughter, even sadder than *No Pain*, if only because there is no Nanny and Nana to provide a sense of order or compassion. Choon and maybe Sook ("it takes an able man to take man") are alone in the world 50 years later with nothing to look forward to:

> Choonilal said, "Just now you go see wot go happen in dis Rag. Everybody in dis island want to go to school. Nobody don't want to work in de cane or plant tomatoes and ting, you know boy. All of dem want big work in govament and ting. All of dem want to be police and postman and ting, boy Rag. Just now in dis island it go have so much educated people, dat dey go have to take dey G.C. E, and ting and wipe dey ass Rag.…"

Perhaps the shortest paragraph in the book occurs when Pandit refuses money and then (with very little persuasion):
He took it.

*Yesterdays* is, like No Pain, a short book, they are both quickly read and in fact facilitate quick reading through the legible print and convenient size, but more than that the style of Ladoo's writing drives the reader. The shortness of the book I believe means less emphasis on the writer's literary style and more on event and symbolic construction; this is certainly the case in Ladoo's work, we don't ever get a 19th century novelist's detailed description of the scene. Most description is done by simile or single incidentally placed adjective, which may add to the inner structure of the work without impeding the pace or action. The few descriptions in *Yesterdays* are of people; they are short and aimed less at giving a detailed picture than at applying symbols to a person. These cameos are more like lampoons.

The lawyer, Poonwa's employer, was a fat black Madrassi Indian.

His hair was trimmed very short and there were a few grey hairs on his head. His gold-rimmed spectacles pinched his nose; perhaps it was causing him pain, for now and then he rubbed his nose with the back of his hairy hands. In his dark suit he looked like an undertaker.

There are also two descriptions of the Pandit which are beautiful comic sketches. We never really get a picture of the person as such, a bald-head here or enormous genitals there; most description is of material properties in the drama. The person could be as faceless as any actor; it's the way he acts and dresses that tells more. Ladoo leaves it to the reader to make judgements from his selective eye.

Other than this point, the book can be divided almost equally into direct speech and narration. There is no doubt at all that one of Ladoo's main stylistic talents is his use of dialogue in creole. Check out this passage, which I think is one of the masterpieces of the capture of Trinidad Creole rhythm and syntax on the page:

> "Boy Choon, dis life eh play, it have trobble nuh."
> "Yeh boy Rag, dis life have trobble too bad. Tailor man, de man shit in me latrine man. God have mercy. Tailor shit fat fat leer in de pit man, boy Rag. Man Rag I does feel to kill meself wen I smell dat pit in de night. Dis world have too much trobble man Rag man. I tellin you boy Rag. Sometimes in de night wen I get up to pray to God man Rag, I does cant pray man. Look eh Rag, Tailor giving me too much trobble man."

The use of 'man' and 'boy' approaches exaggeration but remains perfectly natural and understandable to communicate the speaker's anxiety and earnestness. I know of no Caribbean writer who would have risked a passage like that in print, not even Selvon. It is Ladoo's dialogue that drives his work because he is a master of his language, the energy of our people undiluted by puritanical and colonial editing comes searing through the Trinidadian landscape on to the page. You can hear and feel his characters as if you were right there, that is Ladoo's major stylistic achievement, it is a natural consequence of using the natural language of our people and Ladoo does it better than anyone I am aware of.

If all the dialogue was extracted from the novel and dramatised, very little sense of the novel would be lost. It can stand on its own. This is not to say that the 'ordinary' English prose pieces of narrative detract from the work, far from it, they have to take the place of dramatic action by describing it and what it does in *Yesterdays* is add significance to certain scenes and snatches of dialogue by relating it to the 'yesterdays' of the characters. All the memories of incidents in the past that make up the 'yesterdays' referred to in the title are related in these prose passages, not in minute description but simply in the style of narrator. A short example will give an idea of both of these points:

> "Let we talk little bit nuh man Rag."
> "Look Choonilal, haul you tail and go home. Go now befo I take a cutlass and chop up you ass yeh."
> Choonilal knew that he couldn't joke with Ragbir, because of what had happened once when Ragbir and Sook had had an affair. The queer had promised Ragbir twenty dollars. But after the affair was over, Sook had the boldness to say that he had no money. That drove Ragbir mad. With cutlass in his hand, he chased the queer through the village. When Sook realised that Ragbir had been serious, he was glad enough to pay him the twenty dollars. Shaking his head, Choonilal muttered, "Oright boy Rag. Lemme go and hear wot Poonwa have to say."
> Fingering his loose testicles, Ragbir leaned over the window and said, "Boy Choon, I was just makin a joke man."

In the example Ragbir's 'joke' is explained by reference to the 'yesterday' episode between Sook and Ragbir; this would not come out on stage without much added dialogue. Because of Ladoo's restriction of himself in these passages to dealing with action, the passages in no way intrude by making editorial comment. Ladoo's comment is gathered by analysing the symbolic structure of the work as I have attempted to do above.

The question of Ladoo's implied attitude to what he describes is very important as this is a question that arises when one considers most satire and irony, but I am unable to discern precisely his attitude from his work; he has I think come nearer than any other satirist I can recall to neutrality. We are not sure whether he approves or disapproves, whether he is sneering or praising or laughing. We are only given a clue to his attitude, as I said, after the accumulated evidence of the novel is assessed. The complete lack of intrusion by the author is so effective that one can finally only assess his attitude to the people and events described to be the same as one's own. Compare one of Ladoo's descriptions with the very typical Naipaul description of Mrs. Tulsi in *A House for Mr, Biswas*: "without her teeth she looked decrepit, but there was about her decrepitude a quality of everlastingness." Naipaul interprets the personality behind the figure described, Ladoo leaves the interpretation for the reader. The difference between word and deed is assumed by Ladoo, not judged: "Laughing Pandit Puru explained to the villagers that it was no laughing matter" and motive seems relatively unimportant most of the time except, as in real life, where it is a guide to action in the future.

If we tear ourselves away from the spell of fascination and energy and just plain enjoyment that Ladoo spins, and assess the novel in as objective a way as possible, it would be just to say that Ladoo (in *Yesterdays*) has written comic literature which nevertheless describes the tragedy of our situation. Naipaul has done the same. What then accounts for the tremendously different impression that these two authors give? Ever since the appearance of Ladoo's first work, the temptation to compare him with previous writers who have portrayed East Indian life in Trinidad has been present. Ladoo's vision, while not really appearing that much more hopeful or positive, was in such contrast to that of writers like Selvon and Naipaul that it was almost like a bitter blast of wind clearing our view of a situation which had become so murky, vague and cluttered with stereotypes.

I have attempted above to point to some areas where Ladoo's 'satire' differs from the conventional approach and to Naipaul's. It could be said that Ladoo's very lack of overt authorial comment is a positive reaction to the world but this is of course only so in relation to Naipaul's open scorn. Search as we might, we can only glean little clues as to positive reaction from Ladoo's writing, the theme of compassion in *Yesterdays* and the role of traditional values in *No Pain*. These clues are in fact what saves his work from being outright blasphemy and rebellious nihilism.

Rebellion in fact is a key concept in discussing Ladoo and it may be this that makes his work so exciting to our lives and ties in so well with his obvious gifts of imparting incredible energy to his style. *No Pain* is about rebellion, rebellion against God, the Devil and the world, *Yesterdays* is about the tyranny of the educated. But the works themselves are rebellions against East Indian life and also (and most significantly for Caribbean literature) against previous literary portrayals of this life. Ladoo' s work is as much a literary revolution aimed at the overthrow of Neo-Colonial literature like that of Naipaul as the current political efforts have been since 1970 in Trinidad aimed at political and economic overthrow of neo-colonialism. This is another reason I can give for fascination with Ladoo's work at this time. (His violent death in 1973 of course heightens this aura of rebellion.)

It is not hard to substantiate this interpretation when one compares *Yesterdays* with Naipaul's work, say *A House for Mr. Biswas*. Firstly, Choonilal is fighting to keep the house he built through hard work in the fields, and though he may objectively be a ridiculous figure, as we have seen, he is one of the only human and compassionate persons in the novel. Quite in contrast to Poonwa, who could be Naipaul himself, who though he has never been to Oxford (like the boy Naipaul), speaks with an Oxford accent; who though he wishes to carry his Hinduism into the outside world nevertheless cannot read (the intimate and tender) Hindi; he wants to escape from Trinidad which he sees doomed to the fate outlined by Choonilal to Ragbir above.

Secondly, the only excremental reference in Biswas is the incident whereby Biswas while training to be a pundit was (like Choonilal) worried about doing his puja unrelieved and due to the unfortunate accident of his throwing the shit occasioned by the theft of some bananas onto the Pundit's oleander bush, he (like Choonilal) suffers great pain from a swollen stomach whenever under stress. Incidentally, I don't think it is a coincidence that the white-painted figure of Hanuman occurs in *Yesterdays* to haunt Choonilal. (Mr. Biswas's in-laws lived in Hanuman House which sported a white painted figure of the god.)

If this incidental reference is accepted and Poonwa is seen as Naipaul, then Ladoo's treatment of Poonwa throughout *Yesterdays* could be interpreted as Ladoo's comment on Naipaul and his ilk. Even if the parallel is not accepted, the concept is certainly worth exploring. Ladoo is essentially an ordinary Hindu in Trinidad while Naipaul is the urban Brahmin. The clash of these two outlooks is obvious and adds more fuel to the rebel image. Poonwa is the only person in the book who has a well-documented 'secret self'. Consider this in the light of Naipaul's contention that revelation is vulgar and one must keep one's secret self.

One suspects that one cannot or really should not compare the literature of a brahmin with that of the 'ordinary Hindu'. One should not apply the critical criteria of the traditional novel to Ladoo as one would to Naipaul. Ladoo's work is essentially different in form and style though the content may bear comparison. Ladoo builds a novel on energy and action, Naipaul on a materialist structure of language, character, and authorial comment. There is, as I have said before, no objectivity in Ladoo's characters, the objective world is not important in so far as it directly affects them (the war, or the road) Naipaul's very language is so English and unreal to the situation that this at all times reinforces by its incongruity the ridiculous nature of the things portrayed and the "pathetic underdevelopment" of that world. Naipaul's hopelessness is not tempered with animal joys or possible help from the ancient gods; the Brahmin is too familiar with these gods and has used them so much to live by that they can never mystify him.

Ladoo's achievement has been to seize the time so beautifully. His work is the work of the rebel, maybe even the revolutionary, he is not relating to the colonial but to his own and reacting against the neo-colonial. He is one of the first local writers to do this, to use our literature as a reference, without the achievement of previous writers (like Naipaul) this would have been impossible. His characters act organically in a dynamic of violence and cunning, whether victor or vanquished however, each individual retains his character and does not appear weak or pitiful. His works are capable of ferocious energy which should blast the way for a third generation of Caribbean writers.

APPENDIX EIGHT: Contact sheet for cover phtograph taken by Graeme
Gibson

APPENDIX NINE: Ethnic make-up of the Trinidadian population, 1960

**Population of Trinidad and Tobago according to ethnic group**

| Ethnic group | Census 1960 | |
|---|---|---|
| | **Number** | **%** |
| Indian | 301,946 | 36.5 |
| African | 358,588 | 43.3 |
| Mixed | 134,749 | 16.3 |
| White | 15,718 | 1.9 |
| Chinese | 8,361 | 1.0 |

# INDEX

citizenship, trapped in caste contempt between the plantation and
the independent village, 89; echoes
of the *Ramayana*, 89; pity for Pa
as well as recognition of his de-
vious brutality, 91; wonders about
effects of double loss of his own
father and loss of regular contact
with Such on HL and his revisions
of *No Pain*, 92; Benwa, the stickfighter as a possible hero figure,
92, 99 n. 26, 135; why HL's criticism of Trinidad was acceptable
to him when V.S. Naipaul's wasn't,
93; his reading and review of *Yesterdays*, 112-115, and see appendix 7, 210-221; *Yesterdays* as
comedic tour de force, 112; a swipe
at *A House for Mr Biswas*, 112; on
the language of the novel and the
Trinidadian culture of "shit talk",
113; a novel written without com-
promise to non-Caribbean readers
in its language, 114; criticises
Clement H. Wyke's dismissal of
*Yesterdays* and defends it in terms
of Walcott's recognition of the
Caribbean "tragi-comic" voice,
116; CL's negative conclusions on
whether any other novels existed, but surviving short stories were
submitted to a Anansi but not
published, 127-128; drafts of
unpublished stories and handwritten fragments as sketches for intended novels with interlinked
characters, 128, 131, 135; on HL's
strategies for dealing with family pressures and the expectations
of others, 140-141; on trying to
work out who HL really was and
conflicting views of family, wife,
Canadian friends, over for  instance his treatment of his children and step children, 142-144;
analysis of HL's motivations for
manipulative behaviour, 147; a
summing up of what HL's writing offers and the evidence of how
it was changing in late stories that
return to Tola/McBean, 149-150;
discussion of "Chamar Tola 1940",
153; discussion of "The Quiet
Peasant", and its sensitivity, including towards African Trinidadians,
164-165; evidence that HL was
working towards a family saga
involving Trinidad and Canada,
164; suggestion that this writing
was influenced by father's death
and HL's attendance at the funeral,
166-167; his summing up on HL's
growth as a writer and his sense
of tragedy, 178, 180-181; on the
after-life of HL's writing in new
editions, 181-182

Lee, Dennis, "The Death of Harold
Ladoo", 9; 10, 26, 69, 70, 76; Lee's
recording of his editorial
relationship with Ladoo in his
poem, 83; interview, 84, 90, raises
issue of cutting parts of the wake
scene, 90-91; on Faulkner and
Roch Carrier influence, 97 n. 4;
HL's gratitude to, 106; 107; on HL's
skills with dialogue and Creole in
the narrative voice, 114; on the
chaos of HL's writing energies,
129; on HL's batches of interrelated
stories, 133, 135-136; on HL's
cynical skill in manipulating white
liberals, 146; on HL's vision, ear,
characterisation and story-telling
skills, 149; his final summing up,
176; letter to HL prior to
acceptance of *No Pain*, 191-194;
letters on editorial rewrites
requested after acceptance, 195-
200

Literary emigrants to the UK, 25-26
Lovelace, Earl, 26
Maharaj, Rabindranath, 51; review of
*No Pain* and its perception of the
wounds of indentureship, 94-95

# ABOUT THE AUTHOR

Christopher Laird is a film-maker and producer who has produced over 300 documentaries, dramas and other video productions with Banyan Ltd. over the past 40 years, garnering a score of national, regional and international awards. He has overseen the establishment of what is arguably the world's largest digitised collection of Caribbean culture on video in the Banyan Archive. In 2003, he founded, with Errol Fabien, the region's first all Caribbean free-to-air television station, Gayelle. In 2009 he was awarded an honorary doctorate by the University of the West Indies. In his younger days his poetry was published in a variety of journals and anthologies and he published an innovative literary magazine called *Kairi* in the 1970s.